the
one

USA TODAY BESTSELLING AUTHOR
MARNI MANN

This is for all the women ...
Who crave an alphahole on the outside and a golden retriever on the inside.
Who want a man to worship the ground you walk on and will crawl through fire for you.
Who will love you to eternity with a fierceness that's incomparable.
Rhett Cole isn't just that man.
He's so much more.

PLAYLIST

"Two Hearts"—Dermot Kennedy
"Hurts Like Hell"— Fleurie and Tommee Profitt
"Wheels Fall Off"—Jelly Roll
"Lucky"—Dermot Kennedy
"last november"—Machine Gun Kelly
"I Remember Everything"—Zach Bryan, featuring Kacey
Musgraves
"This Heart"—Corey Kent
"Something in the Orange"—Zach Bryan
"I Am Not Okay"—Jelly Roll
"WILDFLOWER"—Billie Eilish
"The Prophecy"—Taylor Swift
"Scared To Start"—Michael Marcagi
"If You Want Love"—NF
"A Lot More Free"—Max McNown
"The Other Side"—Michael Marcagi
"Just Like Johnny"—Redferrin
"Smile So Much"—Jelly Roll
"Spin You Around"—Morgan Wallen

Music was an integral part of writing this book. It didn't just set the mood while I was in the cave; it became part of the story. It navigated my creativity with a flashlight. When the darkness tried to take over, the mood grim, the notes and melody and lyrics held me with open arms.

I encourage you to listen while you read.

Click here to check out the Spotify playlist.

PART 1

It wasn't water that slipped through my fingers.
It wasn't sand.
Or time.
It was ... you.

ONE

Rhett

One Day Ago

I remembered ...
    Not like it was yesterday.

More like it was less than an hour ago.

Except even that was too much. So was a handful of minutes.

A single second. Yes, that felt like a more accurate amount of time.

That haunting memory, the one I remembered, didn't just come into my head and leave at random.

It repeated.

Endlessly.

A track that skipped—not forward, but back—for almost fifteen years.

Five thousand four hundred seventy-four days of repeats had passed.

Every tomorrow looked like a mirror of the previous day.

And it left me with the most relentless, miserable ache.

One that consumed me. One that refused to let me move on.

My brain was shackled, my hands tensed, fingers bent into fists as though they were locked with arthritis.

That was how I lived my life.

A ball of anger that was fueled by pain.

One thing took it all away.

It made my fingers straighten and my arms outstretch.

It made me expel the loudest, most guttural exhale.

It made the darkness turn to light.

Her.

TWO

Rhett

Present Day

I shouldn't fucking be here.

There wasn't a single ounce of me that had any desire to look toward a stage and see a half-naked stripper dancing across it. Or to celebrate Brady Spade—our business partner—and his fiancée's joint bachelor and bachelorette party. Or to look at my brother and sister—who *should* know what today was—and Brady's brothers, along with their best friends, the Daltons, and try to act like I wasn't slowly dying inside.

Because I was.

Beneath my skin—my muscles, bones, even my blood—felt like it was all dissolving, as though acid had been poured across my body.

Some days were meant to be spent in a room of darkness. On those days, the only energy I wanted to exert was to pull the covers over my fucking head and swallow the whiskey down my throat and exhale the smoke from my joint, hotboxing the bed.

That was what I wanted today to look like.

But I wasn't in bed, high, drunk, lying in total blackness.

I was here.

I'd been dragged to this strip club by Ridge and Rowan, my siblings, and every second I sat in this chair nagged at my nerves and tested my patience—all of it coming to a screaming peak when I felt an arm wrap around my shoulders.

"I never thought I'd say this, but I'd rather be at a club right now." Ridge's hand cupped the edge of my triceps.

A dance club.

I wanted to fucking laugh, but I didn't know how.

A place that would have music worse than what was playing now, where my nose would be filled with the salty scent of sweat every time I breathed.

At least here, all I could smell was despair.

An aroma I knew far too well.

My eyes closed. "That sounds as insufferable as this."

"You all right, brother?" He waited. "I know the last few months—"

I turned toward him and barked, "Don't talk to me about the last few months. Not here."

Ridge was referring to our father, who had passed away. A day I'd like to forget. But a day that replayed, like the other, causing the knife already in my chest to turn faster and deeper, creating an even bigger hole.

"And not now."

"I hear you. My bad." He squeezed my shoulder. "But is that what's bothering you—Dad?"

I rubbed my thumb and forefinger together, my hand

getting ready to tighten into its perpetual fist. "I shouldn't be here."

"Why?"

"You know why." My teeth ground together.

How can he even ask me that?

Why the fuck do I have to spell everything out?

Can't he read between the obvious lines and stop making this harder on me?

"How about you help me out and just tell me the reason, so I don't have to keep racking my brain—"

"The date, Ridge." My head shook. "What's the fucking date?"

As his hand rubbed back and forth across the edge of my arm, the recognition finally showed in his expression. "Do you want to talk about it?"

"No."

"Are you sure?"

He knew I was sure.

I didn't talk about this. I wouldn't even let the thoughts leave my mouth after a fifth of whiskey. Fifteen years to the day was the last time I'd discussed it, and I'd never spoken about it again.

I preferred to keep those thoughts inside—buried.

But they weren't six feet under.

They were in my soul.

And they were so powerful that they rumbled and surged and tried to break through the surface.

But I was stronger. Because I knew once they hit my mouth, I wouldn't be able to stop them from coming out. And then I'd have to talk ... and I couldn't.

I exhaled. "Yeah, I'm fucking sure." I stood. "I need another drink."

"Are you going to take off after you get one?"

"If I do, don't come looking for me."

I disappeared toward the bar without looking back, without even saying anything to my sister or anyone we'd come here with, and I set my fisted hands on top of the wooden ledge. I'd already drained two whiskeys since we'd arrived. I wasn't even close to stopping.

But there were only two bartenders and a slew of bastards in line around me, waiting for drinks.

Fuck that.

A full bottle of liquor and a hotboxed bed sounded better than anything I could get here.

As I went outside, I reached into my pocket for the fob of my R8, groaning, "Shit," when I came up empty-handed.

I hadn't fucking driven here. We'd taken a goddamn party bus.

It only took a few taps on my phone before I had a rideshare coming to get me.

My feet moved while I waited, pacing the walkway between the club and the parking lot. The small white gravel rocks crunched under my shoes with each step.

I never let my siblings persuade me. I didn't know why I'd allowed them to tonight.

Coming here was the worst fucking idea.

This week, every year, followed an almost-identical routine.

My housekeeper would make sure my bar was well stocked, I'd hit up the dispensary and buy as much weed as they allowed, I'd shut off my phone, and I wouldn't go to work, nor would I even enter my home office.

Then what I'd do—the only thing I'd do—was turn off the lights.

Sometime later, around seven days, my family would show up. That was the span they'd give me to drink and smoke myself into fucking oblivion. When it came time to come in, they wouldn't mess with the doorbell—they knew I wouldn't answer it. They'd just use their key and walk in.

Dad usually showed up first.

He was the one who'd flip my lights back on.

But this year, that wouldn't be the case ... because Dad was gone.

Fuck.

My fisted hands dragged across my hair, pressing hard enough that it was as if I were tugging on the strands. Right before I relaxed my fingers to grasp a palmful of hair, a set of headlights flashed across the entrance of the club, and a car pulled in. A neon sign sat in the lower corner of the windshield, advertising the name of the rideshare company.

As I walked to the car, the driver rolled down the passenger window and said, "Are you—"

"Yes."

I didn't know what name he'd been about to voice. If it was mine or someone else's.

I didn't care.

Once I was inside and the backseat door was shut, I barked, "Drive."

I sank into the seat as he pulled onto the road, and I held my phone in front of my face. I could send Rowan a text, letting her know I was taking off, but I wouldn't. Ridge would tell her I wasn't coming back. He'd remind her of what today was if she'd forgotten, like him. She would then know she wouldn't hear from me.

And just like Pops, she'd appear at my house within the week.

In the meantime, I was craving what was waiting for me at home.

That time-out that came with a bit of silence when everything in my head was so fucking loud.

I hit the screen of my phone and pulled up Instagram—the only social media site I was on. I didn't post. I gave zero fucks that the publicist for Cole and Spade Hotels—the high-end international hospitality chain my family and the Spades co-owned—was constantly encouraging me to share shots of our resorts that I visited.

That wasn't me. That would never be me.

There was only one reason I even had an account.

Just like I did every few days, when I couldn't bear the anticipation any longer, I pressed the search bar and typed the first few letters of her name. That was all it took for her account to auto-populate since she was the only name I ever searched.

There were new posts.

There almost always was every time I looked at her account.

Just as I was about to click on the most recent photo she'd shared, I happened to glance up and peek through the windshield. Hell, I needed to make sure the driver wasn't taking me to San Francisco.

Not that it would matter. There was whiskey and weed all over the state of California. I could force a time-out wherever I landed.

But what I saw out the window made me say, "Stop."

The driver looked at me through the rearview mirror. "Excuse me?"

"Pull over. Right now."

"But we're still about fifteen minutes away from your—"

"Did you fucking hear me?" I leaned in between the front seats. "I said, stop."

He turned on his emergency lights and swerved to the side of the road. "Listen, man, if you're going to puke, get it out the window, or it's going to be a two hundred—"

I opened the door and stepped out, growling, "Don't wait for me," before I slammed it shut.

He thought the reason I barked at him to stop was because I had to puke. But the alcohol I'd consumed tonight was going to stay put. I wasn't letting a single drop out.

As the driver pulled back onto the road, I walked along the sidewalk until I reached the entrance, passing through the black wrought iron gate that remained open at all hours.

I knew it was open.

Because I'd been here more times than I could count, normally at this hour or later.

The path was narrow, surrounded by grass on both sides. It ran over two short hills—not steep enough to take my breath away, just a slight incline that caused a tingling in my calves. I was about to approach the third mound when I veered off to the right, my feet stopping on a spot about ten yards from the pavement.

The darkness would make it difficult for most people to see.

Not me.

I relied on the brightness of the moon and my memory.

In this spot, a clearing big enough to fit me, I lay down on my back.

I had so much to say, so much to get off my chest, but nothing was coming to me, except for, "I'm tired."

My temper, which had been roaring at the strip club, was gone. I felt as though a faucet had been turned on and the explosiveness of the pressure had drained from my feet. My hands clenched as the blades of grass tickled my neck, my fingers feeling like they were glued to my palms.

Even with the smell of flowers in the air, I uttered, "I'm so fucking tired."

I focused on the sky, as if I were talking right to it and the night clouds could speak back.

"How has it been fifteen years?" I asked the darkness. "I can't believe it ... yet I can. Because I've felt every single one of those fifteen years, day by day, hour by hour." My eyes burned. "Second by second." When the burning became too much, my eyelids closed. "Do you know how many of those seconds hurt?" I waited for an answer. "All of them." I swallowed, my throat gradually relaxing as the heat began to fade from my eyes. "Every fucking one, and I don't expect that to ever stop."

Tiredness was a weight that I constantly carried. Most nights, I was lucky to get a few hours of sleep. It didn't matter how sleepy I was or how badly I needed rest; my mind would wake me up.

Sleep was the reward, and I was being punished.

But something about being here—my body lying across the grass with the sky above me—caused a heavy wave to come over me. Not a wind. This was a slow crawl that moved inside me and covered me like a blanket.

"I'm so tired of keeping your secrets."

My eyes stayed shut.

My hands unclenched.

My lips whispered, "And I'm so fucking tired."

Enough so that the blackness began to take over and a picture began to form behind my closed eyelids. It didn't imme-diately happen. It was built by the tiny shards moving through the air, landing one by one, piecing together like the puzzles I did with Daisy, my niece.

First, there were feet.

Legs.

A torso.

Arms, fingers.

A neck.

Finally, a face with lips that said, *"Rhett?"*

I smiled.

Because I knew that voice.

Because I knew that grin.

Because I knew her mannerisms, her expression.

As I stood, unable to move, my gaze going from her feet to her face, the burning in my eyes shifted to my chest.

It was churning, forcing on a storm that was thick and so fucking strong that the thunder was clapping over me.

"Rhett?"

Yes, I wanted to reply.

I just couldn't pry my lips apart.

I had so much to get out—and I couldn't.

But she could speak. "Rhett." She could also move, closing the distance between us, placing her hands on my shoulders. "Rhett?"

Yes, I wanted to say again, but my mouth stayed sealed.

Her hands pushed down on my shoulders, and when she wasn't satisfied with that, they moved to my chest and shook me. "Rhett, you're sleeping. Wake up!"

THREE

Rhett

Sixteen Years Ago

If Lainey Taylor had been looking in my direction when she walked into our classroom three seconds after the bell rang, she would have seen my mouth drop open. She would have seen me grab the edge of my desk. And she would have seen a wave of heat move across my face, turning my cheeks dark red.

But she wasn't looking at me.

She was smiling at our English Lit teacher, mouthing, *Sorry I'm late*, before she put her head down and rushed through the aisle, taking the only empty seat in the second-to-last row.

Which was right beside me.

I sucked in the deepest breath while she reached into her bag and pulled out a pencil and notebook, her eyes now pointed at the whiteboard. My hands stayed glued to the desk.

My foot was silently tapping the floor, pushing out all the excess energy suddenly in my body.

What the hell is she doing here?

And why didn't I know she was coming back?

A goodbye a few months into our freshman year that I couldn't fucking forget—that was the last time I'd seen her.

I'd had so much hope when she climbed into her parents' SUV and rolled down the passenger window so she could speak to me while I stood outside the door. I clung to that open window frame and leaned my face in, listening to her promise that she'd keep in touch.

But she didn't.

Once her father made his way out of the driveway, the vehicle disappearing down the street, I never saw or heard from her again.

Wrecked.

That was how I had felt—and still did, even though that had been over two years ago, at the start of our freshman year, and now, there was only a month left of our junior year.

"Lainey ..."

Her back straightened from the sound of my whisper. Her head slowly turned, her eyes widening when they connected with mine. Several seconds passed before she said, "Rhett," in the smallest, quietest voice.

There was a buzzing in my body, like a million bees were flying from my head to my toes, their wings stirring up my blood as if waves were splashing through my veins. I couldn't breathe. Words were failing me, and my thoughts were so jumbled; I couldn't make sense of anything.

I swallowed, hoping that would settle something —anything.

But it didn't.

It only added to the intensity in which everything was spiraling.

"You're here." I kept my voice low so I wouldn't attract any unwanted attention, and I crouched down to hide my face from the teacher. "I thought ..."

What did I think?

Was I even making any fucking sense?

"I know. I thought I was gone forever too. But here I am." She rubbed her finger under her bottom lip, and I could be wrong, but it looked like her hand was shaking.

I couldn't think of anything to reply with. I could only stare at her. At her pretty face and curly light-brown hair and perfect smile with teeth that were no longer covered in braces. Hazel eyes that made my pulse pound. This wasn't a pounding like the headaches I sometimes got after practice when I hadn't eaten or drunk enough. This was a pounding that went straight to my dick. Enough so that I had to adjust myself or Lainey would get quite the sight.

My freshman year, when I'd initially laid eyes on her, I'd felt the same way. It was the first day of high school, and we were in gym class. I was positioned across from her, a volleyball net between us, her shorts riding high up her thighs when she jumped for a block. She was, by far, the hottest chick in our school, and as I stared at her, I decided right then and there that she was going to be my girl.

Within a week, she was eating lunch with me at the football table. We held hands after my third home game when she came onto the field to greet me. We almost made out at the homecoming dance, but we were interrupted by her sister, and the opportunity never presented itself again because she'd moved across the country the next day.

"You're here ... for good?" I asked.

I tried to keep my stare on her face, but my eyes had a mind of their own.

Lainey's brace-less smile wasn't the only thing about her that had changed. Her chest was twice the size, and I couldn't stop gawking at it. And her legs, they were longer, and her waist, even as she sat behind a desk in the khaki skirt uniform, looked curvier.

If she'd been hot back then, she was fucking gorgeous now.

Her bottom lip caved inward, and she bit it, nodding. "Dad was hired to run the whole LA office. We're not going anywhere."

His job was what had sent them to the East Coast.

"And Penelope?" I asked. "She's here too?"

For someone who didn't know Lainey's face as well as I did, they'd have a very hard time telling the identical twins apart. Eyes, hair, mouth, height, and body were mostly the same— aside from Lainey's dimple on her right cheek and a freckle to the left of the bridge of her nose. I thought they looked as different as their personalities. Penelope wanted to be the center of attention. She wanted every eye on her at all times and would do anything to stay in the spotlight. Lainey wanted to blend into the background. She was perfectly happy, going unseen and unappreciated.

"I'm sure you'll see her within the next few periods or hear her in the hallway at least." She smiled and tucked a piece of hair behind her ear, revealing a cartilage piercing she hadn't had before.

I let out a quiet breath. I wanted to talk to her, and I couldn't really do that in here, so I asked, "What period do you have lunch?"

"Mr. Cole," I heard.

Busted.

I slowly looked toward the aisle, where our teacher was standing in between our desks, a stern look on his face.

"Would you like to join the rest of the class?" he asked me. "Or would you like to continue talking through my lecture and spend this afternoon with me in after-school detention?"

I tapped my pencil against my notebook. "Sorry."

"Miss Taylor, why don't you stay after class for a few minutes, and we can discuss what you need to do to get caught up?"

"Okay," she replied.

As the teacher spent the next forty or so minutes boring us from the front of the class, I focused on Lainey, stealing nonstop glances at her. I didn't take a single note or hear anything the teacher spoke about.

All I could think and see and hear was her.

My mind filled with questions the longer I sat here.

Does she still like me in that way?

Did she ever think about me?

Did she miss me the way I missed her?

We had been so young back then. I'd barely even kissed a girl at that age—unless you counted our babysitter, who I'd laid my lips on in seventh grade after my brother dared me to. That was why it had taken me so long to try to kiss Lainey; I didn't really know what the hell I was doing, and I wanted to make sure I did it right. Homecoming was when I finally got the nerve. But Penelope fucked that up, and my whole plan had gone to shit.

I held that regret for a long time.

But now … Lainey was here.

She was within reach.

And I wanted a do-over.

When the bell rang, Lainey looked at me. I could tell she wanted to say something, but her lips stayed sealed as she got up and headed for the teacher's desk. I wasn't going to give up this chance to talk to her. I didn't care if I was late to my next class.

I left the room and pressed my back against the wall right outside the door. I wasn't there long when Ridge stopped by. He had freshman English this period, and we always passed each other in the hallway when I was on my way to Trigonometry.

"What are you doing?" he asked.

I adjusted my bag. "You're not going to fucking believe this."

"Believe what?"

Something caught his attention since he was no longer looking at me, and his mouth opened, the shock clear on his face. "Oh my God, Rhett, is that Lainey Taylor? Or Penelope? Regardless, what are they doing here?"

Lainey was coming out of the classroom, heading in the other direction from where we were standing.

I needed to catch up to her.

"I'll tell you about it later."

I jogged to her side. "Hey."

"Hi." She grabbed the strap of her backpack and held what looked like a school map in her other hand. "I thought I'd remember how to get around this school, but freshman year feels like a million years ago. I'm going to be late for Trigonometry if I don't figure out how to get there. I've got to hurry."

"You don't have Mrs. Lynch, do you?"

"I do."

Another period I got to spend with her.

Fuck yeah.

"So do I. I'll walk you there."

I didn't know how to bring it up. What to even say. I didn't want to sound pathetic and dwell on the past—freshman year did feel like forever ago.

But I'd never forgotten her.

And I'd always wondered what I'd done wrong because she never once tried to contact me.

"Are you happy to be back?" I asked.

She rubbed her lips together, her fingers turning white as she continued to cling to the wide strap of her backpack. "Yes. But, *ummm* ... I've been so nervous about it." She gradually looked at me. "I still am."

"Why?"

She shrugged. "I don't know. To see my old friends and ... *you.*"

"Why would you be nervous to see me?"

"I don't know ... I ..."

I needed that answer.

There was a utility closet at the end of the hallway that was constantly left unlocked, which had become a spot where my friends and I smoked weed between classes. The door was kept a little open, but it could be locked from the inside. As we approached, I gently grabbed her arm and pulled her in, twisting the knob so no one could barge in.

Lainey glanced around the small room. "Where are we? And what are we doing in here?"

"We need to talk, and we don't need the bell or anyone interrupting us."

"Rhett, we're going to be late—"

"I play football with Mrs. Lynch's son. She has a soft spot for his teammates. Don't worry, we won't get in trouble."

She pushed her back against the wall, and even though the open space was compact, the move added some distance between us. "What do you want to talk about?"

"The reason you were nervous to see me."

"Oh ... *that*."

She glanced down, but I reached for her chin and lifted it until her eyes were back on mine. While I held her, something happened to my fingers. There was a tingling, and it moved through my arm to my chest.

"You didn't call or anything, Lainey. You just left. Didn't you miss me?"

"Of course I did."

I felt my head shaking. "Then, why didn't you ever reach out?"

Her expression was softening, like the time we'd walked to the pet store and she played with the golden retriever puppies. "Because I never thought my family would ever move back here. And because of that, I thought it would hurt even more to talk to you every day, you know? I didn't keep in touch with anyone—it wasn't just you."

"What did you think about when you found out you were returning? You could have called me then—and you didn't."

She searched my eyes. "Oh, Rhett ..." She stopped to take a slow breath, and I heard a shyness in her voice and in the way she inhaled. "Does it matter?"

"Yes, Lainey, it does."

She pressed the back of her head against the wall and, with my help, tilted her chin even higher. "I don't know."

"Yes, you do."

She exhaled several times. "I thought about what it would be like to see you again."

"Now that you're seeing me, what does it feel like?"

"I didn't expect you to be in my first-period class—that's for sure." She let out a quiet laugh that felt more nervous than funny.

"That's the only thing that ran through your head? That you didn't expect to see me in English Lit?"

21

"No."

I spread my fingers, stretching from her chin to her cheek. A quick peek at her neck showed goosebumps were rising over her skin.

"I wondered what you would look like. If you'd have facial hair"—she touched the back side of my cheek, where I'd let my patchy scruff grow—"if you'd have an overgrown mop, like you did back then, or if you'd keep your hair short and buzzed. And how much taller you'd be. You're really, really tall now, Rhett." Her chest was rising much faster. "I wondered if working out for football would change your body." She gave a short nod. "It has in a big way." Her eyes briefly closed. "And if you'd have a girlfriend." When I said nothing, her eyes opened. "Do you?"

"If I did, would that bother you?"

She shrugged.

I laughed. "That's your answer?"

"I mean, if you do, what can I do about it? I didn't call, like I'd promised, so I can't exactly be pissed off if you're dating someone."

"I'm not."

She blinked several times. "Oh."

"How does that make you feel?"

A smile came across her face. "Relieved." She took a breath. "And a slew of other things."

"Do you know what I felt when you walked into the class-room this morning—once I got past the shock of seeing you?"

"What?"

"That there's no way I could let you out of my life a second time."

Emotion immediately hit her eyes. "Rhett ..."

"And do you know what I'm thinking about right now?" The tips of my fingers teased the strands of her hair. "That I have to fucking kiss you—something I should have done our freshman year."

I hadn't had the balls then.

I sure as fuck did now.

My other hand moved to her face, and I lowered my head, my mouth hovering above hers. "I'm sure there're a lot of other things I could say and places I could take you to and moments that could lead up to this, but I don't want to waste another second, Lainey. Somehow, someway, we're getting another chance, and all I want to do is kiss you. But first, I need to know … do you still care about me?"

"Rhett"—her hand went to my chest, and I waited for her to push against it, but she didn't—"I never stopped."

The response I'd wanted.

The response I'd needed.

I fit my mouth between her parted lips, and my body instantly exploded. This was what I'd been waiting for. What I'd dreamed about. What I'd been regretting since she'd left.

This feeling.

The one that was catapulting through me, causing everything to harden and ache.

I breathed her in before my tongue slid into her mouth, and I pulled her even closer so I could feel her on me. She tasted of toothpaste and something citrus, like she'd eaten an orange on her way to school or sucked the lemon from an iced tea. And she felt exactly how I remembered—her soft skin, her smallness that got lost against my broad, wide-receiver frame.

But her taste wasn't what stood out the most.

It was the way she wrapped her arms around my neck and melted against me. The way she showed me just how much she cared—because when I went to pull back, she wouldn't let me. And the way this kiss solidified every question in my mind.

Lainey Taylor was once again mine.

FOUR

Lainey

Sixteen Years Ago

"You're wearing that?" Penelope asked as she stood in the doorway of my room. "It's a party, Lain. We're not going to church."

I glanced down my body at the simple boot-cut jeans and peasant-style top that I wore on the shoulders instead of off. "What's wrong with it?"

"Everything." She walked straight to my closet. Anything she touched came off the hanger and was thrown to the floor, followed by a snarky response. "No." *Throw.* "No." Fling. "Hell no." *Launch.* "Definitely not." *Hurl.* "Toss this. Ugh." Until finally, "Okay, I can work with *thisss.*" She turned around. "This is what you'll be wearing tonight."

I eyed the pink dress that she held high in the air, shockingly still on its hanger. It wasn't an outfit I'd bought. I had somehow ended up with it after a sleepover when we were still living in Manhattan. I kept meaning to mail it back to Krissy, whose dress it was, and I'd forgotten.

"That's *not* what I'll be wearing."

"Can you imagine how Rhett will react when he sees you in it? That boy is gonna lose it. He won't be able to keep his hands off you." She sat on my bed and held it in my direction. "Put it on."

She was right about Rhett. His eyes would probably bug out of his head if he saw me wear anything even close to that.

I'd been back in LA for about a week, and the only outfit he'd seen me in was the school uniform. But even when I wasn't wearing the school-assigned khaki bottoms and polo top, I didn't dress to stand out; I dressed for comfort. That was how I'd always been. And in the past, Rhett had never said anything about what I had on.

Why would it be any different now?

So, I replied to my sister, "No."

I liked what I'd picked out to wear. I didn't have any interest in putting on something tight and short that I'd have to pull down all night.

"Because?"

"Because it's not me." I took it from her hand and held it against her. "It's way more you. Why don't you wear it?"

She cocked her head to the side. "You don't want to rock Rhett's whole world?"

Every time she said his name, a tingle shot through my body, like the sparklers we lit for the Fourth of July, their endless stream of embers inside me.

My head shook. "I didn't say that."

"But you did by not wanting to wear the dress." She eyed me down. "Girl, if you don't want him in that way, I'll take him."

"You're ridiculous." I laughed. "I'm just saying, I don't need to wear that to blow his mind." I released the dress, and it fell into her lap. "I've been in love with that boy since the very first time I saw him our freshman year. You know that. But I don't want to be someone I'm not and have him go all wild for that person. This is me, Pen. A girl who wears jeans and peasant tops." I shrugged. "And if he wants me, then he'll accept that."

"What do you mean, if he wants you?" She stood from the end of my bed and started taking off her shorts and tube top, dropping both to put on the dress.

"I don't know ... Rhett and I haven't talked about any of that yet."

Sure, we'd spent some time together at school, in between classes and at lunch, and he'd called me a few times at night while I was doing my homework. But we hadn't had the conversation of what things were going to look like now—if they were going to look like anything at all.

With the dress on, she moved in front of my mirror and looked at me through the reflection. "You haven't?"

"We've only been in school for five days, Pen."

She laughed. "So?"

"So, he might be a little angry that we went over two years without talking, and then I popped back into his life on a random Monday, one month before school ends. He's probably just feeling things out and making sure I don't disappear again. Or maybe he's not interested in me at all."

She snorted. "Have you seen the way he looks at you? Because I have, and I can tell you right now, he's obsessed with you."

"You really think so?"

"Don't tell me you're doubting the connection you guys have?"

He wasn't even in the room, and he was affecting me. As far

as a connection, I doubted nothing. We had one—we'd always had one. I just worried that I'd ruined things, and I wanted to talk to him about it when I saw him at the party tonight.

"Because if you are"—she pointed at her body—"you need to put on this dress right now."

I waved her off. "I'm good." She wasn't convinced, so I added, "I swear."

"You're forgetting, as your twin, I have the ability to feel everything you're feeling. When you're nervous, I know." She turned around and walked toward me. "When you're happy, I know." She put her hands on my shoulders. "When you're doubting yourself, I'm doubting myself."

I laughed. "Pen, you've never doubted yourself in your entire life."

She smiled. "You're right."

"Wear the dress, and let's go. Mom and Dad want us home by midnight, which means we have"—I looked at my watch—"four hours until we have to be home."

"I just need to go find some heels. Give me two seconds."

Once she was gone, I got in front of the mirror and straightened the shoulders of my shirt. I adjusted the top of my jeans, moving the button away from my belly button piercing —something Pen and I had gotten right before we left Manhattan. Since our parents would never give us their signed parental permission, Pen had charmed the piercer so much that he didn't even ask for our IDs. I then ran my fingers through my hair, the curls bouncing as I reached the bottom, and I swiped the edges of my lips to wipe away the excess gloss.

I didn't know how the nerves weren't showing on my face. I could feel them throughout my whole body.

Part of me couldn't wait for tonight to be over with. I wanted to spend time with Rhett. I just didn't want to talk about us. I wanted to focus on whatever happened next—whether that was us together or apart.

"Ready!" Pen yelled from the hallway.

I took a deep breath and a final look at myself in the mirror, and I grabbed my bag and met her at the bottom of the stairs. Our parents had gone out to dinner, so there weren't any questions to answer when I took the keys off the peg in the foyer and walked out to our car.

"Do you want me to drive there?" Pen asked. "Since we both know I won't be driving home."

I hit the button on the fob to unlock the car. "It's okay. I don't mind driving both ways."

She smiled before she climbed into the passenger seat. "God, I love having a DD."

"That's the only thing I miss about New York." I got in and started the car. "I didn't have to cart your drunk ass around."

"Don't act like you do it all the time. This is the first party we've been to since we got to LA."

I pulled out of the driveway and lowered the music. "You're forgetting that I drove home from the mall two nights ago. You know, when you were so high that you were seeing double. Or did you forget that?"

"That doesn't count."

I laughed. "Why not?"

"Because if you had fed me, like I'd asked, I would have come down enough to drive."

I rolled my eyes even though she couldn't see them. "Mall Chinese food gives me a horrible stomachache."

"No one said you had to eat it."

"But you weren't the only hungry one. I was too." I turned at the next light, the GPS on my phone telling me we were only a few miles from the party.

"And your point is?"

I gave her a sideways glance. "I don't even know. You've flipped the story so many times, I can't even keep up."

She turned up the music I'd just lowered. "One of my specialties. So ... do we know who's going to be there tonight, aside from Rhett? Hopefully, he'll be bringing all his hottie friends."

"I'm sure he's not going to be there without them." I looked at her again. "Why? Which one are you interested in?"

"All of them."

I shook my head. "Pen ..."

"Don't *Pen* me. You know I'm only messing with you. In a year, I'll be headed back to Manhattan to go to NYU, so there's no reason to get tied to anything. I just want to have fun. But that doesn't mean I can't appreciate one of his sexy friends in the meantime. Like Timothy—oh my God, he's delicious. I don't remember him being so hot two years ago."

"I feel like everyone has changed since we left."

"How lucky are you that Rhett's single? I mean, a guy who looks like him? Just think of all the girls, especially the cheer-leaders, who have thrown themselves at him. Star wide receiver, getting all the ass—"

"I'd like to not think about that, thank you."

The GPS alerted me that the house was only a few away, so I parked on the side of the road behind another car.

As I turned off the engine, Pen asked, "Does he know?"

I glanced across the front seat and studied her eyes. I didn't know if it was a twin thing or if I just knew her so well, but I didn't have to ask what she was talking about.

I shook my head. "No. He doesn't know."

"Are you going to tell him?"

I chewed my lip, tasting the gloss. "I don't know."

"Tell him, Lain." Her fingers bit into my arm. "It'll matter to him."

"Or it'll make me look completely pathetic."

She nodded toward my door. "There's only one way we'll know the answer to that. Now, get out and go see your boy."

I drew in a deep breath, securing my bag across my body, and I stepped onto the pavement. Looping our arms, we made our way down the sidewalk toward Alyssa's house—a place I'd never been before.

This party wasn't a secret, nor did it have a limited guest list.

During Trig, Alyssa had invited the entire class, and word spread throughout the school. By the time I got to lunch, the whole cafeteria was talking about it. I didn't think much about it until Rhett said he was going and he wanted me to come too.

That was when I knew I couldn't miss it.

And I didn't have to convince Penelope to come. By the time we'd gotten to our car after school, she had already told me we were going.

We headed up the walkway and climbed the front steps.

"Should we ring the bell?"

"Hell no." She opened the door.

My ears filled with music, and there were people everywhere, crowding the foyer and living room—the only two rooms I could see from the doorway.

"Come on." She squeezed my arm as we went inside. "Let's go get a drink."

"You mean, let's go get you a drink. I'm driving."

"Whatever," she groaned.

We weren't more than a few paces past the living room when I connected eyes with Rhett. He was standing at the back of the house with a red plastic cup in his hand and a backward baseball hat on his head. He had on a short-sleeved button-down, the first few buttons undone, and the sleeves were tight around the top of his arms, showing off his muscles. I couldn't see what he had on below his waist—my eyes wouldn't go that far.

They didn't want to leave his.

My stare was as frozen as my feet.

"Lain, come on," Pen said.

I heard her talking, and I felt the tug of her arm. I just wasn't going anywhere.

"*Oh*, I see. He's here, and he's got his eyes on you, girl," she said. "All right, I'm going to go hunt for the keg. You and lover boy go find a nest somewhere. Come find me when it's time to make our curfew."

As soon as she was gone, a half smile came across Rhett's face, like he was satisfied with what he saw, but there was a hint of mystery mixed into his expression. He lifted the cup to his lips, watching me as he swallowed, his throat bobbing after he pulled the plastic away from his mouth.

What is he thinking about?

Even from all the way over here, I could see the color of his eyes. The icy blue glowed, no matter what kind of light he was in. Pieces of his thick black hair stuck out of the back hole of his hat, and the same color scruff was dusted across parts of his cheeks—things I noticed because I had been so overwhelmed by his gaze that I needed to focus on something besides his eyes.

Why can't I breathe?

Why is the most foreign feeling running through my whole body?

And why does it feel completely normal to stare at him while loitering in a room packed full of people as music blasted around us?

I knew that answer.

I'd known it since gym class freshman year, when I first spotted him. He wasn't supposed to be at the front of the net while we were playing volleyball. It was his turn to serve. But I noticed that he switched with his friend, and the next time he was supposed to rotate, he switched with someone else. And when class was over, he came up to me before I got to the locker room and asked my name. The drip of sweat that was falling down my cheek never hit my neck.

Because he'd caught it.

Now, as he gazed at me, he handed his cup to one of his friends and began to walk toward me.

The air suddenly seemed so thick; I couldn't fill my nose. There was a tingling in the back of my throat, and it moved to my chest and my hands. My fingers clenched, released, clenched, and with each pump, sweat bled through my skin.

With the length of his stride, it only took a few paces before he reached me.

But he didn't stop once he was close.

Instead, his fingers linked with mine, causing a spark to shoot through my body, and he led me to the staircase on the other side of the house, positioning me in front of him so I climbed first and he stayed behind me. At the top, he switched our order again, guiding me down a short hallway, opening one of the doors at the end and closing it behind us.

Pitch-black darkness. That was all I saw.

But even in here, the air hadn't thinned. The temperature was cooler, doing nothing to settle what was happening inside me. The nerves were peaking, my chest heaving even though it didn't feel like I was breathing at all.

"I'm right here." He touched my waist, rubbing as high as my ribs, causing my breath to hitch. "Where the hell is the light switch?" His fingers tapped the wall. "There it is." He smiled as it flicked on. "Not that I mind the dark. I just can't see you, and I fucking love seeing you." He took a seat on the bed, which made me realize we were in a bedroom. I hadn't noticed a single detail in here except for him. "You came. I wasn't sure you would."

I shoved my hands into my pockets. "Why?"

"This isn't your scene."

"You don't think so?"

"A party this size? No. A handful of friends hanging out? Yes."

I laughed because he was right, but also because I was so surprised he was right. "Small settings feel better."

"Why did you come, Lainey? If you tell me it was to chaperone Penelope, I won't believe you—although she needs to be chaperoned if she's as wild now as she was a couple of years ago."

"Oh, she is. Maybe even more so."

"Then, I'd bet a twenty that, right now, she's doing a keg stand downstairs."

"I can almost guarantee that she is."

I didn't like where I was standing—or that I was standing at all. I felt like I was on a stage with a spotlight shining over me, and that thought made me shiver. So, I joined Rhett on the bed but sat toward the foot, whereas he was near the head. I folded my hands in my lap, and when that didn't feel right, I set my palms on the blanket.

"I came because I wanted to talk to you."

"Good. That's what I wanted to hear. But if you tell me you're moving again, I'll need about ten more beers before we have that conversation."

My hair fell into my face when my head shook. "I'm not going anywhere until college."

"Then, what is this about?"

I filled my cheeks with air. "I feel like I owe you an apology. You know, about me leaving and never reaching out. I know we talked about it a little on my first day back, but I didn't tell you I was sorry. That I was wrong. That I *couldn't* keep in touch with you ..."

His arms were behind him, holding his weight, forcing his torso to recline back. "Couldn't? Or wouldn't?"

"This is going to sound crazy." While I waited for the courage to come, I chewed on my lip.

"You want to hear crazy? You should hear my thoughts right now ..."

I wanted to ask what they were. But if I did, I didn't know if we'd ever circle back, and I needed to get this out.

"When we moved, I was so furious with my parents. I didn't speak to them for a month. I wouldn't even leave my room unless it was to go to school. I despised them for making me go to Manhattan. And Penelope, she tried everything she could to get me to go out," I said, ignoring his last comment. "She even came into my room one night and spiked my Diet Coke, hoping it would loosen me up enough that I'd leave."

"Did it?"

"The second I tasted the vodka, I flushed it down the toilet and locked her out."

"Hard-ass."

I sighed. "I was miserable, Rhett."

"I don't like hearing that." He extended his leg and rubbed it against mine. "Was it because they had taken you away from everything you knew?"

"It was because they had taken me away from you." My chin dropped, and I looked at my lap. "I know we were together for just a few months, and I was only fifteen years old, and in most people's minds, they'd think that's ridiculous. I was practically a baby. But to me, it was everything." I looked up. "You were everything."

"Lainey ..."

"After a month of my not speaking to my parents, my dad

came into my room to talk to me—which he'd done before, but I wouldn't open up. This time, I was finally ready to get everything off my chest, and I told him I wanted him to let me go home. I'd live with a friend or family member—anyone—but I wasn't going to stay in New York." I wiped my hands on my thighs and wrapped my arms around my stomach. "He wouldn't let me. He said I needed to tough it out, he wouldn't give me any other choice. But he made me a promise and said he'd do everything in his power to prove himself to the New York office so he'd be offered the CEO position in LA. In return, he wanted me to stop sitting around and moping, to enjoy my time in New York."

"Why didn't you tell me any of this back then?"

"I didn't know if it would happen, or if Dad would keep his promise, or if the LA office would even give him the promotion —there were so many things out of my control." I tightened my grip on my stomach. "When it eventually came through, Dad wanted us to stay in Manhattan and finish the last month of the school year and move here during the summer." I let out a huff. "There wasn't a chance in hell that was going to happen. We arrived in LA last Sunday night, and I was at school on Monday morning."

His stare intensified. "You did everything you could to come back to me."

I thought of the conversation I'd had with my sister in the car.

She'd told me to tell him.

But I felt like such an idiot.

This time, when I drew in air, I held it in. "There's more ... I haven't told you everything."

"What do you mean?"

I rocked over the bed, hoping the swaying would ease the feeling in my chest. "The whole time I was there, I didn't date anyone. I was asked out plenty, but I couldn't do it. It didn't feel right. They weren't right." I slowly let out the air through my lips. "They weren't ... you."

As soon as I reached forward, his arms moved from behind him to in front of him, and he grabbed my hand as though he'd been waiting for it.

"The first kiss I ever had, Rhett, was with you in that janitor's closet."

When he scanned my eyes, the movement was gradual. He wasn't just looking at them; he was looking through them. "Hold on a second." He went silent. "You really didn't date anyone while you were there?"

"No."

"And I was really your first kiss?"

"Yes. Really." I wanted to die at the thought of saying the word, but I had to. "I'm a virgin."

He rubbed his thumb over my knuckles. "You were waiting for me."

"I wouldn't be happy with anyone but you." The emotion came into my throat. "I knew that at fifteen, and I know that now at seventeen. I was coming back, no matter what, however long it took. But I wouldn't keep you dangling—because for me, that was torture, and I wouldn't put you through it."

His stare covered my whole face. I even felt it on my ears.

"All this time, all you wanted was me." His head shook. "And all this time, I thought you wanted nothing to do with me." He pulled my hand until he had more of my arm, and then he slid me closer.

With inches separating us, he traced his thumb around my lips. "I'm the only one who's ever had these." He wasn't questioning. It was like he was saying it out loud so it would stick in his head.

"I looked for you"—his voice turned gritty—"in every girl

who talked to me, who walked by, who sat next to me in class. I looked to see if there were similarities, if there was even a tiny resemblance." His stare shifted to my mouth. "Not a single one could live up to you."

I held his wrist while he touched me. "Do you know how many times I dreamed of these fingers on my face?" I wasn't sure if I'd voiced those words or if my thoughts were screaming so loud that it just felt like I'd spoken.

"I want to tell you something." When he exhaled, his breath came out hard.

The nerves didn't settle when I nodded.

Whatever was about to come out of his mouth could either break my heart or fill it.

His fingers stretched out across my cheek, his thumb pressing along the side of my mouth. "It's always been you." He moved his face closer. "And, Lainey, it will always be you."

FIVE

Rhett

Present Day

She was still standing in front of me with her hands on my chest, shaking me, yelling, "Rhett!" Each time she said my name, she got a little louder. "Wake up! Please!"

There was no doubt in my mind who I was looking at. She was missing the dimple on her right cheek and the freckle to the left of her nose. And then there was her voice.

What I couldn't understand was why Penelope had kept telling me to wake up and why she repeatedly shouted my name over and over.

I was awake. I was gazing at her.

Her grip turned harder, her movements rougher. "Rhett!"

Talk to me, I tried to say. *Explain to me what's going on.* But those were no more than thoughts. My lips felt glued together, like they had been since she'd appeared, making it impossible to open my mouth.

"Rhett!"

She looked so good. Tan, like the summer we'd spent on the beach between our junior and senior year of high school. She was smiling the way she did whenever she talked about having fun.

"Rhett, open your eyes."

But they are open, Penelope.

"You're sleeping. You need to wake up."

I'm ... sleeping?

"Yes," she replied as though she'd heard my thoughts. "Now, get up."

Get up—*oh!*

My eyes flicked open, and that was when I realized I'd been sleeping.

I expected the morning light to blind me.

But there was no light.

There was only darkness.

Penelope, the yelling of my name, the shaking—it had all been a dream.

Except ...

Fuck me. Some parts had been real.

Because there was a woman hovering over me. Her hands were on my chest. Her eyes were gazing into mine.

I blinked, making sure what I was seeing was real, that my eyes weren't playing tricks on me, that the shadows of the night weren't showing me a ghost. And while my eyes proved that every inch I was seeing was real, it all came rushing back to me —getting out of the rideshare, walking along the sidewalk, lying down *here.*

The heaviness.

But the fact that I'd actually fallen asleep? That shocked the hell out of me.

"Lainey," I whispered.

When her name came through my lips, something inside me shattered. It broke me to the point where I'd never be the same person again.

"I was getting worried," she said. "I thought something was wrong or you were sick or ... I don't know. I couldn't figure out why you wouldn't wake up."

"I don't ever sleep. When I do, it's deep."

She got on her feet, stepping a few feet away, and I sat up, not taking my eyes off her. If anything, her new placement allowed me to study her even harder. Hints of her light-brown hair showed in the moonlight, along with the outline of her body and a tease of her hazel stare.

Beneath the remnants, there was a beating.

A fucking throbbing that increased every second.

"I can't believe you're here." I didn't know what else to say. Words weren't coming to me. My head was a mess of thoughts and grogginess.

I'd thought about this moment—if it would ever happen, what it would look like—and now that it was here, I sounded like a fucking idiot. What I did know was that it was late. Eleven thirty, according to my watch. It made sense why I was here at this hour, but not her.

"Are you all right?" I tried to understand the look in her eyes, but I couldn't see enough of them. "Seems a little late for you, no?"

"Am I ... *all right*?" She huffed—a sound that told me she was surprised I'd asked that question. "What are you doing here, Rhett?"

If there was a way that my chest could split open from the rapid beating of my heart, that was happening right now.

"I come here a lot."

"Why?"

Why?

To remember.

To reminisce.

To relive.

But what I was doing here wasn't nearly as important as the fact that she was here. That she was only feet away from me. That it would take me just a few paces to reach her.

"It's been fifteen years and—"

"I know how long it's been," she said.

Of course she knew. It had been stupid of me to offer the recap, even if it was a small one.

"I come here when I have things to get off my chest. Given the date, I had a lot to say tonight."

She glanced around as though she didn't know what the area looked like. "Shouldn't you go to a therapist for that? That's what most people would do. They wouldn't come here to purge their soul."

"I suppose you're not wrong. But it feels right, doing it here. It's not like I can call you ..." I pushed off the grass and stood, the bottoms of my shoes feeling round instead of flat, threatening my balance. I grabbed whatever was near, feeling the instant coldness on my skin, and once my feet adjusted, my hand fell to my side. "You know ... it's been fifteen years since I've seen you."

A statement that fucking pounded through my throat and across my tongue.

That day—the last day—was one I'd never forget.

When streams of tears had dampened our cheeks and voices had reached every octave and accusations had flown through the air, like a sky full of jets.

Despite coincidences and fate, I'd never expected this moment to happen. That we'd cross paths again.

That, like sleep, I would get that lucky.

But here we were.

Together in a way I could barely fathom.

And I had so many questions; I didn't know where to start. I went with the obvious and asked, "Did you ever think you'd see me again?" A trembling was happening inside me with the intensity of a goddamn earthquake. "What it would look like if you did? What it would feel like?"

"Rhett—"

"Because I've thought about it. I've thought about it every day, Lainey."

"No." She went quiet, her head dropping, a curtain of hair falling toward both sides of her face. "I never thought about it."

I didn't believe her.

Not when pasts were as intertwined as ours.

Not when there had been so much love between us.

But, goddamn it, all it had taken was one moment with Penelope to blow that apart.

"Lainey ..." I sounded breathless even though I was breathing, my head still wrapping around the fact that she was here, that I was getting to say her name and earn myself a response, like the way she was looking up at me now. "You've never once thought about me?"

"No." Her hands tightened into tiny balls. "I've only hoped for one thing for the rest of my life and beyond."

I drew in as much air as I could hold. "And that is?"

"That I never saw you again."

SIX

Lainey

Sixteen Years Ago

*"I*t's always been you. And, Lainey, it will always be you.*"

It had only been a few seconds since Rhett had spoken those words to me at the party where we were upstairs in one of the bedrooms, sitting on the bed. And as his stare covered me, his words echoing in my head, I could feel my face turning beet red, my lips pulling into the biggest grin.

I was doing everything to stop myself from melting.

Why was he so achingly sweet?

Why was I wiggling, unable to sit still, no matter how hard I tried?

It was the *always* part that was tripping me up. It meant so many things.

And it meant, if I was understanding him correctly, that everything I'd feared while I was in New York was just in my mind, scenarios that wouldn't make it further than my imagination. And if I was reading him right, it didn't matter that I'd left or how much time had passed; Rhett cared about me.

But I still wanted to confirm, so with his fingers spread across my cheek and his thumb on the side of my mouth, I said, "You never stopped thinking about me, the same way I never stopped thinking about you, huh?"

"I sure as hell didn't."

I could smell beer on his breath. A scent that wasn't bad at all; it was actually really hot, especially since it was mixed with something minty, like gum, which he must have tossed before I arrived at the party.

"So, you're saying your feelings haven't changed?"

His eyes were fiery while they focused on mine. "Not even a little."

Wow.

I'd convinced myself that I'd handled everything all wrong, that I should have called him, that I should have somehow persuaded my parents to let me go back to LA—at least for a visit. So, I'd prepared myself for the worst.

"Do you want to know something?" I waited for him to nod. "I didn't think things were going to play out like this. The kiss in the janitor's closet on my first day back, the way you called me the last couple of nights, or that the minute you saw me, you brought me up here so we could be alone. When I'd planned this all out in my head while I was still in Manhattan, I had been so worried ..." My eyes closed as my voice drifted off.

When I felt movement, my eyelids opened, and Rhett was pulling back a little, as if he needed to get a better look at me.

"What do you mean?" he asked.

"You were the most popular freshman in our school, so I figured, by now, you'd be the most popular guy in the entire school. With that title, along with being a football star, comes all the girls." I shrugged. "I assumed you'd be dating one."

"Dating? No. I haven't done much of that at all." I could tell he wasn't done talking. "I'm not going to lie to you and say you're the first girl I've kissed. There were others—and other stuff happened." He took in my expression. "I'm not saying this to hurt you. I just want to be honest. You deserve that."

"I understand."

Even though I hated it and the thought made me hurt, I couldn't exactly expect a guy to have kept his lips and hands and whatever else to himself when I hadn't even talked to him for over two years.

He held my chin. "Those girls are nothing to worry about. It was what it was, and it was over." His voice softened with each word. "They weren't you."

"Are you the kind of guy who just doesn't date at all?"

He laughed. "What would make you think that?"

"You didn't date any of them. You just did ... whatever."

"Lainey"—he gently pressed his lips against mine, and I felt him breathe me in—"I wasn't into dating them. You're a different story."

The tingles were flitting from my stomach to my chest, like they were attached to wings, hitting the walls of my insides the higher they got. "What kind of story am I?"

"What kind would you like to be?"

My shyness definitely took over, and I was almost too afraid to give an answer. "Rhett, I don't know ..."

"Yes, you do."

If I had been red before, I now looked like I'd just run a marathon. "How about you tell me what kind of story you want?"

He smiled. "I asked you first."

"That's not fair."

"I set the rules."

"That's not fair either." I took a deep breath, debating how real I wanted to be with him, even though that was what this conversation was about. I held in the air I'd just taken in and gradually released it. "I want everything."

"What's ... *everything*?"

"Everything when it comes to you."

"You're saying you want to be my girlfriend?"

I was squirming on the inside. "Yes." But then my stomach began to hurt as I thought of our conversation just moments ago. "But from what you said, it sounds like that's something you don't do."

"It's something I didn't do with them. You're different, remember?"

I wanted to feel relief, but it wasn't there yet. "Why?"

He smiled as he moved his face toward mine. "When it comes to you, I want everything too."

"*Everything*, everything?"

He nodded. "As much as you're willing to give me. Whatever that is, I'll take it all." He brushed the hair out of my eye. "And this time, you're not leaving me."

I sighed. "How do you do that?"

"Do what?"

"Make me feel these wild, nutty things. Like, I can barely even breathe right now."

"What if I kiss you?" His gaze dropped to my mouth. "Will that make it better or worse?"

I rubbed my lips together, as though his had just left mine. "Technically worse, but ultimately better."

He slowly came closer until our mouths were pressed against each other, and his tongue slipped between my lips. I wasn't just smelling the beer; I was tasting it, and for a drink I didn't like at all, I loved it on him.

But there was more.

The way he was holding me. The way he was kissing me, like he was starving for me. The way he was exhaling, the sounds he made each time.

Or maybe those noises were coming from me.

Because the tingling wasn't even tingling anymore. It was exploding. My insides felt electric. Rhett had flipped some kind of switch, and everything was on and blazing.

That was something I'd felt during the nights I was in New York, alone, thinking about Rhett and how badly I wanted to get back to him. And then again the first time his lips had touched mine. But none of those occasions were as strong as this.

This ... had me breathless.

When he separated us, he stared into my eyes. "That right there is something I love about you."

"What do you love?"

"That you look at me like it's never enough. That when I pull back, you make me feel that too. That if you could, you'd kiss me forever."

My smile returned. "It's true. I would." My fingers dived into the side of his dark hair before lowering to his neck and then his chest. There had been muscles there when we were younger; they just weren't as defined or hard. They hadn't made me want to unbutton his shirt and see what they looked like when uncovered. "You know what I love about you?"

"Tell me."

"It doesn't matter if you're looking at me in class or we pass each other in the hallway or I'm walking into a party, your stare never changes. You look at me like I'm the prettiest girl in the room."

"More than the room, Lainey. You're the most beautiful girl I've ever seen in my life."

I turned into his hand when his palm shifted to my cheek. "You make me smile so hard. An obscene amount. Just thinking about you makes me smile. It's like I can't stop."

"I don't want you to. Not ever. Promise me that."

"Promise I'll never stop smiling?"

"Yeah, and when we're old and gray, I want that smile on your lips to always be for me."

I grabbed the back of his hand and laughed. "That's an eternity from now. We have to make it through the rest of our junior year and the summer and our senior year and then college and ..." I turned silent when I considered all the time ahead, like college, which could create more distance between us.

"You don't need to worry about any of that." He pulled at my waist, dragging me closer to him. "Or about us."

"No?"

"Fuck no. I told you, you're not leaving me, so I don't plan on ever letting you out of my sight again. I hope you don't get sick of me because you're going to be seeing a lot of me." He winked.

I was sure he was just playing when he said that, but to me, that was a statement I'd dreamed of hearing for far too many years.

I still had to ask, "What about college? Will you be going somewhere to play football?"

"No."

"Why not? You're certainly good enough." I giggled. "I might have checked your stats while I was in New York."

"I like that you did that." He brushed my chin. "If I were interested in going into the NFL, I'd play college ball. That would be my window in. But my dream is for my brother, sister, and me to take over my dad's hotel business. I've worked there every summer for as long as I can remember, and I'll go to work there full-time when I graduate college. Some of the dudes who went on to play collegiate ball have told me how much work it is, balancing practice and traveling and games and off-season workouts while maintaining a certain GPA to keep their scholarship. I don't want that." He shook his head. "I want to have fun before work becomes the majority of my life."

"So, if you're not going after a football scholarship that could take you anywhere in the US, does that mean you want to stay in California for school?"

"I'd like to."

Relief finally flooded through my chest.

I didn't know why. College wasn't for another year. But we would need to start applying this coming fall, and with this school year ending, that didn't feel like much time at all.

"That's what I want too," I said. "Stanford. USC. University of California, Berkeley. Those are my top choices for nursing school ... I think."

"Not NYU?" He smirked.

I rubbed my hands over my jeans before I rested them on his shoulders. "That's Penelope's top choice. She's all about the East Coast. Me? I'm good right here."

"Excellent decision." He pecked my lips. "Do you know what I'm picturing right now?"

"No. What?"

"The two of us at USC, walking hand in hand to class. Moving in together after two years in the dorms. We can get a place just off campus that's big enough for a golden retriever."

My eyes widened. "You want a dog? In our college apartment?"

He laughed. "Out of all the things I just said, the dog is what stood out the most?"

I covered my mouth and laughed even louder than him. "Are you kidding? I'm dying over what you just said." I dropped my hand. "Don't you see my smile?" I paused. "But considering the way college students party and that you want to have all the fun before you go to work for your dad, being responsible for a dog sounded kinda funny."

"I can understand that, but isn't that the kind of dog you want?"

I searched his eyes. "I don't remember ever telling you that."

"You didn't have to. I saw it on your face way back in the day, when we were at the pet store and you were playing with the golden retriever puppies."

My inhale was slow and deep. "Rhett ..." I swallowed, my saliva only adding to the pool of mush my body was turning into. "Yes, it's my dream dog."

"Then, I'm going to make it happen—whether it's our junior or senior year or when we graduate and buy our first place together." He positioned his lips over mine. "Lainey, I'm going to make every one of your dreams come true."

SEVEN

Rhett

Sixteen Years Ago

"It's a good thing we only had a month left of school because I don't think I could have waited much longer to have you all to myself." I adjusted my arm across Lainey's shoulders and pressed my lips against her cheek. The ocean breeze was blowing her hair into my face, tickling my skin.

When I pulled my mouth away, she turned toward me. The sun was causing her to squint, so she used her hand as a visor. "You don't even want to share me with school?" She giggled. "For your sake, I hope the summer goes by slowly."

"Ridiculously slow," I growled. "And I plan to spend every waking hour with you."

Her smile was so big; it made me grin.

"Just so you know, I wouldn't hate it if you were in a bikini during those hours ... like you are right now." My stare dipped.

"Because ... damn, girl." I played with the strings that kept her light-blue bottom on. I wanted to pull them until they were loose, see more of her hot fucking body. But I wouldn't here—not at the beach, not in front of half my football team—but the thought of touching that hidden part, along with her chest, was so tempting.

"You mean every hour, aside from the ones you have to be at work."

I shrugged. "Minor detail."

"Except it's a huge detail. You're putting in a ton of hours, and I'm so proud of how hard you're working."

"Do you miss me while I'm gone?"

She dived her fingers through my hair. "I miss you even when you're here." Her other hand dropped from the top of her eyes, and it went to my cheek. "I can't seem to get enough, no matter what."

"Not even when I do this?"

I kissed her. Not with my tongue, but with my mouth open, using my teeth to tug on her bottom lip.

Her exhale told me she liked it. It even told me she wanted more.

After I pulled away, it took a few moments before her eyes opened.

"Not even when you do that."

"Sounds like I need to cool you off." I nodded toward the ocean. "Let's go get wet."

"You mean, in the water?"

"Unless you're thinking of a different kind of wet. If that's the case, shit, we can leave right now."

"Rhett!" She playfully slapped my thigh.

I grazed her chin. "I'm just messing with you."

Her stare didn't leave mine. "I know you're thinking about

it. I am too." After a solid pause, she added, "You've been really patient with me."

We'd gotten close a few times when she was at my house late at night or when I went to her house after school, her dad at work and her mom out.

But we hadn't gone all the way.

"It's not about patience, Lainey. We have forever. So, it's not something that has to happen right away. Don't get me wrong, if it did, I wouldn't be mad about it." I chuckled. "But I'm good with it happening whenever. I just want you to be ready."

She wouldn't be my first—that had happened while she was in New York. If I'd known how she felt about me, I would have waited. But her silence during those two years had caused me to hook up with a handful of girls—a part of my past I wish wasn't true. During Lainey's second week back, I'd told her. I spared her the details, but I'd felt it was important for her to know since there would be one of us who knew what to expect when it eventually went down and one of us who didn't.

Her hand found mine, and she looked toward the water, where most of our crew was hanging out. Around twenty of us had come to the beach today. Her sister and a bunch of the guys from my team had piled in multiple cars. The spot we'd taken over on the sand was covered in towels and tanning oil and coolers of beer.

"The summer is my favorite vibe." She adjusted the strings behind her head, where her suit was knotted. "Sun, beach"— she looked at me—"you in those shorts, shirtless."

"You're saying I have the best body here? Is that what I'm hearing? That you could stare at these chiseled abs all day?" I laughed as I strummed my stomach.

"Oh, yes, I'm saying every word of *that*."

I wrapped my arms around her and rocked us back against

the towel. As we lay there, we adjusted our bodies to face each other. "The guys are going to want to play a game of football later. The way I just tackled you? Do me a favor—don't let any of them do that to you."

"Because?"

"I don't want their hands on you." I pushed some hair away from her face. "One dude touches you—that's me. No one else."

She poked the middle of my chest. "Same goes for you."

"You don't want any guys touching me?" I smiled.

"Oh my God. I can't with you."

I pulled her closer, laughing. "I hear you, and you have nothing to worry about."

"It's funny, you know I hate beer, but every time I smell it on your breath, I like it a little more."

I'd only had one, and I wouldn't have more than two, not when I had to drive, which I'd done today. I was surprised she could even smell it.

"Tell me what else you like."

Her gaze lifted to the top of my face. "How your hair is so black that it has hints of blue." Her fingers followed her eyes, touching the strands that were on my forehead. "And how, when you kiss me, this roughs up against my skin and burns and tingles at the same time." She was now on my scruff. "And how your lips are always so soft." Her thumb swiped across the top and bottom one. "And the way you smell, a combo that's like wood and liquor, married together in the most delicious way."

"You can thank my mom for that. She puts a few bottles of that cologne in my stocking every year."

"Don't ever change it."

"Keep going."

She leaned up on her elbow. "My favorite part is that whenever your hands or arms are on or around me, I feel like nothing could ever get through. A shield of protection, I guess you could call it. And I love that so much."

"I wouldn't let anything in. Ever." I held my lips close to hers as I spoke. "You never have anything to worry about when you're with me."

"And I love that I feel as though it's just us, regardless of where we are or what we're doing. We're currently surrounded by a beach full of people, and I wouldn't know there's a single person on it." The back of her fingers stroked my scruff.

"My presence alone makes you feel that way?"

"And your eyes. It's more than just a gaze or stare, it's a feeling. When we were in class, I knew whenever you were looking at me. This crazy rush would come through me, and my skin would break out in goosebumps."

I traced up her neck. "Just like it is right now."

"You make it hard for me to breathe." She stayed silent for a moment. "Rhett ... what if I told you I don't want to spend the day at the beach?" Her eyes were changing the longer she looked at me, almost appearing devious.

"I'd say, let's go. I'll take you wherever you want."

"Really?"

I huffed, surprised she even questioned it. "Really."

She filled her cheeks with air, as though she was trying to hide her smile. "I need to make sure my sister can get a ride home. I'll be right back."

She pushed herself up from the towel we were sharing, and I watched her walk toward the water, where Penelope was splashing in the waves with my quarterback. Timothy had dumped his girlfriend for the summer, and I wasn't surprised at all that he'd set his sights on Penelope. According to my team, Penelope was the hottest girl in the school, which meant Lainey was too—they were identical to everyone but me. But my guys wouldn't give Lainey that title

—they knew I'd kill them if they looked at my girl in that way.

I stared at Lainey's ass the entire way to the surf; the small bottoms of her suit covered the middle of her butt, but the outer edge was showing. *Fuck.* The way it led to her sexy, bare back with her long hair hanging down the middle of it was making my dick even harder. I adjusted myself within my trunks and sat up, holding my bent knees close to my chest.

Lainey only had to step a few feet into the ocean before Penelope came running over to her, my quarterback joining them. He listened to them for just a few seconds before he turned his attention to me.

I waved him over, and once he was close enough to hear me, I said, "Take care of Penelope today."

He stood in front of my towel with his hands on his hips. "Why wouldn't I?"

"Lainey and I are leaving, so I'm just asking you to watch out for her. Make sure she gets a ride home and gets there safely." I nodded at him. "You know what I'm talking about."

"I've got her. Don't you worry."

"You promise?"

"Yeah, man, I promise." He turned his head to the side, smiling at me the whole time. "Why are you guys leaving?"

"We're just not feeling the beach today."

He chuckled. "Oh shit, I'm sure that's the reason."

He gave me a wave and took off, passing Lainey on his way to the water as she was coming back to me, the view of her completely different from before.

Hell, she was beautiful. A petite body with lean legs and a slight hint of a curve that led to her flat stomach, decorated with a silver loop that pierced her belly button. A bikini top with a set of hard nipples poking into it. The sun catching the golden highlights in her hair, the ends of her strands bouncing over her tits.

I was one lucky dude.

When she returned, she leaned down and grabbed her bag from the towel I was on. "I'm ready." She slung the strap over her shoulder and smiled.

As I got up, I wrapped the towel around my waist and shoved my feet into my slides. I didn't bother to take the cooler I'd brought. I wanted to leave the beer for the guys, knowing someone from the team would bring it home for me. "Good. Let's go."

As we headed for my car, Lainey slipped a dress on over her head, and once her hands were free, she linked her fingers with mine. "If you wanted to stay, I hope you'd tell me."

"I just want to be with you, whatever that looks like. I don't care if we're at the beach or sitting in my front seat in a parking lot—it's all the same to me." I pulled her hand up to my mouth, smelling the suntan oil she'd lathered on her body.

She patted her chest, teeth stabbing her bottom lip. "Rhett, the sweetness—stop. You're spoiling me."

"You just make it so easy." I wrapped my arm around her shoulders and pulled her close, holding my lips against the side of her head. "Thank God you're back."

Since Alyssa's party, I randomly found myself repeating that statement. I'd missed her the whole time she was gone, but having her here made me realize just how hard and how much.

She'd taken a piece of me with her, and now, I felt like I had it back.

"And I'm never going anywhere again," she said softly.

I hit the button to unlock the doors, and we climbed into the front seat, where I blasted the air-conditioning as soon as the engine was on.

I lowered the radio and asked, "Where do you want to go?"

"Well ... my mom's at my house." She rubbed her lips together. "Is anyone home at your house?"

Ridge and Rowan were both at work—where I would have been if I hadn't taken the day off.

"There shouldn't be."

"That's where I want to go, then." She looked tiny in the big leather seat of my SUV.

"You sure you don't want to grab some of that ice cream you were talking about on the way to the beach? You were bragging about that chocolate sauce like you needed it."

She laughed. "How about we stop there later when you take me home?"

"I can do that." I drove us out of the parking lot toward my place. Because I knew her and because I knew she rarely left Penelope in settings like this, I said, "Timothy assured me he'd take care of your sister. I don't know if you were thinking about it, but I wanted you to know."

"I'm always thinking about her." She glanced out the passenger window.

"In what way?"

She took a deep breath. "In every way."

I stopped at the light and looked at her.

Lainey wasn't straightedge; she just didn't get wasted. In fact, I'd never seen her have more than two drinks before she cut herself off, and she wasn't into weed at all. Penelope was the opposite. She'd been hammered at each of the parties we went to, wrecked when it was time to go home, driven by either me or one of my friends. Lainey would have to help her inside the house since Penelope was usually too fucked up to even walk.

"Do you want me to go back?" I asked. "We can take her home—if she'll even go—and then we can go to my house."

"No." She sighed. "Like you said, she has Timothy. She'll be fine."

"I can't promise he's going to keep his hands off her. I know my boy, and he's single, and the two of them looked like they were on the verge of something."

"Don't worry, she's into him too. I'm sure I'll hear all about it later." Her head tilted to the side, her shoulders slightly raised. "I can't babysit her twenty-four seven. At this time next year, she'll be heading to New York, and I won't be there to help." There was suddenly emotion in her voice. "I just have to accept that Pen is going to do what she wants, and that might be getting shit-faced at the beach and screwing Timothy in the ocean and getting home safely without me."

"Are you okay with that?" I put my hand on her thigh. "You've been in this position for a while from what you've told me." Once she had become my girlfriend, the two years we'd been apart was something she talked about, and many of those stories involved Penelope and her wildness in New York. "I can't tell if you're looking forward to the break or feeling guilty that you want one."

"Both—if that's possible."

I checked the light, seeing that it turned green. My foot moved to the gas, but my hand stayed on her leg. "It is, for sure."

"I love my sister, Rhett. I love her more than life itself. She's everything to me. But I feel responsible for her, and sometimes, it's a role I need a vacation from. And I'm sure she needs a rest from me, too, since I'm the constant bad guy. The one who cuts her off when it's time to go home or tells her to slow down when I sense she's on the verge of getting too far out of control."

I was the oldest sibling in my family. I would look out for Rowan and Ridge forever, especially Ridge, now that we were in the same school. But I didn't parent them—not in the way I'd witnessed Lainey having to do with Penelope.

"It's a lot. I get it."

"What makes it even harder is that every time we leave the house together, my dad tells me to watch out for my sister. But who watches out for me? Who ensures I'm making the right decisions?"

"Me." I squeezed her leg. "I wouldn't ever let anything happen to you, Lainey."

Her hand went to the back of my neck. "I know."

"But I know what you're saying. That's a lot of pressure he puts on you. He obviously feels like you can handle it—and you can because you're strong as hell. That doesn't make it any easier though." I reached for the hand that wasn't on my neck and clasped it. "You're in a hard spot. I'm sorry."

She tilted her body toward me. "Whenever I get into one of these moods, I remind myself that we only have one more school year together, and then, after college, who knows if Pen and I will be living near each other again? If she stays on the East Coast and I continue living on the West Coast, that's a lot of distance." Her exhale came out in slow waves. "And that thought makes me incredibly sad."

I turned onto my street and stole a quick glance at her. "As long as that sadness doesn't involve tears, I'm good with it. But there won't be any tears today, Lainey. Today is only about you and me—you hear me?"

She smiled. "I agree."

I sped up until I reached our long driveway, making my way through the gate, and I parked outside the garage. Lainey joined me at the front of the car, and we went in through the side door, stopping in the kitchen.

I opened the fridge, taking out a Coke. "Want one?"

"No."

I flipped the tab back and took a sip. "Do you want anything?"

She was staring at me, and I couldn't tell what she was thinking about. When she didn't say a word, I pointed toward the backyard even though we couldn't see it from here.

"You've already got your suit on. We can go in the pool or hot tub. Or if you feel like staying dry, we could watch a movie in the media room."

"We could." She came closer until she was standing right in front of me. "But I'd rather hang out in your room."

"Yeah?" I touched her cheek, my thumb near the corner of her mouth, circling the edge of it.

I still had the towel wrapped around my waist with my swim trunks underneath. She pulled the towel loose, and it dropped to the floor, her fingers dipping an inch beneath my waist.

"Rhett"—she swallowed, and even though there was sexiness in her eyes, there was hesitation in her voice and shyness in her touch—"I don't want to wait any longer."

My dick was instantly hard.

But I needed to make sure I was understanding what she was saying since her statement could go so many fucking ways. "Wait for ... *what?*"

She glanced toward my waist and gradually met my eyes again, her hands flattening against my abs. "To have sex."

I drew in a deep breath. "Lainey ..."

"That's what I want to do today. In your bed."

I surrounded her face with my palms and also covered it with my gaze. "I wasn't expecting that."

"I know."

I angled her neck back, pointing her chin up. "Your first time should be something you never forget. I want to make it special—"

"That's why I threw it on you like this and didn't tell you at the beach. I knew you'd want to plan something, like you did for our first date at Disneyland."

"But we talked about it at the beach. Is that why you've decided it should be today? Did I do something to persuade you—"

"Absolutely not. I've been thinking about it pretty much nonstop since we got back together. It has felt like the right time for a while. I was just waiting for the perfect occasion." She scanned my eyes. "And that's now."

I gave her a kiss. "Disney was one hell of a first date."

She smiled. "It was everything."

"I want this to be too, Lainey. The grin that's on your face as you talk about Disney—that's what I want when you talk about losing your virginity. That kind of smile, that kind of memory."

"And all I want is to be wrapped up in you."

My heart was beating away, and my fingers had a slight shake to them. "What if I want it to be more special than my bedroom?"

Lainey deserved the fucking world, and I wanted to give it to her.

Not that my bedroom wasn't a cool spot. But this was a moment that couldn't be duplicated, and I didn't want her to think back on it a few years from now and wish I could have done something more.

"What will make it special is you. Us. Together—finally. I don't need candlelight and music and a hotel room and sexy clothes or anything like that. Maybe later, down the road, when I'm past all the pain." Her eyes were pleading with mine. "But here, now, this is what I want."

I moved my nose above hers. "You sure?"

"I've never been surer about anything in my life."

I didn't lift my hands off her face, nor did I lighten my grip. "You need to know this ... you need to hear it."

"What?"

"I love you, Lainey. I loved you when I was fifteen, and I love you even more now."

She stood on her tiptoes and closed the distance between us, wrapping her arms around my neck and leaning her body against mine. When she pulled away a few seconds later—just her mouth since I wouldn't let her out of my arms—she whispered, "I love you too."

My forehead rested on hers. "I don't want to hurt you ... and today is going to hurt."

"You called me strong in the car, remember?" She smiled without any teeth. An expression that told me she was nervous. "I can take it."

"This is different."

"I know."

"But I'm going to do everything I can to make it easier on you. Believe that, okay?"

"I knew that before you even said it."

My hands dropped from her face, and I reached around her back and lifted her into my arms, her weight no more than a feather. I waited for her to wrap her legs around me before I took my first step.

She laughed when she realized what I was doing. "You're going to carry me all the way upstairs?"

My brows rose. "Do you want me to put you down?"

"No." She tightened her grip on my shoulders.

"Then, yes, I'm going to carry you to my bed."

She wasn't giving me much time to make this extra special, so even the little shit, like bringing her up to my room this way, mattered. And in return, she kissed me—the whole way to the staircase and up the long flight and down the hallway until we reached my bedroom. I kicked the door closed once we were inside and locked it behind me, finally setting her on the bed.

She gripped the edge of the queen mattress while she looked at me, shoulders caved inward, knees bent and pressed to her chest.

"Don't be nervous."

Hair was in her eyes, and she didn't move it away. "I'm not."

I knelt in front of her on the floor and lifted the bottom of her dress, caressing her ankles, which earned me a shiver. "You're sure about that?"

She let out a small laugh. "Okay, maybe a little."

I gently pulled the dress up her body and over her head, tossing it on the floor behind me. It didn't take much effort to get her bikini off; I only had to tug on the strings, and the flimsy suit was in my hand, joining her dress somewhere near the door.

This was the first time she had ever been fully naked in front of me. She'd been topless before, and when I went down her pants, her jeans mostly stayed on.

But this was hardcore.

This was a view unlike anything I'd ever seen.

"When you look at me like that"—she paused to pant—"I can barely take it."

My gaze crawled up her face. "You're beautiful, Lainey." It then dipped as low as it could from where I was positioned. "Every part of you."

She let go of the bed and dived into my hair. "It's hard to breathe again."

"It's only going to get harder, but I need you to keep breathing for me, okay? That's how you're going to get through this."

She gave a slight nod, and I yanked her to the very end of

the bed, spreading her legs apart so I could put myself between them. And while she stayed sitting, her shoulders now back and her spine upright, like when a teacher unexpectedly called on her in class, I kissed her.

But this was different than how we'd made out on the way up to my room.

This was even hotter.

I gave her my tongue, and I cupped her tits and ran my thumbs around her nipples. They were already so hard, and I knew—because I'd done this before—that she liked it when I gently pulled them. Not enough to cause her any ache, just enough to make her moan.

And she did.

With every exhale.

When that sound turned louder, relaxation coming through her posture, I rolled her nipples between my fingers and thumbs.

"Rhett ..."

"I know you like that."

"Don't stop."

There was heat already coming off her body.

I felt it in her mouth and in the spots pressed against me.

Now, I wanted to taste it.

"Are you wet, Lainey?"

"Yes."

"How wet?"

She tilted her head back, and I kissed down her throat, gradually moving to her collarbone and chest so I could take each of her nipples into my mouth.

"Oh my God." She quivered.

Instead of my hands, I used my tongue to flick them.

Tug them.

Bite them.

"Shit," she sighed. "That's ... amazing."

My eyes connected with hers, and I lowered to her stomach, tonguing around the loop in her belly button and to the top of her pussy, spreading her legs around me, giving me enough room so that my face fit in between them.

I'd never done this to her—or anyone. But I'd watched enough porn to know that this was how you made a woman really wet, and that was what Lainey needed to make this hurt less.

But that wasn't the only reason I was doing it.

If she was going to give me one of her firsts, then I was going to give her one of mine.

I wanted to know this part of her body as well as I knew her mouth. And even though I'd touched her pussy before and fingered it, this was a whole different beast. So, I took some time rubbing my fingers around her. Her breathing hitched whenever I got close to the center, and she gasped when I went low. I wasn't even using my mouth, only the tips of my fingers, going far enough to show me just how wet she was.

"What ... are you ... doing ... to me?" She was breathless.

I knew she'd never had this either, not if I was the first dude to ever kiss her. "I'm prepping you for my tongue."

"You're going to put your tongue ... *there?*"

"Yes, Lainey"—I flattened my tongue and swiped from the bottom of her to the top—"right here." I kept it high, wiggling it against her, and I wedged it between where her clit was tucked in.

The second I licked her there, she screamed, "Rhett!"

If my mouth wasn't open and my tongue wasn't out, I would have smiled. But I was too busy, my speed upping with every lick, my finger circling the rim of her pussy until it eventually slid in.

This was for her. That was the plan anyway. I just hadn't

expected to like this as much as I was. For my dick to throb every time she moaned. For the taste of her to be something I was suddenly craving.

"Yes!" she shouted. "Fuck!"

The more I did while I was down here, the more her body began to respond, letting me carefully ease in a second finger. While both were inside her, I turned them, gently pumping and stretching to get her ready for me. And with each rotation, her body moved, her hips greeting me, and she tugged on my hair like she was urging me to go faster and deeper.

I'd gotten her off before.

I knew the sounds, the feel, how she got extra wet, like she was doing now, and how there was a brief tightening and hardening of her clit.

But I also knew how coming would make her relax, and that wasn't what I needed.

I needed her wanting.

I needed her hungry.

I needed her needy.

So, I stopped all movement, like the screeching of brakes.

I gave her a brief kiss and lifted my mouth off her, my fingers slipping out.

"Ah!" She looked at me as though she were feral.

I wiped the sides of my lips, but not the middle. "You want more?"

"I want you to live there. Permanently."

I chuckled, satisfied with my first attempt, and I got on my feet and loosened the waist of my swim trunks, letting them drop to the floor. Naked, I headed to my nightstand and pulled out a condom.

"Do you think it would hurt less if you didn't wear one of those?"

I turned the metal foil in my palm. "I don't know. Maybe? My skin is probably a lot smoother than latex."

"I'm on the pill, Rhett."

"You are?"

"Not for *that*." Her legs returned to the front of her chest, her arms wrapping around them. "My periods were messy and super crampy. The doctor put me on it to regulate me."

I knew what she was saying, but I still needed to hear her voice it out loud. "You're telling me not to use a condom?"

She nodded.

"You're honestly good with that?"

"I've been on it for over a year. I take it religiously. Yeah, I'm good with it."

Then, so was I.

I dropped the rubber back in the drawer and returned to the front of the bed. As soon as I reached her, she focused on my dick, taking it in her hands, running them down the length of me.

"You're going to destroy me."

"I'm really going to try not to." I held the back of her head while she pumped me. "*Mmm.* That feels good as hell."

"My mouth would feel better." She gave me a shy smile and got on her knees so she had a better angle to give me head. "I'm not the only one who needs to be wet."

I combed through her hair. "That's true."

Her lips were at my tip. "And if you get to taste me, I think it's only fair that I get to taste you."

"You don't have to convince me." I held my base to keep me aimed at her mouth. "Do whatever you want to me, Lainey."

"Anything?" Her mouth opened, and she surrounded my crown.

Within a second, I was moaning. That was all it took for her to fill her mouth with half of my dick, sucking so hard that her cheeks added pressure from the inside, and her tongue swirled around the top.

"Fuck." My head fell back once she started bobbing, and I lifted it to see her eyes on me. "You're loving this, aren't you?"

I could tell by her movements.

From the look in her eyes. The way she was working me. Relentlessly.

She didn't answer.

She didn't need to.

But what she needed to do was stop, or this was going to end before it even began.

I popped my dick out of her mouth, letting the cool air calm me down a little before I asked, "Where did you learn to do that?"

She wiped the sides of her mouth. "Girls watch porn too, you know."

"Damn."

She was grinning as I climbed on top of her, shifting her toward the pillows until her head was on one.

"I like making you feel good." She tickled her way across my chest. "Because what you did to me, that was epic."

"You're going to get a lot more of that."

"But first, I need to survive this."

I moved her legs to either side of me, my tip banging against her every time I adjusted. "I'm going to go slow. I want you to tell me if it hurts too much or if you want me to stop." I waited for some type of recognition. "All right?"

"All right."

I added more spit to the end of my dick, rubbing it over my head, and before I pushed my way into her, halting after only an inch, I made sure she was still wet.

Her chest wasn't moving, her face unreadable.

"Breathe, Lainey."

At my command, her chest rose, but it looked like she was holding in the air.

"Breathe," I repeated.

She did, but she said nothing.

Maybe she was waiting to see what I was going to do next, or maybe she was getting her head right and preferred to do that in silence, like me at the start of every football game, or maybe even this small amount was too much.

But I needed to know.

"Talk to me," I said softly.

It took a few seconds, and she finally exhaled what she was holding in and replaced it with another large inhale. I took that as my cue to move, and I went in only a little more. I stayed there, locked, letting her get used to this new width. I was a hell of a lot bigger than the two fingers I'd used on her, so I knew this was going to feel unlike anything she'd experienced.

Since I was met with more silence, I waited until I thought enough time had passed, confident I could continue, and I went in as far as the end of my crown.

"Wow!" She gripped my wrists.

My reaction was the same, but for an entirely different reason.

This was a fucking *wow*, for sure.

She was so tight.

Wet.

Her pussy squeezed me, making me feel like I could come right now.

But I was positive that what I was experiencing was nothing like what she was going through. I assumed it was the exact opposite.

"Are you okay?"

She nodded on the pillow.

"Lainey, I need to hear your voice."

Her lips strained as she breathed through them. "I'm okay."

"Do you want me to stop?"

"No."

"Are you sure—"

"Keep going." She gripped my wrist a bit harder. "Please."

I was using all the control I had to not just slide my way in, and I had to up my restraint even more during my next shift because I was nearing the halfway point and I could really feel her, especially without wearing a condom. I'd never realized how much that layer blocked, but since there wasn't anything separating us, I felt everything.

And, fuck, it felt so good.

But I suspected the latest shift had felt even worse for her.

That killed me. I would do anything to hear her moaning again.

If I couldn't get her body in a place of comfort—at least not yet—then I could attempt to take care of her heart and mind, so I said, "I love you."

There was a change in her eyes. A hint of the smallest smile while she forced herself to breathe. "I love you."

Even if it was tiny, I believed that made a difference.

So, I used that momentum to plow my way in a bit more. That was when her chest froze, her eyes squinted shut, her nails stabbed my skin.

A tear rolled down her cheek.

But she didn't complain. She didn't call this off. She didn't even groan.

I attempted to distract her again and whispered, "I love you."

Her eyes opened, her lips slowly parting. "I love you too."

"Say it again, Lainey."

She swallowed and dragged her bottom lip into her mouth,

biting it while the tension in her legs increased, her knees shaking. "I love you too."

Since she'd had such a strong reaction to my face between her legs, I set my thumb on her clit, giving it soft strokes. Within a few swipes, there was another change in her breathing.

It sounded deeper.

Less tense.

"Lainey ..."

"*Mmhmm.*"

"I love you." I did everything I could to shut off the sensations building inside me and concentrate on anything other than how amazing this felt. But the farther I went in, the more intense it got. My balls were aching for a release. "I fucking love you so much."

"I love you."

"I need you to keep breathing for me."

She didn't respond.

"Take a big breath right now."

As I watched her lungs fill, I arched my hips and gave her the final push. "There. You have all of me."

"Rhett ..." Her eyes widened, hands clutching the blanket she was now holding.

I could feel her pulsing.

Narrowing.

Almost ... straining.

"I'm not going to move until you're ready. You tell me when."

"I think I can feel you in the back of my mouth."

I wanted to chuckle, but I wouldn't.

Not when she was feeling like this.

Her chin tilted backward, exposing her throat, hiding most of her face from me. But what that did was arch her back and spread her legs, her tits sticking out, her body fully displayed.

A sight that was fire.

My thumb had died out while I was gawking at her and was resting on her clit. I started back up, gently brushing across it, and that seemed to cause her to stir.

She looked at me, and I swore there was hunger in her eyes.

It took some time, but her muscles began to relax, and her breathing returned to somewhat normal.

"I'm going to move a little and see if you can handle it." I pushed down harder on her clit. "Okay?"

"Yes."

I went as tenderly as I could, rearing back toward my tip. She was still so wet, so tight, and that didn't change when I worked my way in.

"I wish you were feeling as good as I am right now." I stretched my hand over her side. "I wish you were fucking screaming for more." I traced my fingers over her hip. "It's going to get better. Trust me."

A pattern developed. It was no sprint; it was more like a crawl, but I kept up the movement, waiting for her body to stretch enough that the hurt would fade, the burning would lighten, and a hint of pleasure would come through.

I saw it even more when I wet my thumb and ground it against her clit. If my girl had any chance of getting off, this would do it.

Instead of giving her a full thrust, causing more friction than she needed, I went back only half the length, keeping my pumps short, but my finger adding more pressure.

"I don't know how"—she sucked in an inhale—"but this isn't as bad as it was. And this"—she reached for my wrist again—"feels really good."

"You're going to come."

"I ... don't know."

"I'm telling you, you're going to come."

I wouldn't drag this out forever. I didn't want to scar her. I wanted her to eventually love this as much as me.

I replaced my thumb with the pads of two fingers, and within a few rotations, she was moving. It wasn't a full swing, but it was enough to show me that something was happening. That she was getting there. That it was strengthening, especially when her teeth went to her lip and the softest moan came out.

"I've been fucking dying to hear that sound." I flicked her nipple, carefully tugging it, and that earned me another moan.

"Rhett ... oh my God."

"I was right. You are going to come."

The fact that, through all the pain, I'd gotten her body to this place was all it took for my body to get there too.

There was a swish in my balls, a tightening from a place deep within, a tingling that gradually lifted to the surface.

"Rhett!" Her back rounded as her hips rose off the bed, her stomach shuddering. "Ah!"

Fuck.

It wasn't just the sight of her that sent me over the edge. It was how her orgasm caused her to narrow, sucking my dick from the inside, followed by this heavy wave of wetness.

A feeling I couldn't handle.

And one that I couldn't hold off.

I pulled back on the little control I had left, and while she shouted my name again, I let everything go. "Fuck yes!" While I drained myself into her, I increased the speed of my hand. "Baby, show me how good you feel."

Her exhales were building, and within a few shifts of my hips, I was finally empty. She was still, and we became silent.

I waited for her to say something before I asked, "Are you okay?"

"Definitely okay. I can't believe you were able to get me off."

I was just glad I could. That she'd trusted me enough to even put her mind there.

"Relax your legs for me. I'm going to pull out. And I have a feeling you're going to be sore."

Her knees fell to the sides, and once my tip cleared, I saw the blood. It was on my dick, and there was some on the blanket beneath us.

I was worried it would freak her out, even if she expected it, so I rubbed my hands up her sides and over her stomach, using a calm voice as I said, "Let's get you in the shower."

"Okay." Her eyes bugged when her gaze lowered, and she saw my dick. "Wait, is that my blood?"

I hovered my body over hers and kissed her. My tongue slid in, and I wound our lips together, filling myself with her taste and breath before I separated us. "Your blood doesn't bother me. Not when I'm the reason it was there and that I got to take something so special from you." I pecked her. "But I want to clean you off since I came inside you, and I think the warm water will make you feel better after everything I just did." I kissed her cheek and her earlobe and her collarbone before returning to her lips. "And maybe, if you're feeling up to it, I can give you my mouth again."

She wrapped her arms around my neck and took several deep breaths. "You got me through the pain, and you were so gentle." She smiled. "It was perfect, Rhett. Everything about it." She rubbed her fingers over my lips. "And for wanting to even put your mouth there again after I just bled all over you— you couldn't possibly be any dreamier."

"It's because I love you. Because I would do anything for you. And because I learned today that there's nothing I like more than hearing you moan."

EIGHT

Rhett

Present Day

"*I've only hoped for one thing for the rest of my life and beyond. That I never saw you again.*"

Lainey's words weren't just echoing in my head. They were wrapping around me like a snake and digging into my skin, as though there were spikes attached to its scales.

Even though a few seconds had passed since she'd spoken that statement, she hadn't moved. She still stood only a few paces away. Close enough that I could smell the scent of her in the air.

Rose.

Fuck, it hadn't changed.

I wiggled my fingers, surprised they weren't balled into a fist. "I want to talk to you—"

"No."

"Lainey, I have so much I need to explain—"

"No!" She held out her arm, her hand pointed up, like she didn't want me to come any closer.

But I wasn't. My feet had stayed planted.

"We can go somewhere," I offered. "We don't have to talk here. There's a coffee shop a couple of blocks away that's open all night." The quietness was thicker than a dense fog. "Please."

"Rhett ..."

My eyes closed after she said my name.

I'd fucking dreamed of this.

Of hearing her voice those five letters.

Of watching her mouth part as the sound came through her lips.

"Yes," I whispered.

"I can't."

My sigh didn't even dent how badly her response hurt. "You can."

"No, I can't."

"Aren't there things you want to ask me? That you want to know about? Answers to questions you've had all these years?"

"I told you, I—"

"And I heard you, Lainey. But with the kind of past we had, I have a hard time believing you've never thought about me once. That you didn't wonder, question—*something*." I clasped my hands together, not knowing what the fuck to do with them. "I know, for me, I've waited a long time for this opportunity."

"Don't call it that. This isn't an opportunity. That gives hope, and that doesn't exist between us." She shifted her weight. "This is a coincidence. You and I, at the same place, at the same time. Nothing more."

"Talk to me."

Her head shook. "No."

"Please, Lainey. Talk to me."

"Stop asking me. I'm not going to change my mind. I came here for one thing. I would like you to leave so I can do what I need to do."

"I can wait for you." I pointed to the closest hill. "I'll stand right over there. I won't say anything. I won't bother you. You won't even know I'm here. And then I'll walk you to your car—"

Her laughing cut me off. "I can't believe you would think I would want any of that."

When I swallowed, it felt like my spit was fuel, adding to the fire in the pit of my stomach. "I just don't want you to be alone."

"I didn't have to come here alone. I chose to."

"Lainey, please, just give me a chance—"

"A chance? Are you serious?" She crossed her arms over her chest. "What you did is unforgivable. I told you that fifteen years ago. I would have thought you'd understand that by now." She nodded toward the way I'd walked here. "Go."

NINE

Lainey

Sixteen Years Ago

A s I sat across from Rhett on the other side of his dining room table, I could no longer hear his fingers typing on his laptop or the deep sighs, followed by, what I assumed, was the pounding of the Delete key.

His silence wasn't the only sign that told me he was staring at me. I could feel his eyes on my skin. On my face. A stare that I could sense even in the dark, which would cover me in goose-bumps, which would make it almost impossible for me to be still.

It had that much of an effect on me.

I glanced up, the screen of my laptop hiding my smile, but it was there, bigger than ever.

"What are you doing?" I asked.

His hands went behind his head as he leaned back in his chair. "Staring at you."

Noises outside drew my attention to the window, where I could see Penelope, Ridge, Rowan, and several of Rhett's teammates splashing around in the pool. We should technically be out there with them. Rhett's dad was out of town this weekend, and since his parents were divorced, he'd opted to stay here with no supervision rather than go to his mom's place. And since he'd had a game last night, he had today and tomorrow off from football. So, his house was now a free-for-all until we had school on Monday.

"But by staring at me, you're not getting anything done. We promised we'd finish up these college apps and then shut off our computers and have fun."

We were going into the third week of our senior year, and it was already hitting hard. I had more homework than I knew what to do with, which was why I wanted to attack the college stuff on the weekend, wrap it all up, and get it submitted.

The glimmer in Rhett's eyes told me his plan was much different from mine, regardless of what he'd agreed to.

"I should be doing that, yes. I'd much rather be looking at you."

I wiggled in my chair. I couldn't help it. "Have you finished any of the applications?" I checked my watch. "We've been at it for over an hour."

"Nah." He grinned. "But we really only need to complete one. We're going to USC. We decided that over summer break." He licked his lips. "So, there's no need to apply to Stanford or the University of California, Berkeley."

Aside from having an epic summer that had been spent at the beach, in his pool, and with all our friends, we'd narrowed down our top school choice.

"Except what if we don't get in?" The worry was in my

chest, beating away, keeping my hands on the keyboard of my laptop, refusing to lift until I was done. I couldn't imagine what would happen if one of us got in and the other didn't. That thought had been haunting me. "It's a tough school, Rhett."

"Don't worry, we'll get accepted."

"But what if we don't?" I looked at my screen, the cursor blinking on the third paragraph of my college essay, which I'd already rewritten a handful of times, each draft continuing to get worse. I shut the screen and rested my hands on the back of it, the metal cold against my skin. "We need to apply to each of the schools, Rhett. Because I don't care what you say, there's always a chance."

"False."

I let out a short laugh. "How is that false?"

"We get good grades, and we have high SAT scores. You're involved in extracurricular activities, and I'm on the football team. On paper, we look sick. We're a shoo-in, baby."

"Same for almost everyone else at our school."

"But they don't have my dad. He'll pull strings if he has to—and I'm not saying it'll even get to that, but he has the power to make it happen. All it'll take is a phone call. I've already talked to him about it."

"You have?"

He nodded.

The thought of Rhett sitting down with his dad, talking about our future plans and how we wanted to go to college together, had me asking, "What did you say to him?"

"I told him I was going to college with my girl. That I don't want to be apart from you and that I had no doubt we would get in, but if we needed some extra help, I'd let him know."

"He was cool with that?"

"Sure was."

When I'd had the same conversation with my parents, they

hadn't been surprised to hear I wanted to attend college with Rhett, considering he was the reason I'd pushed so hard to move back to LA. But they didn't want him to be the reason I attended a certain college over the other. They'd reiterated multiple times that their biggest concern was my education and they wanted that to be my top focus.

Dad was a graduate of Stanford. He preferred I go there instead of USC. Rhett's father, Ray, was a huge fan of USC football and donated to the team, which probably had something to do with Rhett wanting to go there.

"What about your parents?" he asked. "You never told me what they said when you talked to them about it."

I slowly filled my lungs.

"Shit," he groaned as he studied my face. "It went bad?"

"Not bad."

"But not good either?"

My head dropped, no longer holding eye contact. "They want me to put school first."

"And me second."

I pulled my arms back and wrapped them around my stomach. "Something like that."

"Is this going to get messy, Lainey?"

"No."

"You sure?"

I let in more air and exhaled it out. "There's no question in Dad's mind that I'm going to college with you. He just wants me to make the right choice school-wise, you know? Like, if you want USC and I want Stanford, I won't settle just to go with you."

"Are you settling?"

"Definitely not."

"Then, you'll just have to make Dean's List every semester, so he stays happy and off our backs."

I laughed. "That would please him, for sure." I glanced out the window, where Penelope was play-wrestling with one of the offensive linemen. A tower of beer cans—from what the group had already drunk today—was next to them. "I still think we should apply to the other two schools. Not as backups, but as possibilities. In case ... I don't know."

"In case what?"

My stomach did a flip. "What if, at the last minute, we decide Stanford is a better fit?" Or if my dad threatened not to pay for school, but I wasn't going to bring that up. "Or what if UC Berkeley is more our mood? I don't want to be stuck, and I don't want you to be stuck. I want to do this right ... it's a big decision."

"Come here." He pushed away from the table and tapped his lap. When I didn't move, he repeated, "Come here, Lainey."

A tingle suddenly moved its way through me. "Why do I feel like the second I reach you, you're going to try to get me naked?"

He laughed. "Because you know me, and that's normally the case." He nodded toward his patio. "But I wouldn't do that here, not when my teammates or siblings could see you. Even the thought of that makes me fucking crazy." He leaned his elbows on the table and pushed his chest into the edge of the wood. "Come here."

I rose from the chair and walked over to his side of the table, wrapping my arms around his neck, my lips positioned in front of his. "I'm here."

He kissed me, softly at first and then with much more hunger. "This is what I wanted."

He buried his face in my neck. I rested my face on top of his head, my eyes briefly closing as I breathed in his cologne. The woodsy and liquor combo was a scent I still couldn't get enough of.

"Can I tell you a secret?" I whispered.

A secret I wouldn't tell my parents.

A secret I wouldn't even admit to Penelope.

"Of course."

"I don't care where I go to school as long as I'm with you."

He lifted his head, which made mine do the same, and I gazed into his eyes.

"I fucking love you." His admission earned him a smile. "College is going to be so much better than high school. Just wait. You'll see."

"Why do you think so?"

He pecked a spot close to my ear before he moved on to my cheek. "There won't be football on my schedule—no practice, lifting—or even any work at Dad's office to occupy my time. You won't have a curfew either, so if we're not in class, we'll be together, and you'll be spending every night in my bed."

Now, there were so many things that got in the way of us hanging out. Many evenings a week, Rhett worked at his dad's office, and with it being football season, he had practice and lifting after school. Besides that, my parents wouldn't let up on my midnight curfew, and I couldn't stay the night at his house under any circumstances.

The little time we had wasn't enough.

I found myself constantly missing him throughout each day, craving the summer when he hadn't been as busy.

Which was why, when I'd found out Rhett and his siblings were going to be left alone this weekend, I had come up with a fib to tell my parents so I could spend both nights at his house. I hated not telling them the truth, but I also hated the thought that a ton of girls would show up, who would want nothing more than to be all over the hottest guy at our school.

"Every word of that sounds so amazing." I pressed my forehead against his. "I'm ready to go. Right now."

His hands went to my face. "We still have a shit ton to look forward to this school year. It's going to fucking rock, and I wouldn't fast-forward time even if I could. That would mean I'd miss out on my last season of football and skip out on us walking across the stage for graduation." He nuzzled my neck. "I'm already dreaming about taking off your prom dress."

I giggled as his lips tickled me. "You're right. This is going to be the best year ever."

"Make me a promise?"

"Okay."

"You'll stop stressing about us getting in."

No matter what, I wouldn't be able to relax until the acceptance letters were in my hand.

But I still replied, "I'll try my hardest."

The sound of shouting and laughter caused me to look outside. Penelope was in the pool, on the shoulders of the linebacker, and Rowan, Rhett's little sister, was on the shoulders of the running back. The girls were trying to knock each other into the water.

"I love how they're all outside, drinking their faces off, having a blast, and we're inside, working on college stuff." I took in his expression. "And you haven't bitched about it once."

"You wanted to get this done before Monday. This was the first chance we got. I've got all night to get hammered with those fools." He winked.

Still, he hadn't complained when I told him I wanted to finish our essays and applications before we partied. Not once had he tried to rush us through it so he could go outside and join his friends. He seemed perfectly content in here, with me, which made him my favorite person in the world.

And it made me love him even more.

"Just so you know, you've blown my mind."

"Yeah?" His head cocked to the side. "Does that mean I've earned myself a beer? And some pool time?"

"Have you finished a single application? And your essay?"

He laughed.

I tapped his chest. "I know you think this is a riot, but let's just get it done, Rhett. I don't want to put it off any longer and miss the deadline—we'd be screwed."

"You're underestimating the power my father has."

"That's not it at all. I'm just hoping we won't have to use him and we'll be able to get in on our own. I want the admissions department to love me on paper. It'll be the most rewarding feeling to know all my hard work has actually paid off."

"That's fair."

"So, we finish, and then we go join the group." I paused. "Cool?"

He smiled as he shook his head. "Lainey ..."

"Yes?"

"Lainey, Lainey ..."

"Yesss?"

His face was warming, and there was a bit of mischief in his eyes. Before I could ask what he was plotting, he was lifting me in the air.

"Rhett? What are you doing?" My legs wrapped around him, and I held on to his shoulders.

He moved us through the dining room and living room to the sliding glass door. "Probably what I should have done an hour ago."

"Which is?"

The door opened, and he brought us outside. "Get you wet."

"Wet—" The word was barely out of my mouth before he was running us across the patio and jumping into the pool.

87

With my legs and arms still around him, we sank under the water.

I didn't have a bathing suit on, just a pair of cutoff jean shorts and a T-shirt, both sticking to me as I surfaced, pushing my dripping hair off my face.

Rhett's arms stayed around me as I bobbed. He chuckled as he looked at me. "Sorry. I had to. It was the only way to get you to focus on fun instead of obsessing over these applications. We'll get them done, don't worry."

"You're the worst."

"But I thought you loved me?" His smile was bigger than I'd ever seen it.

I wiped the water out of my eyes. "I did. Past tense."

He tugged my bottom lip into his mouth, releasing it to say, "I don't believe you." He kissed me. "And what I believe is that you know I'm right."

"Right about what?" Penelope asked as she swam over, pulling me out of Rhett's grip and giving him a playful push before she surrounded me in a hug.

"That I need to stop working on college apps and start having fun," I groaned to my sister.

"You're so fucking right about that." She gave Rhett a pound. "Lain, I've been waiting for you and your hottie to come and join me out here, and you've been taking *forever*. Shots! We need shots! Where's the tequila?"

I tried to keep us afloat in the deep end while holding the weight of my sister. "No shots for me."

"Come on. You never get wasted with me." She dragged me to the edge of the pool, where there was a bottle of tequila close by that she could grab without even having to get out of the water. She poured some into three plastic cups and handed a cup each to Rhett and me, holding hers high in the air. She then wrapped her arm around Rhett's shoulders, using him to stay above the water. "To spending the weekend at lover boy's house"—she tapped her forehead against Rhett's cheek—"and to hooking up with that sexy linebacker." Her gaze shifted to the shallow end. "Oh my God, he's so hot."

"You're done with my quarterback?" he asked Pen.

She sighed. "He was summer. I've moved on to fall."

"And both of the guys know that?" he pressed.

"Who cares? It's not like things are ever serious or I'm going to marry one of them. And once I'm done with the linebacker, I'm moving on to the lacrosse team. Those boys know how to party, and I love that."

"They're also nothing but trouble," Rhett said. There was an edge of concern in his voice that I didn't miss.

I wondered where it had come from, considering the football team had a reputation for getting rowdy too.

Did he know something I didn't?

"It's our senior year," Pen replied, pulling him even closer to her. "You're the one who's harping on having all the fun, not me. Maybe you should take your own advice." She released him and held the edge of the pool, putting her glass in the middle of us. "Oh, and don't be surprised if I climb into your bed in the morning and cuddle between you two. Lain knows I like to spoon." She laughed. "Cheers."

Rhett moved slowly, but he met her cup, and I did as well.

Then, the two of us said, "Cheers," in unison.

While they leaned their heads back and downed the liquor, I pretended to do the same, except the tequila went into the pool instead of my mouth.

The last thing I was going to do was get drunk.

Someone needed to watch out for Penelope this weekend and make sure Rhett's party didn't get out of control—roles no one had asked me to take on but that I'd assigned to myself.

TEN

Rhett

"What's up, Penelope?" I said as I walked through the living room of the girls' house, getting closer to where she was lying on the couch.

I hadn't bothered to ring the bell since their parents were out for the day. She didn't look at me or respond, but her eyes were open, and her arms were raised high, her hands moving like they were dancing but no music was playing. The sight was odd enough that I paused in front of her.

"Pen?" I stood over her, making it impossible for her to miss me.

But the weird thing was, she didn't appear as if she was seeing me at all.

"Penelope?" I waited. "Yo!" I shook her shoulder. "Pen ... hello? Why aren't you answering me?"

When I pulled my hand away, she sat up like a bolt of lightning, reaching for the dark blue glass on the coffee table, and while she guzzled several sips, her eyes finally connected with mine. When they did, she almost choked mid-swallow.

"Rhett!" She wiped her mouth, returning the glass to the table. "I didn't even see you! What are you doing here? Oh, never mind. I know." She pointed behind her, to no place in particular. "If you're looking for Lain, she's up there. Somewhere."

"I know Lainey's in her room."

"Then, why are you here with me? Unless you came over to see me ..." Her teeth skimmed her lip. "Ah, Rhett, you're finally coming to your senses." She smiled as though she'd just scored a point. "Sit." She patted the spot next to her. "Tell me all the reasons why you think I'm the better twin."

I studied her blown-out pupils and the way her hands wouldn't stop moving. How there was something about the way she'd positioned her body and how her jaw was swinging that just didn't feel right.

And what she was saying—that shit felt so off too.

What the fuck is going on with you, Penelope?

"I was just making sure you were all right. That's why I'm standing here." I nodded toward her. "You're looking a little fucked up, Pen, and it's only eleven in the morning."

"I'm looking hot. And you"—her eyes dipped down my body—"are looking all kinds of hot." She took another drink and almost dropped the cup when she returned it. The glass was too dark of a blue to tell what was inside. "Besides, I'm the best ever. Just like you're the best ever. Just like"—she smiled and pointed up—"she's the best ever." She started to dance again, this time her shoulders moving, her neck sliding left and then right. "Did you hear?"

I shifted my weight and crossed my arms, wondering why I

was giving her any attention rather than going upstairs to find Lainey. In my gut, I knew something was up, and I wanted to get to the bottom of it. "Hear what?"

"I'm celebrating."

"Celebrating what?"

"All the things. For all the reasons." She turned her head, giving me a side angle of her smile. "This badass"—she thumbed her chest—"got into NYU. I'm going back to New York. Where I belong. Wanna come with me?"

"Congrats—"

"Penelope," a guy called out.

I hadn't known anyone was here; there hadn't been any additional cars in the driveway when I arrived. He wasn't in the living room; it sounded like he was in the kitchen. Whoever it was, his voice was vaguely familiar.

"I'm getting a pizza delivered. Do you want pepperoni or sausage?"

"And kill this buzz? Don't think so." She winked at me.

"Baby, I have plenty more to keep that buzz roaring." He poked his head into the living room. "You're really not hungry —" His voice cut off when his eyes met mine.

Anthony Potter.

The captain of the lacrosse team.

A dude who had rubbed me the wrong way since our freshman year. I didn't like his cockiness. His fucking attitude. And I didn't like how he thought he was invincible. Rumor was, he'd wrecked his car over the summer, and his dad paid someone the right amount of money so Anthony wouldn't get charged, and the DUI had disappeared.

"Rhett." He nodded toward me.

"Anthony." I shifted my gaze to Penelope.

Her body was still moving like she was at a club. Whatever was going on here, it wasn't right.

"You should listen to him and eat something."

"You can daddy my sister, not me." She smiled and playfully kicked my leg. "Go. She's waiting for you."

"I know you're not telling my girl what to do," Anthony said as he walked over to the couch, sitting next to Penelope. He put his arm around her shoulders and pressed his mouth against her cheek. "You need to go," he said toward her, but it was directed at me.

I didn't give a fuck what he said. "Pen?" When I gained her focus, I added, "Are you sure you're okay?"

"Never been better," she replied.

She faced him, and they started to make out.

I'd seen enough.

Whatever these two were into, it was nothing but fucking trouble.

"Holler if you need me—or if you need anything," I said.

I headed for the stairs, taking two at a time until I reached the landing. At the end of the hallway, I knocked on the last door.

"It's me." I opened it without waiting for a response.

"Where have you been?" Lainey was reclining across her bed and sat up, getting on her knees so, as I got closer, it was easier to wrap her arms around my neck. "It feels like it took you forever to get here."

I kissed her, holding her face steady, and while the softness of her cheeks rubbed against my palms, my nose filled with her rose scent. It reminded me of my mother's rose garden, but Lainey's perfume was richer and so much sexier.

And her taste—fuck, it was good. Like she'd been eating some type of gummy candy before I came over, my tongue watering as I pulled back and hugged her against my body.

"I had to drop Ridge off at a friend's house, and I was in your living room for a few minutes, talking to your sister."

Her back stiffened; her breathing stopped. "Is Anthony still here? They were hanging out earlier, and ... I had to come upstairs."

"Yeah, he's still here."

She leaned back to look at me. "I don't like him, Rhett."

"He's not my favorite dude either."

"And I don't like them together. The way he was acting bothered me so much that I couldn't be around him." With her mouth closed, she rubbed her tongue over her top teeth. "And Pen wasn't herself. She's so different around him."

I had an idea what that *different* could be. I just wasn't going to out her sister, not until I had solid proof that the two of them had been doing more than drinking. Plus, Lainey was stressed enough, and I wasn't going to add to it.

"What could she possibly see in him?" Her arms dropped from my shoulders, and she slumped onto the bed.

I climbed in next to her, wrapping her up against me. "A good time. That's what I'm thinking."

"I was sure things were going to work out with the line-backer, and then, like she'd promised, she was suddenly working her way through the lacrosse team. You'd told us they weren't good guys, and you weren't kidding."

At the start of the school year, I'd warned the sisters that the guys on the lacrosse team weren't people you wanted to mess around with. They weren't like my teammates. They were a group of guys who took partying to a whole new level, and instead of trouble accidentally finding them, they hunted for it, and they fucking craved it.

"Good thing is, you know it's not going to last." I brushed some hair out of her face. "Not when she's going to NYU next year. I doubt Anthony is going there—he doesn't have the brains to get in."

"She told you she got accepted?"

I nodded. "Just now. Downstairs."

"You don't think he could get in on a lacrosse scholarship?"

"I don't think NYU has a lacrosse team."

She sighed, and her hand went to my chest. "Even better."

I didn't want to mention that if Anthony's dad had enough money and power to get him out of a DUI, then there was a chance he could get his son into NYU. But with the way Penelope flew through guys, she'd probably be done with Anthony next month.

I held her chin, waiting for her stare to lock with mine. "There's no reason to worry—and I know you are. Your sister is obsessed with that school, and nothing or no one is going to stop her from going there. Certainly not Anthony Potter."

"Just as obsessed as you are with USC."

She turned quiet, and I wondered if she'd heard back from the three schools she'd applied to. Because there was a piece of paper in my back pocket that was burning a hole in my jeans.

"I got something in the mail today." I reached behind me and pulled out the sheet, holding it in the small space between us. "It's from USC."

"I got something from them too." She pointed across the room. "It's on my desk. Well, actually, there are a couple of things on my desk. I heard from all three schools."

"And it took you this long to tell me?"

The truth was, I hadn't applied anywhere else despite Lainey telling me to do so. USC was where we were going. There was no reason to waste my time with applications and schools I had no interest in. But when Lainey had asked if all three of my applications were in, I'd avoided answering her. Therefore, I hadn't lied; I just hadn't said anything.

I slipped the paper in her hand. "Open it."

Her brows furrowed. "You don't know what it says?"

"I didn't want to look until I was with you."

She sat up and crossed her legs in front of her. "I'm so nervous, I'm shaking."

I chuckled. "Why?"

"Because this is the moment, Rhett. The one that's going to decide so many things. What if—"

"Just open it. Please."

There were no ifs here.

Not when it came to this.

She held the paper in her lap, staring at it, and slowly unfolded until it was open in front of her, her eyes scanning the words. She filled her lungs and gazed at me, holding in the air, a smile creeping across her face. "You're in."

I know. That was what I wanted to say since I'd had no doubt I'd be going there.

"I'm so happy for you. Rhett, my God, you're a superstar. The school of your dreams and, like you said, a total shoo-in."

Without voicing a word or even showing a reaction, I got off the bed and went over to her desk, opening the envelope that had come from USC, facing her while I said, "You're in too."

Something else I knew would happen.

Whether my father had made a call, I didn't know. He had just assured me that both of us would be attending USC if we wanted to. When Ray Cole made a promise, his word was his bond.

But seeing it in writing and getting to tell her? It was the best fucking feeling.

Her hands went to her chest. "I am? Seriously?"

I couldn't stop grinning. "Yes."

"For a Bachelor of Science in nursing? Just like I applied for?"

I didn't have to look at the paper—I was that sure. "Yes, baby. Just like you applied for."

"Oh my God." She tucked herself into a ball and rocked

over the bed. "What about the others? There are still two envelopes to open."

"You want *me* to open them?"

She nodded.

I thought about my words carefully before I asked, "Because you're curious?"

"That's one of the reasons."

"And what are the others?"

"Rhett, please, the suspense is killing me." She paused. "I knew you were coming over—that's the only reason I haven't ripped open the envelopes."

I could understand the curiosity, but did that mean she was actually considering going somewhere besides USC?

A question I was going to ask once I found out if it was even a possibility since the worry could all be for nothing.

I set down her acceptance letter and picked up the next envelope. This one was from the University of California, Berkeley. I only had to read the first sentence since the wording was almost identical to the letter from USC. I picked up the final envelope and opened it, reading the first few lines before I set all the paperwork back on her desk and joined her on the bed.

She wiped her hands on her knees. "And?"

"I don't know why you questioned it. You're a badass, Lainey. Of course you got into all three schools."

"What? Stop! I did? Really?" She shook my shoulders. "You're not bullshitting me, are you?"

"Congratulations, baby." I pulled her in for a hug.

She squeezed me back. "I didn't think I'd get into all of them. I really didn't. Especially Stanford—I thought that was a long shot."

"I'm sure your dad is going to be pleased when he finds

out." I pulled back to look at her face. "I know he's been pushing you to go to Stanford."

"Yes." She bit her lip. "He has been."

I didn't want to ask. And I hated that I had to even question this. "Is that where you're going to go?"

She traced her hand across my face, starting with my eyes, moving to my nose, and stopping at my mouth. "I've thought about this so much, Rhett. What's best for me. What *I* want rather than what everyone else wants me to do."

Why don't I like the sound of this?

What the fuck caused her to change her mind?

"I swear it's been keeping me up every night," she continued. "And that was before I knew where I'd been accepted, so I was just playing all the different scenarios in my head, and it was eating away at me." She swallowed, like her throat hurt. "Would people be happy with my decision? Could they accept it?"

"What are you saying, Lainey?"

She put her hands on top of mine. "I'm saying I've made a choice. I know what's best for me and what I want."

"And that is?"

I found myself holding my breath, my insides churning, as if I was on the verge of being sick.

If she was at Stanford and I was at USC, we'd be about six hours from each other, and I feared it wouldn't work. I'd want it to, but I knew the distance wouldn't make us closer. Neither would the partying we'd do separately and the booze we'd be drinking with our friends and all the shit that came with college that would test our relationship in every way.

We could try. But four years and over three hundred fifty miles? That was a lot.

She shook my fingers, her lips gradually pulling into a grin. "USC." She winked. "Duh."

"Jesus Christ, you're killing me." I tugged her so hard against me that she let out a tiny scream, which was quickly followed by a laugh. I rolled us sideways against the bed, and I wouldn't let her go. "I really thought you were going to tell me Stanford." I needed to feel her, so I gripped her even tighter. "I was getting ready to lose my shit."

She tilted her head back from my neck and kissed me. "I know. I couldn't help myself. It was the perfect opportunity to tease you a little—something I never get to do."

"I don't like it, but I get it." I pressed my lips on hers. "Why were you so curious about whether you got into the other two colleges?"

"It's hard to explain. I guess I needed to see if I was good enough, to see if all the time I've put into school had paid off."

"Makes sense. Everyone needs their ego stroked. I have football for that, you don't."

She rolled her eyes and laughed. "And then there were certain things I needed to do to keep Dad off my back. It's up to me if I think Stanford will be a good fit. But I don't. I have no desire to go there, and he can't force me to. Besides, Pen is going to NYU. She applied to Stanford, but everyone in this family knows she wouldn't go there even if she got in. So, it wouldn't be fair if he pushed me and not her."

"What if he doesn't pay? Will that change your mind?"

Her hand lowered to my neck and then my chest. "I'll take out student loans. I'm not afraid of that."

I rubbed my thumb over her lips, breathing in the rose scent with every inhale. "Christmas is next week, which means we're leaving in only eight months." I hovered my mouth over hers. "We're doing this, Lainey."

"We are, and I cannot wait."

ELEVEN

Rhett

Present Day

I was buried under a blanket with a full glass of whiskey in one hand and a lit joint in the other, the smoke hotboxing my bed, just the way I'd dreamed about when I was at the strip club earlier tonight.

Except so much shit had happened between then and now.

And not a goddamn thing I was sucking down—not the liquor or the weed—was helping.

I couldn't get Lainey out of my head.

Her voice.

Her scent.

The way her face had looked once she shook me awake.

Being back in her presence wasn't something I had been prepared for. Neither were the feelings it'd triggered inside me.

But she'd made it clear she didn't feel the same way. She didn't want me around her. She didn't want me waiting for her.

She wanted me gone.

That didn't mean I listened.

Once I retraced my steps down the sidewalk and over the small hills, I hid behind a tree in the back of the parking lot. Not my proudest moment. I just wanted to make sure she got to her car safely.

Shit, that was what I told myself anyway.

But I also wanted to see more of her, and I'd take whatever I could get even if that meant a few seconds of watching her walk through the parking lot and climb into a Jeep and drive away.

I wondered if that vehicle was hers or if it was her parents'.

One of the many questions I had, adding to an endless list.

Once I watched her disappear, I took a rideshare home, and I'd been in this spot ever since.

It was one thing to go all those years without seeing her in person. Without hearing her voice. Without experiencing her touch.

But tonight, all three had happened.

Seeing the taillights turn to small specks of red had left me grieving in a way that consumed every ounce of me. I was empty. Lost. Desperate for something I hadn't had in a long time.

I couldn't numb the feeling.

I couldn't fill the holes that had been left behind.

I couldn't get out of my fucking head.

Every time I swallowed, every time I put my lips around the end of the damn wet paper, every time I closed my eyes— she was there.

She was looking at me.

Talking to me.

Touching me.

I couldn't stop my hands from clutching, squeezing what was in them, wishing it were her face.

This bed felt like a fucking prison, and mentally, I'd been in one for too long. I needed out. I needed to piece together why Lainey had been there tonight.

I wouldn't get that information by wasting away in this hellhole.

Since I wasn't sober enough to drive, I'd called my assistant a little bit ago, woken her out of a dead sleep, and told her to come pick me up. I could have asked Ridge or Rowan to do the same. I just wasn't ready to go there with them. I didn't want to tackle the questions that would pour from their mouths. In fact, I didn't really feel like talking at all.

Trista was the safest option. She didn't know my past—at least I didn't think she did—and she would do what she was told.

TRISTA

I'm outside.

My phone glowed as I read her message, and I kicked off the blanket, stubbed out the joint in an ashtray, and stumbled toward the door. I heard it close behind me before I climbed into her passenger seat.

"You reek," she said softly.

"Of fucking misery, I know." I took a drink from the glass I'd brought with me.

"What if I get pulled over?" She nodded toward the mostly full cup.

"It'll be gone before you even get out of the Hollywood Hills."

"And what if there's a cop waiting outside your driveway?"

The only cops in this area were the ones hired by my

celebrity neighbors, and they weren't there to pull someone over for a goddamn open container.

"I'll pay the ticket," I barked. "Drive."

"Do you want to tell me where I'm going?"

I held out my hand. "Unlock your phone and give it to me."

When she set her cell on my palm, I opened the Maps app and typed in the address, hitting Go. As the spoken directions started to play through her speakers, she pulled out of my driveway and followed the next set of instructions.

She wasn't more than fifteen yards from my house when she said, "You don't have to tell me why you called me in the middle of the night or why you're drinking straight booze in my car at this hour, smelling like you just woke up from the floor of a bar, but I need to know if you're okay."

I held the glass to my lips and swallowed until it fucking burned. "You don't need to worry about me."

She gripped the steering wheel with both hands, stealing quick glances at me. "It's part of my job."

"It's not."

"Then, consider it a friendly gesture from a person who cares about you."

I sighed as I stared out the window. "I'm all right."

Because today, I had seen the woman I was so fucking in love with.

The woman I'd been dreaming about for the last fifteen years.

The woman I compared everyone else to and not a single one measured up.

"For someone who's all right, you sure don't look it. Or sound it." She paused. "Or smell it. I'm on the verge of dry-heaving over here."

I downed the rest of the booze and put the glass in one of the cupholders. "Better?"

She laughed. "Definitely not." She went quiet again. "If you feel like talking about it, I'm a great listener."

"I don't."

"That's fair. I just want you to know you can."

Our eyes connected at the red light, and I said nothing.

I'd talked enough.

Conversation, at this point, was just getting in the way of my thoughts, and right now, I had a shit ton to think about.

I reclined the seat back a few inches and watched the view through the windshield. The drive wasn't far, no more than a few miles. A trip I could do in my sleep. But the moment Trista turned down the Taylors' street, I wasn't prepared for the memories.

They came flooding right into me.

Images of us kissing in the driveway.

The times I'd gotten her naked in her bed.

And then there were the bad ones.

The ones that made me fucking shake, like all the tears that had been shed inside those walls and the words that had been screamed and the pain that had been inflicted.

There was anguish.

Resentment.

Hatred.

All of it had been caused by me.

"Go slow," I warned.

Trista drove at a walking pace, and as she got deeper down the street, nearing the cul-de-sac where their house was situated, there was a buildup inside my chest and a fucking knot wedged in my throat.

As soon as their home came into view, I saw the Jeep in the driveway. The same one Lainey had driven tonight.

My pulse hammered away. "Turn off your lights."

"But I'm still driving—"

"Turn them off!"

It was the middle of the night. I was sure most, if not all, of these homes had exterior cameras. I didn't want her headlights to cause any alarm or bring unwanted attention.

"It's the white one." I pointed at the house even though her app was telling her how much farther to drive and when to stop. "Park here." My finger shifted to the house directly before theirs.

She pulled over along the grass, the angle not only showing the front, but also the side.

While I was memorizing the Jeep's license plate, Trista said, "Are you going to get out?"

"No."

"Then, why are we here?"

I hadn't told her where we were going or why I was having her pick me up in the first place, so I could understand how this could seem a bit odd.

But that didn't mean she deserved an accurate answer.

"Because I need to be here."

She turned off the car. "Okay."

I moved the seat up, forcing my back to straighten, and I took in the exterior of the two-story house. I didn't know what I was looking for. What I expected to find. Why I'd thought coming here would settle anything in my mind.

The only thing I got was, the presence of the Jeep told me that Lainey was staying with her parents.

But for how long?

And when had she gotten back?

I certainly wouldn't find those answers in the flower beds on each side of the front door or the stucco exterior, but as my gaze rose to the second floor, something caught my attention. A light had just turned on. Since I knew the whole layout of the home, I knew the room was Penelope's.

But the person appearing in front of the window wasn't her.

It was her twin sister.

Lainey.

She stood in front of the glass, looking outside.

"Shit, I don't want her to see me." I ducked, hiding as much of myself as I could behind the dashboard.

"Don't worry, she's gone, and I don't think she saw either of us."

I first looked at Trista and then out the windshield, confirming the first part of what she'd said. The light stayed on, and within a few seconds, Lainey reappeared. But rather than standing in front of the window again, she was pacing by it, giving me a glimpse of her face and then her back.

She didn't stop; she just kept going.

"You know ... she looks as torn up as you," Trista whispered.

How did she know that?

We were too far away to see the details of Lainey's face. What we could see was the placement of her hands, how they dug through her hair and how they gripped the back of her neck and how they rested flat on the top of her head, constantly moving, as though she couldn't find a comfortable position.

There was only one reason you paced in the middle of the night with hands that couldn't stay still.

She was as fucked up as me.

"Do you want to go?" Trista asked. "Or do you want to wait until she turns the light off and then head out?"

I didn't look at Trista. There was only one place my eyes needed to be, and that was on Lainey. "We're not going anywhere. Light on or off—we'll be here for a while."

"I had a feeling you were going to say that."

TWELVE

Rhett

Sixteen Years Ago

"You're shivering." My hand left Lainey's thigh to turn on the heat in my car. "Don't worry, it'll be warm in here in a minute."

She rubbed her bare arms. "I don't know why I'm so cold."

I held the back of her neck, hoping the feel of my skin would speed up the process even more, and I turned at the light. "Probably because it's freezing outside."

"But you're not cold."

I laughed. "I'm never cold."

"You grew up in LA. How is that even possible? The minute it dips below seventy, most people don't even know what to do with themselves. And then there's you, a sauna twenty-four hours a day, twelve months a year."

"What can I say, baby? I'm just hot." I winked at her.

"Yes, you are." She giggled.

I gave her a sly smile and focused back on the road. "Which comes in handy, considering you're always chilly."

She lifted her phone from where it had been resting on her lap. "Pen won't stop texting. She's at the party already." She took a deep, loud breath. "She wants to know when we're coming."

"After dinner"—I quickly looked at her again—"as long as you're good with that."

I heard her nails typing a reply.

"Let's see how long it takes her to tell me that's too late and we need to get there now—yep, I was right, that text just came in."

"Damn, she's fast."

"You have no idea." She groaned. "She said we can eat at the party."

The party was at Travis's house, a guy on the soccer team who had a New Year's rager every year, and since this was our last year of high school, it was bound to be the biggest one he'd ever held. All of my football dudes were going to be there. And because I knew how Penelope rolled, the lacrosse team would be there as well.

Besides the fun we were going to have, it was bound to be an interesting night.

When Lainey and I had been deciding what we wanted to do for New Year's Eve, I'd wanted to make sure that if we ended up at a party, we'd at least have some alone time together. Because once we got there—if we decided to go to Travis's—I knew that would be impossible. So, I'd ended up making us a reservation for dinner.

But my girl was consumed with guilt whenever Penelope gave her shit, like she was doing now. Lainey would become so torn, and I didn't want her to feel that way or put her in that position.

"I can turn around and drive us to the party. I swear I don't mind."

Her hand went to my forearm, the one that was still behind her head, and she squeezed. "That's not what I want. I just don't know what to say to her. She's not taking no for—" Her phone was ringing. "It's her. Of course."

"Are you going to answer it?"

"I don't have a choice." She held the phone to her ear. "Hi, Pen."

I couldn't hear what Penelope was saying. I could only hear that Lainey could barely get a word in besides, "Mmhmm," and, "Okay."

After a couple rounds of responses like that, she held the phone out to me. "She wants to talk to you."

"Me?"

She waited for me to release her neck, and she set the phone in my hand. "Good luck."

I put her cell up to my ear. "Pen—"

"Lover boy."

I chuckled. "Yeah?"

"It's completely ridiculous that you're not here yet, and since you're the one driving tonight, I'm blaming you. What could you possibly be doing to my sister right now that's making her not want to come here until later? *Ahhh*, wait, I know ... you're going down on her, aren't you?"

Jesus Christ.

Nothing appropriate ever came out of her mouth.

"Pen—"

"Rhett, you're so dirty. Where do I find a hunk like you, huh? A guy who's all about pleasing me. You don't know any, do you? Aside from yourself, of course." Her laugh sounded evil. "One day. Sigh."

I glanced at Lainey, who was staring out the passenger window. "Listen—"

"No, you listen. I want your ass here now. Got it?"

"I heard you loud and clear, Penelope."

"See you soon, lover boy."

I placed the phone in Lainey's lap. "She's a tough one."

"I know this."

My hand stayed on her leg and rubbed up and down her thigh. "I promise, whatever you want to do, I'm cool with. I don't want you to feel like you're in the middle. We can do dinner any night—"

"Pen is getting what she wants, and that's us going to the party. So what if we don't get there for a couple of hours? We'll have all night with her. That's more than enough."

I slowed for the red light. "True."

She turned toward me. "And the funny thing is, once we get there, she'll either be too fucked up to even care or she'll be off with some guy and she won't see us for the rest of the night."

I nodded. "Also probably true."

"So, all of this nagging is sorta for nothing." She played with the back of my hair. "She just needs to control every situation and loves to get her way. Most of the time, I don't mind. But sometimes, it drives me batshit crazy."

"Like right now."

She sighed. "Like right now."

"That's what happens when you have siblings. Mine are no different. It's our parents' fault for not stopping after one kid. I guess in your case, they couldn't exactly stop."

"What if I want the control?" Her voice was soft, like she was weighing the possibility. "What if I want to get *my* way?"

"The only person who's preventing that is you, Lainey."

She went quiet for a minute. "You're right." Her hand looped through more of my hair and stilled. "Will you pull over?"

"Now?" My brows rose high.

"Yes."

I glanced at her as I made another turn. "We're still about ten minutes from the restaurant. Are you all right?"

"I'm all right. I just want you to pull over ... I don't want to go to the restaurant yet." She pointed to a strip mall up ahead. "Go in there. Most of the stores look closed. Drive around the back."

I had no idea why she was asking me to do this or where her head was at, but I drove into the entrance and slowly made my way around the building.

Her hand shot up again, aimed at a spot in the center of the parking lot, far from any lights and cars. "Park there."

I backed in between the two lines and turned the car off.

She unclasped her seat belt, her body fully facing mine. "You must think I'm nuts for asking you to do this."

"Nuts? No. Curious? Yes." I pulled my hands off the steering wheel.

"Fair." She set her phone on the floor in front of her. "I guess I just need to show you my idea, then." She climbed over the armrests and straddled my lap. "I'm taking back control." She wrapped her arms around my neck.

My dick was instantly hard, my hands rubbing up and down her sides. "You want to fuck me in the front seat of my car?"

If there were light back here, I was sure I'd see that her cheeks were exploding with redness.

There was a naughty side to Lainey, and she was open to just about everything. But she was extremely shy when it came to vocalizing what she wanted.

This was huge for her.

"Is that okay?" The timidness was clear in her voice.

"You never have to ask me if that's okay." I kissed the top of her chest. "I always want to fuck you, Lainey. It's all I think about." My lips moved to her throat. "What I dream about." I pulled her face against mine. "I will never get enough of you."

The second our mouths touched, she moaned.

Her hands were in my lap, unbuttoning my jeans and lowering my zipper, reaching inside to pull out my dick.

The way she rushed through each step showed me how badly she wanted me.

It was the hottest fucking thing ever.

When she had her legs spread around me, her dress lifted toward her waist, and I slipped my hand underneath. I didn't bother trying to remove her panties or shift them to the side, where they'd get in the way or rub against us. I just ripped them off.

"Well, I wasn't expecting that." She laughed.

"You'd better be careful where you bend over at the party, or someone is going to get quite the view." I held her tighter. "A view that's only mine."

"Rhett—" Her voice cut off when I ran my finger over her pussy. "Yes!"

I didn't dip it inside her; I just used my thumb to pet her back and forth, spreading the wetness already there.

And while I teased her, she pumped my dick, going as high as my tip and as low as my base.

"Lainey ..." My moan told her how good she was doing and how she was making me feel.

With her dress tied around her neck in some complicated way, I didn't attempt to take it off. I cupped her tit over the fabric instead and tugged at her hard nipple.

She panted, "I need you."

It was like she was reading my thoughts.

She lifted up, steering my tip toward her pussy and sinking her body down the length of my shaft until I was fully inside her.

"I guess you do need me. You're so fucking wet."

And tight, squeezing me from the inside, pulsing around me.

I cranked the seat back and reclined a bit, giving her more room to move.

To fucking take.

Which she did, immediately riding me, wasting no time to buck her hips forward, rising and falling against me.

"Jesus, Lainey." I swiped her clit and instantly heard her inhale, followed by an increase in speed. "That feels good, doesn't it?"

"Yes!" Her hands were on my shoulders, her head leaning back toward the steering wheel, her whole throat exposed. "I want more!"

I could tell.

She was riding me like she wanted to come now.

Given that we were in my car—a position slightly cramped compared to what we were used to—and that we had a dinner reservation that wasn't far from now, I assumed she wasn't going to draw this out.

By the way she was taking me, working me, it wasn't going to take long. A few more flicks of my thumb while she was in this position, and she would be fucking screaming.

Shit, I would be too.

I massaged her clit, and she tightened around me, dipping down even faster than before, clutching me from the inside.

"Fuck!" she gasped. "Ah!"

She was close. I could feel it.

And what that was doing to me was making my balls tingle.

Especially as she swallowed my whole dick, her swivels adding pressure to each side, sucking all the way to my tip before she dropped again.

"Lainey!" A surge was moving through me. "You're going to make me come."

"I'm already there."

I gripped her waist, not to guide her, but to hold on because what was about to shoot out of me was the most overwhelming intensity and it was building fast.

I fisted the back of her hair and led her lips to mine. "Fuck yes." I tilted my hips upward. "Ride that fucking dick."

A wave of wetness came through her pussy, covering me as I slid through. And just when I thought she couldn't get any tighter, she began to narrow even more.

"Rhett!" She drew in air. "Yes! I'm coming!"

We moved together, our bodies slapping against each other, and while I ground her clit, I emptied myself inside her.

"Hell yeah." My tone was gritty as I rode through each ripple.

Within a few more drives, our thrusts softened; they slowed, and they completely died out until there was only stillness and breaths between us.

I hugged my arms around her, my hands lifting until they were on her face. "You can tell me to pull over anytime you want, baby."

She laughed. "You're saying you won't ever complain about it? Is that what I'm hearing?"

"That's what you're hearing."

She smiled. "Good to know."

I kissed her. "I loved it."

"I know."

"And I love you."

"Same." She pecked me. "Now, let's go to dinner."

THIRTEEN

Rhett

Present Day

My cell rang as it sat on top of my desk in my office at the headquarters of Cole and Spade Hotels, Ridge's name appearing on the screen.

What the fuck? Why won't everyone just leave me alone?

I held the phone to my ear and barked, "What do you want?"

It was seven thirty in the morning. The last thing I wanted was fucking chatter.

I couldn't believe I'd even answered.

"I've been texting you since you left the strip club on Friday night," he said. "Since you didn't write me back, I wanted to make sure you were still alive."

That felt like a hundred years ago.

My life, since then, had done a one-eighty, leaving me dangling on the edge of a cliff.

"It's only Monday," I replied.

He knew the one-week rule when it came to this time every year. Why the fuck had he even expected me to pick up, never mind reply to his text?

"Which is too long to go without hearing from you. Are you doing all right?"

Am I all right? Is he serious?

Even if I hadn't run into Lainey, my fucking brother knows better than to ask me that.

I wanted to laugh, but the sound wouldn't generate in my throat.

I no longer found anything funny.

"How about I ask this instead: do you need anything?"

I pounded my fist against my desk. "I need a lot of fucking things."

"Rhett—"

"Unless you're a magician, then don't fucking ask."

The air from his exhale hit the speaker and caused my ear to tingle.

"How about we meet up for a drink later—"

"Are you on your way to the office?" I asked, interrupting him.

It would be easy for him to come into my office and shut the door and ask to talk. But at least I wouldn't have a couple of drinks in me, like he was wanting, where my walls could fall and I'd tell him everything that had recently happened.

At some point soon, I'd have to tell him, especially because I'd assigned our assistant to follow Lainey, but I wanted to hold off having to say anything to him or Rowan for as long as I could.

I just didn't want to fucking talk about it.

"I'm headed to Jana's."

His baby mama. They were no longer together and hadn't been for a while, but they co-parented like pros for Daisy's sake.

"To pick up Daisy?" I asked. "What, are you bringing her into the office?"

"We're bringing her to school together."

Her first day of first grade.

I'd forgotten.

Fuck.

"Aren't you just the perfect parents?" I huffed. "It's too bad she has school. I wouldn't mind ditching work and spending the day with my girl."

If there was anything in this world that could get my mind straight, it was Daisy.

"I get her back this weekend. Why don't you swing by on Saturday morning and take her out for the day?"

I needed far more time than just a day.

"How about I bring her back on Sunday morning? You cool with that?"

"I'm cool with that."

Relief trickled through my chest.

It only lasted a few seconds, but at least it came.

"I'll see you when you get to the office." I hung up.

My phone hadn't even reached my desk when a text came across the screen.

TRISTA
She left the house and went to a coffee shop.

ME
Is she alone?

TRISTA
No.

Trista's assignment had been to not let Lainey out of her sight. I didn't care what that meant or what that involved; I wanted my assistant's eyes on her at all times. And while doing that, she wasn't allowed to have her cover blown. The last thing I needed was for Lainey to know I was having her followed.

ME

Who is she with?

I held my fucking breath, my thumbs hovering over the letters.

TRISTA

Another woman.

More relief passed through me. I didn't know why. She could be dating or married, and I had no right to feel anything if she was. It had been fifteen years since she had been mine. But I had a feeling if she was in something long-term or had gotten hitched, she would have posted a picture of the guy on Instagram. Since she'd opened the account, she'd only ever shared solo photos or ones with other women.

ME

Let me know when she leaves.

TRISTA

What about work? Don't you want me in the office today?

ME

I told you what I want you to do.

TRISTA

Who will assist you and Ridge?

ME

The only thing you need to worry about right now is making sure you don't lose Lainey and that she doesn't see you.

TRISTA

She's at the mall.

ME

Alone?

TRISTA

Yes. But before she went to the mall, she had lunch with someone. A guy.

ME

You didn't tell me ...

I need details. Who is he? What does he look like? What's his fucking name?

TRISTA

I took a few pictures. That's all the information I have.

The first photo that came through showed Lainey and him at a table, sitting across from each other. She wasn't smiling; they weren't touching either. It looked like they were just talking. The second picture she sent was a much better angle of him. And as I studied him, I realized I recognized him.

He was Benny, her cousin, whom I'd met several times.

ME

Keep me updated. I want a text every time she goes anywhere new and pictures of who she's with. Got it?

TRISTA

Yep.

ME

And if, at any point, you get the sense she's heading to the airport, I need you to get ahold of me. I don't care what you have to do— find me.

TRISTA

She just left the rental office of an apartment building, and there was a key in her hand. Pretty sure the key wasn't for her car.

ME

Where?

TRISTA

West Hollywood.

ME

Send me the address.

Where is she headed now?

TRISTA

Looks like she's on her way to her parents' house.

TRISTA

She picked up a few empty boxes, and she's carrying them into her parents' house. All signs point to her moving from their house to the apartment building in West Hollywood.

ME

When she does, I need to know.

TRISTA

You still don't want me at the office?

ME

I need you doing exactly what you're doing.

TRISTA

I just got an email from HR. Every day I've spent away from the office as your private PI, they've deducted it from my vacation time. Rhett, please do something.

ME

I'll take care of it.

TRISTA

Maybe I should just come back to the office? And start working my real gig instead of this?

ME

Trista, you're the only one I can trust with this. Don't fail me now. I need you.

TRISTA

I just don't want to get in trouble with HR.

ME

I'm one of the owners of the company. HR is not going to argue with me when I tell them to reinstate your vacation time. Stop worrying.

> **TRISTA**
>
> I got an email from HR. Thank you, Rhett. I feel a lot better now.

> **ME**
>
> Any updates on Lainey?

> **TRISTA**
>
> She's with a friend for happy hour. I'm sending a pic in a second.

> **ME**
>
> Male? Female?

> **TRISTA**
>
> It's a woman who looks so much like her that they could be twins. They even smile the same, it's wild.

My stomach churned as I read her last message, my hands balling into fists. There was a burning in my chest, like someone had dropped a lit match in a pool of gasoline and the flames caused the acid to rise from my gut and rush to my throat.

With my closed fingers, I pounded on the center of the fire, telling the food I had inside of me to stay in.

My eyes were closed when my phone vibrated with another message, telling me the picture Trista sent had come through.

I couldn't look at it.

I couldn't even be around it.

I left my phone on the desk, rolled back my chair, and walked out of my office.

As I passed Ridge's door, I heard, "Hey, Rhett, are you leaving? I need to talk to—"

I didn't turn around.

I didn't answer.

If he said anything more, I stopped listening.

I just kept going until I reached my car and slid into the driver's seat. I shifted into first gear, and I peeled out of the parking lot.

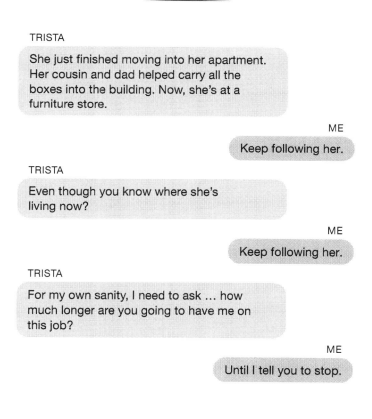

TRISTA

She just finished moving into her apartment. Her cousin and dad helped carry all the boxes into the building. Now, she's at a furniture store.

ME

Keep following her.

TRISTA

Even though you know where she's living now?

ME

Keep following her.

TRISTA

For my own sanity, I need to ask ... how much longer are you going to have me on this job?

ME

Until I tell you to stop.

"Uncle 'Ett," Daisy said, turning her upper body toward me while she sat in the pedicure chair, "you need pink sparkly toes, just like me. I want to be twinsies."

Her feet were in the water, and flowers were floating around her ankles while the nail tech wrapped her shins and knees in something gold and leafy.

Daisy only got the best.

I made sure of that.

"You want *my* toes to be pink?"

Every time I hung out with my niece, which was as often as Ridge would let me have her, she somehow convinced me to get my toes done. When I tried to just be a spectator and not participate, that wasn't good enough. If Daisy was getting a pedicure, she wanted me to get one too.

"Not just pink. Sparkly pink." She smiled and giggled.

I looked at the chick who was sawing my heels with a stone. "We'll have matching toes."

She whispered something I couldn't hear to the woman doing Daisy's feet, and the two of them laughed.

I didn't blame them. I didn't exactly give off pink-toe vibes.

While Daisy sipped her strawberry milkshake that was left over from lunch, I said to her, "I can't believe you started first grade. You're growing up way too fast, my girl."

She pulled back from the straw, and a smear of pink ice cream was somehow above her top lip. "I'm so old."

I wiped it off, dunking my hand in the soapy water after. "Yes, you are. Don't get any older on me, all right?"

"I want to be a big girl, Uncle 'Ett, so Daddy can buy me a car, and I can go to the beach whenever I want."

"You're never driving—do you hear me? You're also never going to the beach without your father or me. Or dating. Or—" I cut myself off, positive I'd made my point.

But it wasn't enough because the thought of my little one being around dudes—dudes like me—was something I couldn't fucking handle.

"Uncle 'Ett, but I want to have matching cars with you. I'm going to paint mine pink, and you're going to paint yours pink, and we're going to go everywhere together."

"A pink car?"

I hoped to hell she never asked for that. As much as I'd like to think I wouldn't drive a car that was that color, she could convince me to do just about anything.

"Pink everything." She giggled again.

There were curls—in her eyes, bouncing on her forehead, sticking to her cheeks.

God, she was adorable.

"Do you think, someday, pink won't be your favorite color?"

"Nope."

"What about purple?"

"Ack."

"Green?"

"Ugh."

I shook my head. "I give up. Tell me about school. How's your teacher? How are your classmates? No one's giving you a hard time, are they?"

"School"—she wiggled in her seat with a huge smile—"it's all kinds of awesome-blossom. My teacher is named Miss Lark, and I love her. She's extra pretty."

"Yeah?"

"And she also loves the color pink, and she listens to Taylor. Like, how cool is that?"

"Taylor?"

"Swift, Uncle 'Ett. You *knooow* who Taylor is."

I laughed. "I was just testing you." I glanced down at the nail tech as she wiped my toes with cotton, getting ready to paint them. "Do you have a best friend in your class?"

"Yep. We eat lunch together, and she gives me her sandwiches sometimes, like on the days Daddy makes me lunch." Her eyes went big, and she cupped her hands around her mouth, whispering, "Don't tell him, okay?"

"Your secret is safe with me."

"His sandwiches aren't like Mommy's. They're ... jiggly."

"Jiggly?"

She nodded, more curls bobbing into her eyes. "I don't know what he does, but *ewww*." Her nose scrunched, and her little lips curled.

"So, your bestie gives you her sandwich?"

"They're so yummy, like the ones we get at that sandwich place you sometimes take me to."

"That's a really good bestie to have, Daisy. Whatever you do, don't lose her."

"She hates bread." She held up her hands. "She's a weirdo like that, but I love her to pieces. I give her my crackers. The ones Daddy packs me have these spices on them, and they make my tongue stinky."

My brother tried his hardest, and he was one hell of a parent, but it sounded like he needed improvement in the packing-lunch department. Which didn't make much sense, considering we shared a private chef.

"She doesn't mind having a stinky tongue?" I asked.

She shrugged. "But I hate talking to her for the rest of the day 'cause I can smell the crackers, and"—her jaw dropped further—"it's so bad that I cringe."

"Maybe you need to bring your bestie a piece of gum."

"*Ohhh.* I didn't even think of that! One of those big balls from the gumball machine in your theater room. That's what I'm going to do." She paused. "Uncle 'Ett, why aren't there more pink balls in the gumball machine?"

"You ate them all."

A devilish look came across her face. "I did not!"

"I pulled the camera feed from a few weeks back, and I saw you reaching into the glass and sneaking out all the pink balls. Caught you red-handed, girlie."

Her lips formed an O. "You *saaaw?*"

"I saw."

"Am I in trouble?"

"You're in all the trouble. You're going to bubblegum jail."

She laughed as though that was the funniest thing she'd ever heard. "Uncle 'Ett, I want you to have a baby."

My head snapped back, and my eyebrows went so fucking high that they hurt. "A baby?"

"I want you to have one like Auntie Rowan and Uncle Cooper so I can play with it and dress it up and do its hair in cute little bows if it's a girl."

I couldn't believe this kid.

Sure, I was the only one in the family who didn't have a child now that my sister was with Cooper Spade and they'd had their daughter, Rayner.

But being the single one out meant nothing.

I wanted children. I wanted them more than anything.

But there was only one person I wanted them with.

And that woman wasn't mine.

"You have a better chance of convincing your father to give you a sibling than for me to give you a cousin."

Given that Ridge was as unattached as me, that was going to be almost impossible.

"I asked Daddy for a sister or a brother before you came to pick me up, and you know what he said?"

"What?"

"That I should ask you for a baby."

I reached across the small space between our chairs and held her chin. "Tell your father he needs to stop encouraging me to have a baby."

"Why, Uncle 'Ett?"

"Because people like me don't have kids."

Her tiny eyebrows pushed together. "Why would you say something silly like that? You're the best uncle ever, and that means you'd make the best daddy ever."

There was nothing I worked at harder in my life than being good to this girl. And once Rayner was a little bit older and able to hang like Daisy, I'd do the same with her.

But hearing this come from my Daisy, shit, my fucking heart was melting.

"Uncle 'Ett?"

"Yes, baby?"

"Promise me something?"

"All right, I'll make you a promise."

"One day, you'll give me a little cousin to play with, even if it's a hundred years from now?"

"A hundred? I don't think I'll be alive to have any kids in a hundred years."

"*Okaaay*, then fifty."

"Fifty years is a stretch too, Daisy."

She gave me the widest smile, followed by the sweetest giggle. "Whenever it happens and if it's a girl—and I really, really hope it is—then she'd better make you take her for pedis and have you paint your toes pink."

I couldn't help the grin that pulled at my lips. "Yeah?"

"You know why?"

"Why?"

" 'Cause I wouldn't ask just *anyone* to take me for a pedicure and to paint their toes pink. I only ask people I love extra much. Like you."

As soon as my phone started to ring, I turned it to silent and quietly held the cell up to my ear, hearing Ridge say, "How's my girl?" the moment the call connected.

"Are you really checking up on us?"

I kept my voice down even though I didn't have to. Daisy could sleep through a goddamn hurricane.

"Checking up? No. If that were the case, I would have called a lot earlier than nine at night. But am I inquiring? Yes. I fucking miss her, all right? Jana had her all week, and you have her tonight. I feel like I haven't seen my baby in months."

"We had a hell of a good time today. She kicked my ass in Putt-Putt and *somehow* convinced me to go for pedicures because she simply couldn't survive another minute unless her toes were pink and sparkly—"

"Hold on. *You* got a pedicure?"

"Do you honestly think she gave me a choice?"

He laughed. "Man, she has you whipped. Keep going."

"Dinnertime hit, and the princess demanded tacos, so that was what we had, followed by a movie. She made it a solid ten minutes before she fell asleep in my theater room, and that's where she currently is, passed out on my chest."

I popped a red Starburst into my mouth since Daisy had eaten all the pink ones. My home theater was stocked with all her favorite candy since, apparently, this was as much her house as it was mine.

"Don't tell me you made the tacos?"

"Fuck no. You know me better than that." As her head lay on me, her tiny snores vibrating against my chest, I gently brushed the curls off her cheek.

"Wait until she asks for an egg burrito for breakfast—that's been her favorite lately. Or French toast—her second choice with warmed-up syrup and cinnamon butter."

"Jesus," I groaned. "Tell me you're fucking kidding."

"The kid likes good food. What can I say? She has my palate."

I thought about the conversation I'd had with Daisy over pedicures, when she'd called my brother's sandwiches jiggly.

What the fuck is jiggly?

"It's a good thing our chef will be here in the morning," I said, reminding myself to have a talk with him and make sure he was the one who took over lunch-making duty. "That's a project he can tackle, not me."

"What time do you want me to pick her up?"

I paused the movie since this conversation was lasting longer than I'd thought it would. "I can drop her off. I'll text you in the morning and figure out a time. It won't be early. Daisy and I will be sleeping in."

"If you can get her to sleep past seven, it'll be a miracle."

"You don't know the power of Uncle 'Ett."

He laughed.

But there was other noise in the background, sounds that told me he was on the road.

"Where are you?" I asked. "I can tell you're driving somewhere."

"A place I probably shouldn't be."

A place he shouldn't be?

I thought about a conversation we'd had at work not too long ago, when he told me about the woman he'd met at the strip club the night of the bachelor and bachelorette party.

That motherfucker was going back for round two—I would bet my life on it.

"Are you at the fucking strip club?"

"I'll see you tomorrow," he said and ended the call.

TRISTA

> She's at a bar, sitting at the bar top, having what looks like a vodka tonic.

ME

Who's she with?

TRISTA

She's alone.

Fuck.

I glanced down at the top of Daisy's head; she'd been asleep on my chest for a couple of hours now. I wouldn't wake her up, nor could I exactly bring her to a bar. Although I'd probably have a better chance of Lainey talking to me if I showed up with a cutie like Daisy.

ME

Let me know if she leaves.

As I hit Send, I almost regretted it.

Because if Trista told me a guy joined Lainey or bought her a drink, I'd fucking lose it.

And if she told me she went home with one?

Shit.

I wouldn't be able to control my jealousy.

A jealousy that would turn to rage.

FOURTEEN

Lainey

Fifteen Years Ago

As I stood in front of the full-length mirror in my bedroom, my cell began to ring from the back pocket of my jeans. Penelope's name was on the screen, so I answered and brought it up to my ear.

"Hello—"

"Where are you?"

I glanced toward Rhett as he sat on the end of my bed. "Home. But only for a couple more seconds. We're leaving—"

"You're coming here, right?"

"Coming where?"

Rhett's arms were stretched out behind him, his long legs extended in front of him, his heels resting on the carpet. I could tell he was curious about the conversation I was having with my sister as his head cocked to the side. I just couldn't get over how hot he looked. The first two buttons of his shirt were undone, showing hints of his chest. His backward baseball hat made his smile pop, and then there was the thickening of his scruff that, in the last couple of months, had grown to cover even more of his cheeks. Especially now since he hadn't shaved in a couple of days.

But it was his position that was really setting me off.

It was like he was inviting me to climb on.

"Elijah's house," Pen said, reminding me we were on the phone. I'd almost forgotten. But I was holding it away from my ear and she had talked loudly enough that Rhett could hear. "The party. I told *youuu.*"

What she had told me was that she was going to the mall with a couple of girls who were dating guys on the lacrosse team and they were going to do some shopping with one of the guys' credit cards. And I had told her Rhett and I were going to the movies. I'd just finished getting ready, and we were going to grab some pizza and then head to the theater.

"You're at Elijah's house now?" I asked.

I already knew the answer to that question. Unless the mall was blasting music, which I highly doubted.

"Yes. You need to be here. It's so fun, Lain. Everyone is here."

"Who's everyone?"

"Everyone," she repeated, drawing out each syllable, almost making the word into a long sentence.

Do you want to go? Rhett mouthed.

I shook my head.

Then, tell her we're not going, he mouthed.

It was a statement I wanted to say; it was just hard to get out. Because the thought of turning her down caused dread to spread through me.

I never said no to my sister.

I didn't have it in me because I needed to look after her—no one else would.

I swallowed, forcing the words to the surface, shutting my eyes as my mouth opened. "We're not going to make it, Pen. We have plans. If I'd known about the party—"

"What? You're really not coming?"

My eyes opened. "No."

"Lain, stop it. I know you're joking. I'll see you in an hour. Or less. It'd better be less."

"Pen, I'm not joking. We're going to sit this one out. But you have fun and please be careful."

There was a tightening in my chest as I thought of her there without Rhett or me. One of us—usually both—always attended the parties my sister went to so I didn't have to have this conversation with her. So I could make sure, with my own eyes, that she and everyone else was safe. Something so important to me. I couldn't wait to be a nurse so I could do the same in a hospital.

"Don't forget to be home by curfew, or Dad will have your head."

She laughed. "Right. 'Cause I'm so good at doing that."

"Be careful," I emphasized again. "Seriously."

"I always am."

I laughed. "That's not the truth at all, but do it this once. For me." I paused. "Okay?"

"Yeah, yeah."

The phone went dead, and I shoved it into my back pocket, taking a few seconds to catch my breath. The feeling in my chest hadn't gone away. If anything, it was worse now that I could no longer hear her voice.

"If you change your mind, we can go to the party," he said. "Whatever makes you happy, I'm down for."

I hadn't even said anything, and he knew.

I walked over to him and climbed on top of his lap, strad-dling him with my knees on the bed, my arms resting on his shoulders. "I love you for that, but no. I want to do what we planned."

He held my hair off my face. "You sure?"

"The only reason I'd want to go to the party is to make sure she's safe. Which is crazy, I know. It's March, for Christ's sake. She's going to be leaving for college in five months. It's time I stop babysitting her."

And it was time I stopped worrying. Penelope could take care of herself—I was positive about that. She got straight A's, she had gotten into NYU, she had a perfect driving record, she'd never even had a cavity.

So, why do I feel the need to constantly watch out for her?

He gave me a kiss before he said, "The way you care about her is something I love about you."

I narrowed my arms around his face. "Really?"

"That motherly, nurturing side of you is adorable. How you can't go to sleep unless you know everyone is okay. How you look out for everyone at parties. Yes, Lainey, I love it."

I took a deep breath. "Good, because I don't know if I can change that about me, but what I do know is that I haven't changed my mind about going to the party. Dinner, movies—that's what I want."

He smiled. "Then, let's go."

"Stay here," Rhett said as he shifted the car into park, unlocking his seat belt and opening the driver's door. "Don't move, okay?"

This was our first stop after leaving my house, and I'd assumed we'd reached the pizza shop, although this wasn't the plaza where the shop was located unless he was taking me somewhere new. Either way, I couldn't imagine why he didn't want me to get out of his car and join him.

"Are you up to something, Rhett Cole?"

He laughed as he got out, looking at me through the open doorway. "Never."

He smiled and closed the door behind him, and I was suddenly alone in the idling car.

I checked out the plaza again, reading the signs to see if there were any I recognized. I hadn't really paid attention to where he was driving. My mind had been on Penelope.

It still was.

Even though Rhett had said he loved this about me, I hated it. I couldn't entirely focus on everything we talked about on the way here because all I could think about was Pen at the party and what she was doing and how she'd get home.

How was I going to survive four years away from her?

Maybe it would be easier than I thought. She'd be so far away; I wouldn't know what she was getting into—or what she wasn't getting into—and she wouldn't constantly be at the front of my mind.

But until then, she wasn't only front; she was center too.

I dug inside my purse to find my phone and pulled up our last text.

ME

How's the party?

PENELOPE

Puuuuurfect. If you were here, you'd know. Asshole.

ME

I'm going on a date with Rhett. That's hardly asshole-ish.

PENELOPE

You guys have all of college together. We don't.

ME

I've lived with you for 18 years, Pen. I even shared a womb with you. You act like we've only had minutes together.

PENELOPE

We're not 18 for a few more days. 😉

ME

Close enough.

PENELOPE

Stop texting me and go have fun on your date.

ME

Love you. 🖤

PENELOPE

Love you way more. (You're still an asshole though.)

The sound of the door opening caused me to look up, and I slipped my phone back inside my purse. Rhett was placing a big bag in the backseat, making sure it was secure before he climbed into the front.

I turned around to inspect it. "What's that?"

"Food." He reversed out of the spot and pulled onto the road.

"I see that, silly." Even though the bag was large, there was no way it was holding a pizza box. "I thought we were getting pizza?"

"Change of plans."

"Change of ... plans?"

He slowed at the light and looked at me. "I wanted to do something a little different tonight. I didn't think you'd mind."

It was dark outside and in the car, so I couldn't really see his face. The traffic light and the adjacent vehicle lit random spots, giving me hints of his expression. But it was enough that I could see his smile and how huge it was.

One so big and addictive that my lips tugged wide. "I don't mind at all."

He reached for my hand and brought it up to his mouth. "You see, there's a certain someone in this car who's turning eighteen next week."

"I wonder who that could be."

He kissed my thumb. "It can't be me. My eighteenth birthday was last month."

I giggled. "I guess that leaves only one other person."

"We're going to be in school over your birthday, Lainey. I thought we could celebrate tonight. Not with your sister and our friends and family. Just us."

I didn't know how it was possible, but my grin was even bigger.

"Does that mean we're not going to the movies?"

He kissed the tops of my other fingers. "No, we're not going to the movies." He nibbled on my middle knuckle. "Unless you're dead set on seeing—*shit*, I don't even remember what you said you wanted to see."

I laughed. "I just wanted to be with you, Rhett. I never cared about what movie was picked."

"My girl." His voice was soft. "The good news is, you won't have to wait long to find out what I have planned. We're almost there." I felt his eyes on me. "And I know you love surprises, which is why I didn't tell you about any of this."

"I do. I love them so much."

He squeezed my fingers. "And you're going to love this one."

He pulled into a lot and turned off the engine. This time, I knew where we were. I'd only been to this park once before, and it had been years ago. What stood out the most was the scenery. The whole area sat up high with LA below, the lights of the city so bright that they illuminated the entire park.

Rhett grabbed the bag of food from the backseat and a few things from the trunk.

As I joined him outside, I held out my hands. "Let me help."

"I've got it. Just find us a good spot to sit on the grass."

I led us toward the back side, as close to the cliff's edge that I could get us, where the view was the best. "I think right here." We were so high up; it almost felt like we were in a plane and I was looking at all the lights out the window. "Definitely right here."

He set down everything he was holding, except a blanket, and he spread it out over the grass. After we sat, from a small cooler, he took out a Diet Coke, placing it in front of me, and a Coke for him. From a canvas bag, he removed some silverware and napkins and paper plates.

I watched in awe. "You're kinda cute."

"Yeah?"

"You thought of everything. I'm impressed."

"I even thought of this." He placed a small votive candle between us, the scent of vanilla strong when he lit it. "I stole it from Mom's house. I thought it would be a better idea than the candlesticks from my dad's dining room table. I was afraid those would fall and set the blanket on fire, and that was a situation I didn't want to deal with."

"Good call." I put my hand on his arm. "This is so perfect."

He was quiet for a moment. "Do you know why I chose this spot?"

I tried to trace back and think of every possible reason. "No."

"The first time I saw you and talked to you was in gym class freshman year, but the first time we hung out was right here at this park."

"It was?"

He nodded. "I told you that a bunch of us were coming here to hang, and you showed up with Penelope. It was a Friday night, after one of my football games." He pointed to the left, on the other side of the grass. "We were over there, the whole group of us, and I got you to walk with me over here." He pointed down as though where we were sitting were the same blades of grass as before.

The memories were slowly unraveling, and I whispered, "I remember."

"We talked right here until you had to go home. And that night was the first time I touched you." He was gripping my fingers. "It was only your hand, but back then, that felt like a lot." He gave my fingers a squeeze. "I guess this place will always be special since it's where it all started for us."

"Rhett ..." I swallowed, the emotion thickening in my throat. "I was wrong. You're way more than cute."

He chuckled. "Didn't think I was sentimental, did you?"

"*Hmm*, I don't know. I wouldn't put anything past you."

"There's more where that came from, but right now, it's time to eat." From the large bag, he took out several to-go containers. "I got a bunch of Italian. My dad swears by this restaurant. They just opened, so I haven't had a chance to check it out, but Dad says it's as good as what we've eaten in Italy. There's calamari and meatballs for an appetizer"—he set those two containers in front of me and opened them—"and for the main course, there's chicken parmesan, spaghetti with meat sauce, fettuccini Alfredo, penne with vodka sauce, and of course, garlic bread." Every time he mentioned a new dish, it would appear from the bag, the plastic top coming off and a whole new scent filling the air.

"I think I might be drooling." I wondered how we were going to even make a dent in all this food. "This is incredible, Rhett. I don't even know how to thank you."

"And there's tiramisu for dessert."

My head shook as I looked at him. I couldn't stop the movement; I was just totally blown away by all the effort he'd put in. "I can't believe you did this all for me."

"This is just food, in a park that overlooks the best view of LA."

"Not just any park. The park where we had our first meetup."

He smiled. "One day soon, when your parents are no longer controlling how late you stay out and where you spend the night, I'll take you to Italy, and you can compare the meals."

"Italy?" My brows rose high.

"My father has a hotel in Rome, and we went last summer. It's gonna blow your mind how sick that city is."

"I'm sure that would be incredible. Really. But so is this, Rhett." I reached for his hand. "In my mind, this is as good as Italy."

"I'm glad you like it."

I turned toward him, knowing the food was getting cold, but I needed to get this out before I even considered putting any of it in my mouth.

"I dreamed of this, you know. Of being in a place like this with you. Of getting to hold your hand and kiss you. Of giving you things I've never given anyone else." The shyness was creeping through me, and I was thankful it was dark and there was only candlelight and city lights so he couldn't see how red I was getting. "And those dreams have now come true. And it's getting even better because I get to go to college with you." I took a breath, the emotion building in my eyes. "I just feel so lucky that this has worked out better than I could have ever imagined. And the best part is, I get to tell you *I love you*. Every day, if that's what I want."

"And every day, I get to show you how much I love you." He leaned closer to my face. "I was going to wait until after we ate to reveal my next surprise, but I don't know if I can."

"What is it? I'm dying!"

He kissed me and sat up straight again. "When I was a kid —we're talking eight or nine—I overheard a fight between my parents. It was a bad one, and even then, I knew their marriage was done. I left them downstairs and went up to my room. I was listening to music when my dad came in and sat on the bed with me." He ran his hand over the top of his head. "He looked defeated. Tired. For a kid who knew nothing at that age, I knew what I saw. And what he said to me that night was something I never forgot. He said, 'Rhett, you are my why.' "

Rhett's head dropped, and it seemed like at least a minute passed before he lifted it and began talking again.

"It took a while before I knew what that statement meant. Freshman year, I got hints of it when I met you. The happiness you made me feel, the way my stomach tightened whenever I thought about you. But since you've been back, I've understood it on a whole different level, and Dad's statement makes perfect sense to me."

He cupped my face. "Lainey, *you* are *my* why."

His lips met mine and stayed there, softly kissing me, and when he pulled away, he undid a few more buttons of his shirt —the top was already unbuttoned—and he slipped his arm out, extending it horizontally to show me the inside. He picked up the candle and held it near his skin, where words were tattooed from his armpit to his elbow.

YOU ARE MY WHY, LAINEY.

My heart exploded as I read the words again and again.
My name is really inked on his body?
He loves me that much?
I'm his why?
"Rhett, oh my God." I wrapped my fingers around the tattoo, curious if it would feel different, if the ink would have texture. I learned that the black words were as smooth as his skin. "I'm obsessed with it and in shock and losing my mind over this. It's everything." I gently traced the letters. "When did you get it?"

"Last week. That's why I've been wearing long-sleeved shirts to school. I wanted it to heal a bit before you saw it."

"I can't believe you did this. For me." I slowly glanced up at him, and even though his eyes were dark from the night, I could feel the intensity of his stare. "I love it. I love you. So much."

He slipped his arm back into his shirt. "There's something else."

"No." I put my hand on his chest. "There can't be. This is all more than enough."

He laughed as he reached into his pocket, pulling something out that he held in front of me. "Happy eighteenth birthday, Lainey."

"I can't."

"You can." He set a box on my hand. "Now, open it."

The box was wrapped in paper, the bow on top flattened because it had been in his pocket.

"Open it," he repeated.

I carefully tugged at the ribbon and tore the side of the

wrapping paper, sliding out the velvet box. As I lifted the lid, he held the candle nearby so I could see the jewelry inside.

My hand went over my mouth. "Rhett!"

There was a thin, dainty silver chain with the letter R hanging in the center, made of all diamonds.

"Oh my God, it's so gorgeous!" I rubbed my finger over the letter the same way I'd done to his tattoo. "You bought me diamonds ... are you insane?" I couldn't hold back the excitement. "It's the most beautiful thing I've ever seen in my life and definitely the most thoughtful gift anyone has ever given me."

He set the candle down and took the necklace out of the box, holding it around my neck and clasping it. "You're permanently on my body, and now, when you wear this necklace, I'll be permanently on you."

The second the R hit my throat, I wrapped my fingers around it, my eyes filling with tears, and I leaned forward and kissed him. "You are my why, Rhett." A tear left my face and dripped onto his, the single drop glistening under the moonlight. "And you will be for the rest of my life."

FIFTEEN

Rhett

Fifteen Years Ago

When Lainey and I left the park and got into my car, the diamond R necklace now hanging from her neck and the tattoo on my arm no longer a secret, the clock on my dash showed she still had thirty minutes before her curfew.

We weren't far from her house; it would take me no time to get her home.

Before I turned on the car, I looked at her. I knew she'd had the best time tonight, that she had been surprised by everything I'd planned. She appreciated that I'd taken her to the park and brought food and her gifts. But underneath her happiness and the way she'd loved up on me, there was something eating at her.

It was Penelope.

No matter how hard she tried, she couldn't get her sister off her mind. She was worried about what Penelope was doing at Elijah's party, the unknowns endless since she wasn't there to keep her eyes on her twin. And she was nervous that Penelope wouldn't get home in time for their curfew.

Before we had gotten to the park, I had given Lainey the choice of going through with our date or going to the party. She had chosen the date, and I believed that was what she'd truly wanted.

I also knew that if Lainey got home and Penelope wasn't there—and she wouldn't be—she'd feel sick until her sister showed up.

I had the power to ease that.

"Rhett, what's wrong?" Her voice was soft, her hand moving to my face as I continued to stare at her silently.

It was obvious something was going on since I still hadn't started the car.

"We're going to stop by the party and check on Penelope. I'll give her a ride home if she needs one."

"Really?" I could hear the surprise in her voice even though her tone hadn't gotten any louder.

But what had changed was her grip. It became more loving, if that was even possible, her thumb rubbing the side of my mouth.

"Yes, really."

Even though it was dark in the car and we weren't under a streetlamp, I could sense the relief in her expression.

"Thank you," she whispered.

I linked our fingers together, and I pulled her hand up to my mouth, kissing the tops of her knuckles as I started the car and drove out of the parking lot.

"All you had to do was ask, and I would have taken you. You know that, right?"

"I know."

Then, why didn't you ask?

Lainey was doing everything in her power to stop mothering Penelope. She was trying to insert space between them, hoping that would help when they separated for college and Lainey wasn't there to oversee every move Penelope made.

That was why she hadn't asked.

The size of her heart and her caring nature were two things I loved the most about her.

Lainey wasn't the type of girl who just held my hand, like we were doing now. She was the type who stroked my skin at the same time because she knew it soothed me, because it showed even more love.

She didn't have to try; it just came naturally to her.

"We have to leave Elijah's at about ten to twelve to make sure I get you home in time." I'd never been late dropping her off, and I sure as hell wasn't going to start now. "I'm saying this because once we show up, everyone is going to be throwing drinks at us, trying to get us to stay and party, and it could turn into something wild."

"And they're going to be so wasted."

"Exactly."

"Do you know what it's like getting away from a wasted person? They're like an octopus, they cling, and they don't let go."

I laughed. "Which is why we need to be fast. We'll divide up so we can cover double the ground in the same amount of time. When one of us finds Penelope, we'll text the other person. If she needs a ride, then she'll leave with us. We'll slip out the back if we have to in order to draw less attention. Cool?"

"Perfect plan. But what if she's not there?"

I quickly glanced at her. "You really think she's not there?"

"Anything is possible when it comes to her."

"True." I pulled into Elijah's neighborhood. "But something tells me she's there."

There were cars on both sides of the street, parked on every inch of spare curb, which told me Penelope's description had been right when she called Lainey and said everyone was there.

"Penelope wasn't kidding," Lainey said. "It looks like the whole school is here."

"You're in my head. I was thinking the same thing." I was still holding her hand up to my face, breathing in her skin, and I nipped the back of her palm. "But I'd much rather have been at the park with you than here with them. I'd choose you any day over this."

I heard her smile when she said, "Same."

I found a parking spot several houses past Elijah's, and we climbed out and hurried toward the front of his mansion. As I opened the door, the blasting music hit my ears, and all I could smell was weed.

And people—they were everywhere.

Lainey walked in first, and I shut the door behind us, turning her toward me.

I put my hands around her ear, hoping to block out some of the noise as I said, "Most of my football team is here. The second they see me, it's going to be hard to pull away from them. That's why I'm going to go upstairs, where I assume it's much less crowded, and check the bedrooms and bathrooms for Pen. Why don't you stay down here, look outside by the pool, go into the parents' bedroom and bathroom, dining room, living room, and media room? I even think there's a wine cellar. It's a big place. We have a lot of ground to cover."

When I pulled away, she nodded.

My lips went close to her ear again, my arms wrapping around her, my hands on her ass. "Have your phone out and text me if you find her."

"You do the same."

"See you in a sec—"

"My two favorite people," Timothy said, cutting me off and stopping us from leaving.

The guy had come out of nowhere, his arms going around my shoulders and Lainey's shoulders, holding us all close together.

I could smell the booze on him, and the weight he was bearing down on me told me he was having a hard time standing up.

"I was losing hope that I was going to see you fools tonight," he said. "Don't tell me, you went on a date and told each other how much you love each other."

I didn't take my eyes off Lainey when I replied, "I told her that a long time ago, but nice try."

"I don't blame you for keeping her away from this party." His gaze was fixed on Lainey. "I wouldn't bring her around these fucking vultures either."

He readjusted his position, and his hand dangled past her shoulder, hanging over her chest.

I didn't like it.

And if he wasn't a friend, I would have broken his fucking wrist.

"Watch your fingers there, Timothy," I warned.

He pulled back, locking those same fingers on her shoulder. "You're worried I'm going to touch her titty?" He laughed. "Nothing I haven't felt before."

"You haven't felt hers," I barked.

"Her sister's. Same thing," he said.

"*Ewww*. Gross, Timothy," Lainey moaned.

They weren't the same thing.

Not at all.

"Have you seen Penelope?" I asked him.

"Earlier, I think. I'm not sure. I stopped keeping track of that one a while ago. She's nothing but fucking trouble." He huffed at Lainey. "No offense."

Before I could respond, he was gone.

In his wake, Lainey's expression turned extremely somber.

Shit.

I would get her head straight and apologize for Timothy being a dick, but right now, I needed to focus on finding Penelope and getting us the hell out of here so Lainey would be able to sleep tonight.

I pulled Lainey against me and said into her ear, "I'm going upstairs. Be careful of the vultures around here, as Timothy put it."

After she nodded, I gave her a kiss and took off for the staircase. It wrapped around the whole side of the foyer with a catwalk across the middle that separated the two wings. From the upstairs landing, I had a direct view of the party downstairs —not all of it, just the living room and kitchen and hints of the patio.

It was packed, wall to wall, with people. Lainey was going to have a hard time making her way through.

I began my search on the right wing, rushing toward the end of the hallway, where there were at least eight doors on both sides.

I didn't knock. I didn't have time to wait for a response. I just opened the door.

What was inside didn't surprise me.

There were three people on the bed—two chicks and a guy. Naked. All getting it on. They didn't even notice that I'd opened the door or that I was standing there.

Since I was positive each of these rooms had their own bathroom, I needed to go in.

Fuck.

As I went past the bed, I looked at the faces of the girls just long enough to prove that neither of them was Penelope before I checked out the bathroom.

It was empty.

As I was making my way around the bed again, I heard, "Rhett, come join us," from one of the girls.

I didn't turn around. I didn't even stop long enough to respond. I closed the door behind me and moved on to the next room.

The vibe in here was completely different. There were about eight people, either sitting on the bed or standing around it. There was a full-length mirror resting across the bottom of the mattress with a large mound of white powder on top of it. Some of them were busy dividing the powder into lines. Some were snorting the lines that had already been cut.

I studied each of their faces as I got deeper into the room, and once I confirmed Penelope wasn't in the bathroom, I got out of there.

But as I left, a part of me was surprised she hadn't been in there.

The third room was much quieter than the last two.

There was a dude in the bed without a shirt on, holding his phone, looking like he was typing on the screen.

I knew him.

He was on the lacrosse team.

"Is Penelope in here?" I asked.

He slowly glanced at me, my voice gaining his attention but the opening of the door hadn't. "Who?"

"Penelope Taylor."

He was staring at me like he didn't understand what I was asking, and he wasn't saying a fucking word.

I didn't have time for this.

I went around the bed and peered inside the bathroom.

Even though the light was off, there was enough coming from the bedroom that showed a shadow of a body bent in front of the toilet.

I flipped the light switch, and long hair and a thin frame came into view. So did the bareness of her back and arms and legs.

There was no question in my mind ...

It was Penelope.

I had known she'd be at the party. I just hadn't wanted to find her like this.

Damn it, Pen.

She was such a pain in my ass. I hated the way she always guilted Lainey into stuff that my girl didn't want to do, but she was Lainey's sister, and Lainey loved Pen more than anything. My girl would forever worry about her, so I handled Penelope the best way I knew how.

And now, that was getting her out of this bathroom.

As I approached, I smelled the vomit. It was on the floor where she was sitting, on her legs and arms, and on the seat of the toilet, where she was resting her face.

Since she was only wearing a bra and panties, I grabbed a towel from the rod by the shower and wrapped it around her.

"Penelope," I whispered.

"Leave." She tried to push me, but there was no force or energy in her hand. "I'm sick."

"It's me. Rhett. I'm going to help you and take you home."

"Rhett?" she whimpered. "*Mmm.* My lover boy."

Hair was stuck to her forehead and cheeks, which were pale and sweaty.

"Are you okay?"

"No." Her eyes stayed closed, but her mouth was open as little bubbles formed on her lips. "I hurt."

"What hurts?"

"Head. Stomach." She moved her mouth off the seat and into the openness of the toilet. Nothing came out when she heaved. "Spinning. Everything is." She dry-heaved again.

"Where are your clothes?"

She attempted to raise her hand and point.

"I'll be right back." In the bedroom, I said to the guy, "Where are her clothes?"

He didn't respond.

"Where are her fucking clothes?"

He gradually looked from his phone to me, and like before, he just silently gawked at me.

What the fuck is wrong with this guy?

I didn't bother waiting for the motherfucker to answer.

I searched the room instead and found a heap of clothes on the floor, almost under the bed. I grabbed the whole pile and brought it into the bathroom, dropping it on the counter, sorting through them until I found a dress. Before I could put it on her, I picked up a towel by the sink and soaked it under the faucet, adding some hand soap.

I knelt beside her. "I'm going to clean your face, all right?"

She let out a groan as I dragged the towel over her lips and cheeks, trying to clean off some of the puke that had dried before rubbing the coldness over her forehead. I hoped the water would cool her down a little. I was sure she was hot based on how clammy she felt. I then washed her arms and legs.

"I see why she loves you."

As she looked at me, her pupils were blown, her expression pulled, like she was half with it and half gone.

"Come on, Penelope. Let's get you dressed."

I pulled at the neck of the dress and positioned it over her head, helping her guide her arms through.

"My body is better than hers, isn't it? My tits are bigger. My ass, better."

I tugged at the material until it was covering her back.

"I'm never jealous of her." Her voice was scratchy and thick. "But I'm jealous that she has you." She was wobbly as she released the toilet. "I should have gotten to you first."

This was the booze talking and whatever else she'd ingested tonight.

I wasn't listening to a word of it.

I put her arm around my shoulders and helped her onto her feet, yanking the dress as low as it would go. "Can you walk?"

She turned her body, putting her other arm on my shoulder, and she stood in front of me. "I wish you were mine."

"Penelope, can you walk?"

"I wish you were going to NYU for me ..."

If I tossed her over my shoulder, turning her upside down to carry her, something told me she'd feel even worse and probably puke on me. So, I put my arm behind her knees and one on her back, and I lifted her against me.

She folded her arms around me and rested her face in my neck. "Right where I'm supposed to be." She sighed, and it sounded like it was full of pain. "I love you." The scent of vomit was almost too much for me to handle. "I love you so much ... Rhett."

Jesus Christ.

As I got us into the bedroom, I said to the dude, "You're a fucking asshole."

"I'm the asshole?" He folded his arm behind his head. "Looks like you're the one who's taking her for round two. She likes it doggy style, if you don't already know, and her ass slapped nice and hard."

I flipped him off as I walked us out of the room and down the hallway to the stairs. As I reached the bottom, Lainey was almost at the first step.

"You forgot to text me when you found her." She held Penelope's bare feet. "Is she okay?"

Too much shit had been happening, and I'd forgotten.

"I found her in one of the bathrooms. She's sick, Lainey."

I'd give her all the details—most of them anyway. I just wasn't sure telling her the things Penelope had said to me was such a good idea—but not here.

Lainey rubbed her hands over Penelope's shins. "You're going to be okay. We'll get you home and get you straight to bed." She looked at me. "Should I go look for her shoes?"

"You're absolutely not going up there," I told her. "Lead us to the car. I need to get you both home."

Lainey turned toward the door, and as I followed, Penelope whispered, "My hero," in my ear.

SIXTEEN

Rhett

Present Day

W hen I heard the knock on my office door, I had a feeling who was behind it. A feeling that was confirmed as the knob twisted and Ridge's face appeared in the crack. He was the only motherfucker in this universe who had the balls to come in without waiting for permission. Rowan was behind him, the two walking in like they fucking owned this space. They closed the door and took seats in front of my desk.

My hands left the keyboard of my computer, my arms crossing over my chest as I eyed down my siblings. "What?"

"You know what," Ridge said. He waited, and when I gave him nothing, he continued, "When you dropped Daisy off, you wouldn't stay to talk. You're not answering any of our calls or text messages. This can't continue, Rhett. We need to know what the hell is going on with you."

"Talk to us," Rowan said.

Concern was etched across their faces.

It should make me feel bad.

But it didn't.

In fact, it did the opposite. It pissed me off.

"What do you want to hear me say?" I pounded my palms on the desk. "What's going on with me should be fucking obvious."

"The date, the anniversary—we get that," Ridge said. "But is there more?"

"We're assuming there is," Rowan said softly. "And that Trista has something to do with it because whenever we reach out to her to ask where she is, she tells us that we should ask you." She chewed her lip. "So, we're here ... asking you."

I'd told Trista to keep her mouth shut about her assignment. It pleased me to no end that she'd followed my order.

"What's going on?" Ridge asked.

I had known this conversation was coming. That didn't mean I wanted to have it. But I wasn't taken by surprise, and that mattered when it came to this.

"Lainey's back."

My gaze shifted between their faces as the words registered with them. Their reactions were exactly what I'd anticipated.

They were shocked as hell.

"You mean ... *back*, back?" Rowan asked.

I nodded. "She rented an apartment in West Hollywood."

"Damn, she really is back," Rowan voiced.

"How do you know that?" Ridge asked.

"I ran into her the night of Brady's bachelor party," I told them, avoiding Ridge's question.

"Hold on a second." Rowan leaned forward onto her thighs. "You left the strip club and just randomly ran into her?"

My teeth ground together. "Yes." I glanced down at my lap.

"She stumbled upon me. I was over on Murphy Drive ... asleep." I let out a loud exhale and faced them.

"Murphy Drive ... *oh*." Ridge exchanged a look with Rowan, the two of them knowing the spot I was referring to.

"You were asleep?" Rowan was careful with the way she asked her question.

Because this was territory they knew I wasn't comfortable speaking about.

A layer that they never got me to discuss.

All they got out of me was a nod.

"How did it go when you saw her?" Rowan asked. "Did you get a chance to talk to her?"

How did it go?

That was a memory I'd been replaying in my head since it'd happened.

The details on fucking repeat, a continuous loop that wouldn't let up.

"You mean, did she throw her arms around me and tell me how much she missed me?" The anger was bubbling in my goddamn chest. "Hell no. It went the way you'd imagine. She didn't want to talk to me."

"I just thought—"

"That after all this time, she'd have a change of heart?" I shot back as Rowan tried to justify her reply. "No. Quite the opposite."

"Rhett ..." Her voice was so soft, her head shaking.

"Have you seen her again?" Ridge asked.

I rubbed my hands over the top of the desk. "No."

"Then, how do you know she moved into an apartment in West Hollywood?" Rowan asked.

I had a feeling that question was going to come back around.

"Oh shit, don't even tell me you're having Trista follow her and that's what she's been up to?" Ridge paused, reading my face. "Rhett fucking Cole, what is wrong with you?"

"Everything," I replied. "Fucking everything."

"What are you going to do with the information that Trista's collecting?" Ridge asked.

My phone vibrated from my desk, a text from Trista on the screen.

TRISTA

She's at a high school, walking the track outside.

ME

Which high school?

She sent another message with the name of the school.

My stomach was suddenly in fucking knots.

It wasn't just any school.

It was the high school we'd attended.

And it wasn't located anywhere near West Hollywood, which meant Lainey had gone there for a reason.

To remember?

To reminisce?

I was sure there were many reasons.

ME

When she leaves, tell me immediately.

SEVENTEEN

Lainey

Fifteen Years Ago

I couldn't handle how hot Rhett looked in his graduation suit.

He'd gone with a dark gray one and a white button-down with an icy-blue tie that was the same color as his eyes. Most of his outfit was hidden under his long navy gown. I was positive if I put my face in his neck, I would smell a mix of his soap and the woody scent of his cologne—a combination that practically made me pant. It was certainly making me jittery, my legs pressing together in my dress, the tingling below almost too much to handle.

He'd shaved this morning, and from here—where I stood in line alphabetically with the T's while he was up front with the C's—I could see the smoothness of his cheeks with just the tiniest hint of dark whiskers trying to break through his skin.

Up until today, the tuxedo he'd worn for prom had been my favorite outfit on him. The black suit and matching bow tie and cummerbund, along with the red rose boutonniere and polished black shoes, had looked explosive on him.

But it didn't compare to this.

This was business Rhett. A man who, in four years, would graduate from USC and then help run his dad's hotel business.

A life that was waiting for us on the other side of college.

I couldn't wait to spend those four years with him, and I couldn't wait to come back here and start a whole different kind of life together.

As if he could sense me staring, he glanced over his shoulder at me, and the buzzing between my legs was now taking over my whole stomach.

God, he was so delicious.

His sexy grin. The way his eyes, even bluer than normal, felt like they saw right through me.

"This is ridiculous," Penelope groaned from behind me.

Her complaining forced me to break contact with Rhett and look at her. "What's ridiculous?"

"I don't understand why we have to be lined up thirty minutes before graduation starts. We know we have to be here. We know we have to walk. We don't have to be treated like children. So, there's no reason why we can't be here *five* minutes before it starts."

"Because then half our class would be late to graduation." I nodded toward a girl who had just arrived and was rushing to get in line. "See what I mean?"

"She's one of the smart ones." Pen rolled her eyes. "A lucky one who doesn't have a sister like you, dragging my ass here even earlier than everyone else." She grabbed my wrist and looked at my watch. "I feel like we've been here for hours."

"Try ten minutes."

"Same thing." She sighed.

"You'll miss this about me when you go to NYU." I joined her against the wall, leaning my body on the sturdiness instead of balancing my weight on my heels. "You won't have anyone to wake you up in the morning, or make sure you get to class on time, or pick you up from parties when you feel like death."

Which the perfect way to describe how ill she had been after she got home from Elijah's party. She'd spent the entire next day in bed, unable to keep anything down.

Prom hadn't been much better.

Rhett had gotten us a bunch of rooms at his father's Beverly Hills hotel, and after the dance, that was where we went, and it turned into an all-night party. I'd never seen Penelope that drunk before.

Or that sick.

And when I tried to warn her and get her to slow down, she wouldn't listen. She didn't care about anything I had to say. She just kept going, and she wouldn't stop.

Until her body couldn't take any more. That had been when the puking started, and it had gone on all evening and into the morning.

"I have an alarm clock," she replied, her arms crossing over her chest. "My classes won't be far from my dorm, so it'll only take me minutes to walk there, and I don't need a chaperone at parties." An arm dropped so her finger could tap my shoulder. "I'm doing just fine, thank you very much."

I gave a quick peek at Rhett, his head turning at the same time as mine, our eyes locking.

I want you, he mouthed.

I felt my face turn every shade of red.

That boy couldn't ever get enough of me.

I loved it.

Get over here, he then mouthed.

I can't, I silently replied.

Lainey ... now.

Not now. I shook my head. *Later.*

I returned my attention to Pen, wiping off some of the black liner that had bled from her bottom eyelid. I didn't know how it had run already; we'd just got done doing our makeup minutes before I drove us here. But she was somehow looking a little disheveled, and when I finished touching up her liner, I adjusted her white cap so it sat straight on her head.

"You're still going to miss me."

"During the moments when you're not a pain in my ass." She nudged me. "Yes, I probably will."

I could sense Rhett's eyes on me, and I once again glanced toward the front of the line.

Ugh, that smirk is so handsome; I can barely breathe.

The minute his lips parted to mouth something else to me, I looked at Pen.

"I really want to ditch all this waiting and go smoke a joint," she whispered. "Can you cover for me if anyone asks where I am?"

"That's a horrible idea. Like, the worst ever. And, no, I can't cover for you."

"Why not?"

"Because this is our graduation, Pen. Something you've worked incredibly hard for. You need to be sober. And you need to be here even if it's not starting for"—I checked my watch—"twenty-four minutes."

"Rule follower."

"You say that like it's a bad thing."

She eyed me down. "It is."

"How so?"

"You need to live a little, Lainey."

"I am. I'm doing everything I want, when I want. But that

also means following orders and staying in this line until we're called up onto the stage to receive our diploma."

Her mouth opened, her head shaking. "What exactly are you doing besides graduating, like the rest of us?"

"Well, in two days, we're going to the beach house to spend a couple of days there with friends, and the following week, we're headed to Europe. I don't know, Pen. That sure as heck sounds like living to me."

I absolutely couldn't wait for the next couple of weeks and all that was planned.

A group of us was going to Timothy's beach house, where we'd spend a few nights. An invite I'd scored for Penelope even though Timothy wasn't happy about having her there. And then the same group was going to Ibiza and Mykonos for two weeks—the trip a graduation gift from our parents.

Since most of us were dividing up and going to different colleges, it was probably going to be the last time we'd all be together for a while.

"That's not living. That's following what's planned." She pushed off the wall. "This is living." She moved out of line and began walking toward the exit.

"Where are you going?" I called out.

She looked back and held her fingers to her lips, like there was a joint between them, and continued walking.

What the hell?

Is she serious?

"Where's she off to?" Rhett asked, suddenly beside me.

I shook my head, still in shock, as I stared at the back of my sister. "To go smoke a joint," I whispered. "I can't believe her right now."

"That's perfect."

"Perfect?"

"Yes, because you're coming with me."

He found my hand and pulled me out of line, taking me past the hallway and into the main lobby of the auditorium.

"Where are we going?" I asked.

Instead of answering or going through the main entrance, he turned and went through a back door. This was just another hallway, but as we got to the end, he opened the last door on the right, and we were inside a stairwell.

Rather than take me up the stairs, he brought me underneath the first flight, where there was an opening, almost cubbyhole-like and private so anyone who came into the stairwell wouldn't see us.

Which immediately told me what his plan was.

That little shit. He really did want me, and he didn't want to wait.

"Rhett—"

"You're mine." He moved me to the wall that was blocked off by the stairs and placed my back against it, his hands going to my face and down my neck to my chest. "You're wearing way too many clothes right now."

My back arched as his fingers hit my sides. "We're about to graduate. I should be wearing way too much." I gasped in a breath of air as he clutched my butt. "Don't you think—"

"No. I don't think we should wait, and I know that's what you were about to tell me. I think the timing of this couldn't be better." He lifted the bottom of my long white gown and went under my dress, where he touched the outside of my panties.

I could no longer find any air.

It was gone—from my lungs, from around me.

He felt *that* good.

"You do realize we're about to walk across the stage in approximately twenty minutes?" I didn't want to push the back of my head against the wall; I didn't want to mess up my hair.

But once his fingers dipped below the silk of my panties, I couldn't help myself.

I was pushing.

And squirming.

"That gives me plenty of time."

My hands reached up, flattening above my head. "And our families are going to be in the crowd, so we can't walk out there looking all sweaty and sexed up."

He laughed as his lips skimmed my neck. "Sexed up?"

"Yeah, you know, red and sweaty and—"

"Oh, you're going to be red." He kissed across my jaw and my neck, his knees bending so he no longer towered over me, even in my heels, and he got himself in a kneeling position. "And you're going to be fucking sweaty."

My eyes widened as he put the gown over his head, disappearing beneath it. From there, he moved quickly, lifting the bottom of my dress and going underneath that too.

I was instantly consumed with the feel of his hair, the presence of his face, the pressure of his fingers.

"Rhett ..." I was looking down, but it was pointless. I couldn't see anything, aside from the movement of his head.

But I could feel his lips against my inner thighs.

The heat from his breath.

The swish of his tongue.

The—

Oh God.

"Rhett!"

"I want my face to smell like you when I walk across that stage."

This was bad.

He was ... bad.

Yet it was all so good.

"I want ..." My voice died off when his tongue hit that

spot, the one at the very top that he was now stroking. But that wasn't the only thing he was doing. He was using his fingers as well, circling them around me before he dipped inside. "You."

He stilled. "I know. I can taste how wet you are."

The redness was already there, but I felt it seeping through my pores.

"Baby, you taste so good."

I tried to swallow.

I tried to lower my arms and hold the top of his head.

I couldn't.

I was frozen.

Stuck on this wall, swelling with pleasure.

He'd done this a couple of times before. He'd go slow, licking all around me, like he wanted to get me extra wet. And once I was, he would surface and immediately slide his dick into me.

But this was different. That didn't seem to be what he was doing here.

Because there was nothing slow about the way his tongue was moving, which was focused on that one area while his fingers took care of the other area.

"Rhett!"

And his licking—it was more like a flick, the same way he rubbed me sometimes when we were having sex and he wanted me to come. But instead of massaging me with the pads of his fingers, he was beating across my clit with the point of his long, wet tongue.

How could something feel so good?

How could it cause this kind of reaction from me?

One where I wanted to pull at his hair, and I wanted to scream, and I wanted to collapse because I wasn't sure my legs would continue to hold me.

"Fuck," I said as quietly as I could. "What are you doing to me?"

"I'm making you come."

His lips surrounded me, and he sucked, the friction so hard, like he was pulling something out of me. I'd never felt anything like it, and I found myself banging my head against the wall.

As though he knew how close I was, his lips pulled back, and he released my clit. The licking returned, his fingers moving even faster than they had been, his breaths hitting me, adding to whatever was stirring.

It was a combination I hadn't been ready for. "Oh! Yes!"

A mixture that was creating something I couldn't fight.

He wanted me to get off.

And he was about to get it.

With each pat of his tongue, I was getting closer. A build that was swishing across me, like he was plugging me into a socket, sending electricity through my whole body.

Every end was sparking.

But together, those sparking ends created something.

A rush.

A scream of, "Rhett," came shouting through my lips. "Fuck! Yes! Ah!"

If there was a peak, I was there, dangling over the edge, unsure if I would ever come back.

But each lick brought me down further, and it brought me back to reality, sending the shivers, which had been roaring, to a dull simmer.

"Oh my," I breathed, attempting to fill my lungs again, "God."

"You gave me just what I wanted."

There was a calmness in his tongue, a lapping he hadn't yet given me today, and then a stillness as he gently kissed me. His fingers slid out, and his head surfaced from my dress and gown. Then, he was standing in front of me, his hands on my face.

"Kiss me, Lainey."

I sighed as I looked at the wetness on his mouth that I knew was all me. "What did you just do to me?"

"I fucking ate you." He ran his teeth over his bottom lip.

"Yes. You did a lot of that."

He smiled. "And there's a lot more where that came from. But right now, we have to go graduate. Later, you're going to get the rest."

"Fair."

"Kiss me." His tone turned to a growl.

I checked out his lips again, unsure I even wanted to go there. "On the mouth? Really?"

"I want you to know what your cum tastes like."

Before I had a chance to respond, his lips were pressed against mine.

And in that moment, I tasted myself.

There was a sweetness I hadn't expected.

A kind of satisfaction I hadn't been prepared for.

And when he pulled away, our faces still close together, he said in a deep, gritty voice, "What's it like to know I'll do anything to taste you?" He put his hand on the wall above my head. "To know that my need for you runs so deep that I took us out of line to graduate." His lips were almost touching mine. "That I brought you here, a place I'd sought out when I arrived because I knew I'd have to have you." He kissed me again. "That you have the power to get me on my knees."

EIGHTEEN

Rhett

Present Day

I was parked in front of the field at my old high school, watching Lainey make her way around the large oval track. She wasn't running. Her speed was a brisk walk, and when she passed the spot closest to my car, I could see the white earbuds firmly pressed in her ears.

I wondered what she was listening to.

What she found entertaining, whether it was a podcast or an audiobook. Or maybe she was on the phone, and I just hadn't seen her lips move.

I had questions.

How had she spent the last fifteen years, aside from what I'd seen on Instagram?

Why was she suddenly back?

And out of all places, what was the reason she'd chosen to walk here?

Our senior year, we'd spent a lot of time on this field. This was where every home game was held. Lainey would be in the stands, watching me play ball. She'd rush to the grass when it was over, jumping into my arms. She hadn't cared that I was dirty and sweaty. Her lips would find mine and stay there until I pulled away.

Fuck, that felt like a million years ago.

When times had been good.

Unlike now.

I turned off the car and took out my phone.

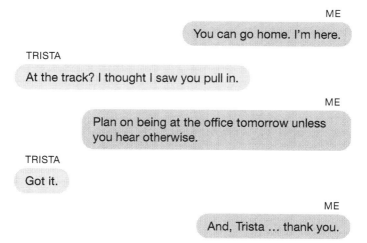

ME

You can go home. I'm here.

TRISTA

At the track? I thought I saw you pull in.

ME

Plan on being at the office tomorrow unless you hear otherwise.

TRISTA

Got it.

ME

And, Trista ... thank you.

I slipped the phone into the inside pocket of my suit jacket and got out of the car, walking to the bleachers that were on the right side of the track. The metal should have felt cool beneath me when I took a seat in the third row, but the truth was, I could have put my ass on a block of ice and I wouldn't have known.

There was too much fire inside me.

Each flame caused my stomach to churn. My head to pound. My hands were damp enough that I rubbed them over my gray pants, and they immediately turned clammy again.

It didn't matter if I was walking up the rows of bleachers or trying to find a position that didn't ache, my eyes stayed on her.

Dressed in a pair of tight, bike-style shorts and a zip-up that clung to her torso, she was three-quarters of the way around the track when she stopped. When her fingers, which hung at her sides, wiggled before they clenched into fists.

If I hadn't already felt her gaze on me, then the way she'd halted would have told me she'd spotted me. But the intensity of her stare was hitting me in a way where I could feel it on every inch of my body.

This wasn't the look she'd given me when she was on the other side of the volleyball net and my eyes locked with hers for the very first time.

That was untarnished.

Too innocent.

A time before I knew the sound of her voice. Before I knew the feel of her skin.

Before I'd ever caught one of her tears.

The look that passed between us now was of two people who had experienced some of the hardest parts of life.

Even if it wasn't together.

I stood from the metal bench, shoving my hands into my pockets. "I just want to talk."

I knew my voice was loud enough.

Hell, Lainey would have heard me even if I'd whispered.

Her head dropped. Her chest was rising and falling, which had nothing to do with her trying to catch her breath from the walk. Lainey's body was fit; she could handle any pace.

The reason for her heavy breathing was me.

"Please, Lainey."

She glanced up.

The fire in my chest moved into my throat. "I only need a couple of minutes."

That was a fucking lie.

It was certainly going to take more than a few minutes to say everything I needed to, but I'd start with a couple and see how many more I could get out of her.

"Rhett ..."

Her head shook.

Her shoulders slumped forward.

And she slowly headed toward me and came to a stop at the base of the bleachers, her arms crossing over her stomach. "What could you possibly have to say to me?"

Every word that came out of my mouth from this point forward held a massive amount of weight.

My eyes closed for just a second, and I exhaled, "Everything."

A hand rested on her chest, the placement close to her heart.

I understood. Mine was pounding something fierce.

She glanced toward the parking lot. "That's too broad. I don't want to go back. I don't—"

"I want to tell you what happened."

That earned me her stare. "I know what happened."

But she didn't know the truth from my mouth. I'd only told that to four people—Rowan, Ridge, my mother, and my father.

Everyone else knew an entirely different version of the story.

But I was tired.

Tired of the secrets.

Tired of the lies.

I pulled my hands out of my pockets, and they clenched for her. For all these years, that movement had been constant—squeezing, releasing, squeezing, releasing—just like they were doing now.

"No, Lainey. You have no idea what really happened."

NINETEEN

Rhett

Fifteen Years Ago

"So, don't kill me," Lainey said as I answered the phone and held it to my ear, "but I have some bad news."

I was halfway down the stairs of my house and halted. "What kind of bad news are we talking about?" I focused on the front door and how I should be walking through it rather than standing in the middle of the staircase. "I'm literally on my way out to come pick you up. Does that mean ..."

My mind was spiraling.

Going to Timothy's beach house had been the plan for a couple of months. We were going to spend a few nights there before we all flew off to Europe for two weeks.

But by the sound of Lainey's voice, something told me that at least half of that plan was going to change.

"Don't laugh, okay? But my hairdresser just called, and

she had a cancellation, so she can squeeze me in. Like, right now. If I don't take this appointment, she can't get me in until after we leave for USC, and I don't want to wait that long to get my hair done, Rhett. I want my highlights fresh for Europe."

Highlights fresh for Europe—check.

But that didn't answer any of my questions, so I said, "I'm not sure what you're telling me?"

"Instead of going with you in the boat, Pen and I will meet you at Timothy's beach house. I'll just drive us there, which means I'll be driving us home, too, rather than taking the boat back with you."

The logistics weren't something I cared about. I'd been driving Dad's boat since I was a kid, and I was more than comfortable going alone.

"So, you're not canceling the trip?" I pressed.

"Heck no. I would never do that. But it does mean you'll be going there and back alone, and even worse than that, I won't be there to help you pack the boat with all our stuff or unpack it once you get to Timothy's."

I exhaled a long sigh of relief, and I rushed down the rest of the steps. "That's nothing. Don't worry—"

"I'll help," Penelope said in the background.

I immediately stopped walking.

"*Ohhh*, yes. I like this idea a lot," Penelope said. "Instead of waiting around for you to drive us to Timothy's, I'll meet Rhett at the dock. I'll help him pack the boat, and I can help him unpack it at Timothy's. He shouldn't have to do all that work alone."

Fuck.

That wasn't what I wanted at all.

"Rhett?" Lainey said. "Are you okay with that?" When I didn't say anything, she continued, "Pen was going to be coming with us anyway, so you'd only be missing me instead of both of us."

How could I tell her I fucking hated her plan?

The last time I had been alone with Penelope, she'd confessed her love to me. I knew the chances of her being fucked up today were high, and I didn't need a repeat of that night in any way.

But I wasn't going to mention that to Lainey. Just like I hadn't told her about what Penelope had said to me.

Maybe one day, I would, when we were deep into our years at USC and enough time had passed and I could blow it off.

Not now though.

"Rhett, are you cool with Pen going with you?"

I exhaled. "Yeah, yeah. Whatever." I walked out the door and got into my car.

"Are you headed to the boat now?" Lainey asked.

I started the engine and put on my seat belt. "I'm pulling out of my driveway as I speak."

"Pen, he's leaving now," Lainey shouted, like she was standing downstairs and Penelope had just run upstairs.

"Is that Rhett on the phone?" I heard Lainey's dad ask.

"Yes," she replied.

"I'd like to talk to him," he said.

My hand tightened on the steering wheel, my breathing deepening.

Her dad?

Wants to talk to me?

Now?

"Rhett, Dad wants to talk to you, so I'm going to give him the phone," Lainey said. "Call me before you guys take off on the boat, okay? I'll just be sitting there with foils on my head, so I'll be able to talk."

I sucked in more air. "All right."

Prom was the first time he'd let his daughter stay the night with me, and Timothy's beach house would be the second. But before we'd left for dinner, which we went to right before the dance, he had pulled me aside and laid down the law, letting me know I was responsible for his daughters and that I wasn't to let anything happen to either of them.

I didn't tell him that one of the twins was completely out of control and no one was capable of being responsible for her.

I made him a promise instead, and I'd kept my word.

"Rhett," Mr. Taylor said, "I'd like to speak to you about this trip to Timothy Barden's beach house. Lainey told me you'll be staying two nights and there will be approximately eight of you there, the same group who will be going to Europe—am I right?"

"Yes, sir." I slowed at the light.

"And from what I understand, you'll be taking my daughters there by boat—your father's boat, I assume?"

I adjusted my hand since the steering wheel was getting sweaty. "Those plans have changed a little. Now, Lainey is meeting us at the beach house, and I'll be taking Penelope by boat."

"Will there be drinking?"

I glanced in my rearview mirror as if I could see the trunk, where there were at least five cases of beer and four handles of booze packed away. Of course, that didn't count all the weed I'd stashed in my bag and whatever else the others were bringing.

If I told him what was in my trunk, there was a chance he wouldn't let Lainey go. The dude was extra strict when it came to his girls. Which was funny as hell to me, considering how wild Penelope was when it came to partying.

But there was a workaround to his question because he hadn't specifically asked if there would be drinking at the party or on the boat.

His statement was broad.

So, I replied as if he'd asked if there would be drinking on the boat, and I said, "No, sir."

"That's the answer I wanted to hear."

I accelerated through the green light, feeling like shit that I'd semi-lied, my pulse going as fast as my speed.

"I want to remind you, son, that I only have three angels in this world, and you're going to be responsible for two of them at the beach house and again when you all go to Europe. We'll talk more about that trip later, but while you're at Timothy's, do not—I repeat, do not—let me down."

"I won't, sir."

"I know."

TWENTY

Rhett

Present Day

No, Lainey, you have no idea what happened.
As those words hit her, her head slightly shook, like she was fighting against them. Like she didn't want to believe what I'd just said.

What she wanted to believe was the version of the story she knew. The one that had been living within her mind for the last fifteen years.

Every tale needed a villain.

I was that person.

I couldn't blame her for giving me that title, not after all the information that had been fed to her. But what had been omitted were details that changed everything. That didn't just shift the story, but flipped it on its back.

That side—my side—was long overdue.

And I had no plans on leaving these bleachers until she heard it.

I tapped the spot next to me, filling my lungs before I said, "Please sit." I waited for movement, and when there was none, I added, "Or come closer and just stand here." I pointed at the row in front of me. "I need to get some things off my chest."

"I don't understand what there is to say at this point. What could you possibly tell me that I don't already know?"

I pulled at my tie. The knot was pushed against my skin in a way where it felt as though it were trying to choke me. "The truth."

"I already know that."

I nodded. "You do, yes, but not all of it. There's much more that you haven't heard."

Curiosity was getting the best of her—I could see it in her expression—and she slowly took a seat on the bottom bleacher, putting a row between us. She turned until her feet were on the metal in front of her, her arms folded around her knees. She focused on the parking lot, where my car was, and when an excruciating amount of time had passed, she finally looked at me.

"Tell me how you found me. I doubt you live near here, and"—she nodded toward me—"dressed in that suit, you definitely didn't come here to work out."

If I was going to come clean about the past, then I'd have to confess the present.

I would put everything on the table. I would show her every card.

What she did with that information was up to her.

So, I said, "I know you don't live near here either. Not your parents' place. I'm talking about your new apartment."

Her eyelids narrowed as she looked at me. "Have you been following me?"

"I haven't. But my assistant has. I asked her to."

She gazed at me as if I'd just slapped her. "Why?"

"Why?" My voice was softer than normal. "That's a good question." I took my jacket off and set it on the bench beside me. "When I saw you at ..." My voice trailed off, and after a few seconds, I tried again. "When I saw you, I couldn't believe you were there or that you were back. I still can't. And I know I've said that to you many times in the past, but each time, I've meant it more, and this time certainly takes the fucking cake." I pressed my palms together and held them between my legs. "I never thought I'd get the chance to talk to you in person. There were times I thought about getting on a plane and coming to you, but ..." I went quiet again. "Obviously, I didn't." My throat was dry, my chest pounding like I'd been the one walking the track. "Now that you're here, in LA, I wasn't going to waste the opportunity. I guess I was just waiting for the right time, even if that meant going to the airport and having a discussion with you before you entered security."

"But to have someone follow me? Just to figure out when would be the right time to talk to me? That's some stalker-level shit, Rhett."

I nodded.

I couldn't disagree with what she'd said.

The whole thing was fucked—I wasn't denying that.

"I couldn't exactly go to your parents' house and ring the bell and ask your dad if I could talk to you, could I?"

She rocked over the bleacher. "Still, that's some unhinged behavior. I hope you know that."

"I do."

She looked away. "God, this is so ... I don't know what this is."

"It's fucked," I said, repeating the words that I'd just voiced in my head.

"Yes."

"I know you won't get it—hell, I'm not sure I even get it— but having my assistant follow you made me feel closer to you." I briefly focused on my hands before I glanced at her. "I wanted that."

"Rhett—"

"I told you ... you wouldn't get it."

As she rubbed her lips together, her eyes softened. Her body almost curling into a ball. "What is it that you want to tell me?"

I took my time saying, "It's about Penelope."

Her head leaned back; her eyes closed.

Her throat bounced as she swallowed.

"If you're going to go into detail about what happened between you and my sister"—she paused as she drew in a shaky breath—"I don't want to hear it."

"Lainey—"

"And if you're going to tell me you weren't high when it happened, don't bother. I already know you were."

TWENTY-ONE

Rhett

Fifteen Years Ago

Penelope set the case of beer at the bow of the boat and turned toward me, her hands on her bare hips. "Is that the last load, lover boy?" She wore her cutoff shorts unbuttoned and rolled down so low that I wasn't sure why she'd bothered wearing them at all, considering she only had on a string bikini on top.

Whatever her reasoning was, I was relieved she'd decided to wear them. Enough of her was showing as it was.

I set another case of beer on top of the one she'd just carried. "Yep, that's it."

She used her finger to count all the booze we'd piled up in the corner of the bow and looked at me with a scowl. "Five cases of beer and four handles of vodka? That's all you got for the beach house? Tell me you have a secret stash hidden in your backseat that I just didn't see?"

I adjusted my baseball hat lower on my face. "We're only going for two nights."

She smiled. "I don't think you realize how much I can drink."

I realized.

I'd seen her drink more times than I could count.

But I'd also witnessed her hugging the toilet when all that liquor caught up to her.

"Timothy has a fake ID," I said. "I'm sure if we run out, which would be a miracle, then he could make a booze run."

She rolled her eyes. "Timothy ..."

"What about him?"

She stared at the edge of the marina, where a sailboat was on its way into the dock. "Been there, done that. And *so* over it."

I cleared my throat. "It?"

"Yeah ... *It*."

It was nice enough to let us stay at his parents' beach house. And *It* felt the same way about her, so Lainey and I had to convince him to allow Penelope to get an invite.

But I wasn't here to argue with her. She could think whatever she wanted about Timothy. No matter what I said, it wouldn't change her mind.

I crossed my arms over my chest. "Well, you're about to be spending a lot of time with Timothy during this trip and in Europe, so—I don't know—play nice, I guess."

She sat on the side of the bow, swinging her legs in the air. "I just wish there were some new guys coming to his beach house and not the same old crew you guys always hang out with."

"Penelope, that crew, they're our friends."

"And your friends are all taken. *Blaaah*."

"Why is that a problem?"

I swore she was trying to stick out her chest when she said, "Because they're all married up and there's no room for me to squeeze in." There was suddenly a smile on her face. "Especially you. You're, like, beyond taken, and that's just annoying."

I squeezed the visor of my hat with both hands. "Stop."

"Stop what? Confessing my love? Don't deny it—you love hearing it."

I shook my head. "I don't."

"Now, you're just lying to me." She nodded toward the duffel bag I'd packed my clothes into. "You wouldn't happen to have anything in there that's stronger than booze, would you?"

"Just some weed."

She waved me off. "I'm not talking about weed, Rhett."

"Then, you're shit out of luck."

She laughed. "No, you're shit out of luck because I don't share."

I had no idea what she meant, but I wasn't going to ask. I didn't need anything she had or wanted or was or wasn't willing to share. Weed and alcohol were good enough for Lainey and me, and I knew my girl, and she probably wouldn't do much of either at Timothy's beach house.

"Are we getting out of here anytime soon?" Penelope asked. "I'm ready to hit the water."

I scanned the boat to see if everything was in place and what was left to do.

My dad had gotten the forty-two-foot center console about two years ago, around the same time I'd gotten my driver's license, so while I was learning the rules of the road, I was also learning the rules of the water. She had four 400s on the back and a decent-sized cuddy that was under the bow—a place I'd slept a few times over the years, especially before Lainey came back into town—along with a head that came in handy whenever Lainey was on the boat since the girl drank more water than anyone I knew.

"I just have to untie the lines," I told her, "and we can get going."

She used her hand to block the sun out of her face even though she had a pair of sunglasses on her head. "Whatever you need, I've got you, captain."

"I've got to call Lainey first. I promised her I would before we took off."

"Yes, get my sister on the phone. I'm dying to tell her how much of a snore you are." She grinned.

I wanted to chuckle; I just didn't have it in me.

I took my phone out of my back pocket and hit Lainey's number, holding my cell up to my ear.

"Hi," Lainey answered.

"Hi, baby." I peeked at Penelope, who was now doing something on her phone, and I turned my back to her, walking toward the stern.

"Are you on the boat with Pen?"

"Yep."

"How's everything going? Are you all packed up and ready to go?"

I tapped the top of an engine. "Once I hang up with you, we'll get going. It should take me about thirty minutes to get to Timothy's. We'll be there waiting for you." I watched a twenty-five-foot bowrider pull out of the marina, its wake far larger than it should be.

"I'll be leaving here in about an hour," she said. "Hopefully, the traffic won't be too bad, and it won't take me long to get to the beach house."

"Will you call me when you leave?"

"Of course. In the meantime, will you take some pics of you

and Pen on the boat? I want to document every second of the next couple of months before we leave for USC."

I gripped the edge of the plaster, next to one of the cleats, and attempted to keep my voice down. "You want pictures of me with Penelope?"

"Is that okay?"

Jesus, I could only imagine how much Penelope would love that.

"Lainey—"

"I know. It's not your thing. But this one time, will you do me a favor and snap some for me?"

I sighed. "Really?"

Lainey didn't know how I truly felt about Penelope and how I was getting so tired of her behavior. I kept that to myself. But my sounds made it clear that her constant presence was wearing on me, and I was sure Lainey was picking up on that.

"Rhett, she's going to be in New York soon, and I won't be able to get these moments back. Who knows if she'll come home for summer breaks or even holidays?"

There was emotion in her voice, and I couldn't handle hearing it.

"I'll take some," I told her. "Don't worry."

"Thank you."

Penelope had mentioned wanting to talk to her sister to tell her how much of a snore I was, so I turned toward the bow to get her.

"Hey, Penelope, do you want—" My voice cut off when I saw what she was doing.

What the fuck? Is she fucking serious?

I couldn't believe my eyes. I couldn't believe Penelope.

I ground my teeth together, attempting not to sound pissed when I said to Lainey, "Never mind, she's busy. Don't forget to call me when you leave the salon."

"I won't. I love you."

"I love you, Lainey."

The phone went dead, and I squeezed the rubbery cover, my brain scrolling through all the things I wanted to shout at Penelope while she sat on the floor of the boat.

Her legs were folded in front of her, and she had one of those makeup compacts in her hand. Lainey had them all over the vanity in her bedroom, so I recognized what Penelope was holding.

But Penelope wasn't putting on makeup.

She held the compact upside down so the mirror lay flat on her palm, and she was using a credit card to chop up a mound of white powder that she'd dumped in the middle of the glass.

With each pass, she formed a new small, thin line.

And the dollar bill that was balanced on her lap told me those lines were about to be snorted up her nose.

TWENTY-TWO

Rhett

Present Day

"If you're going to go into detail about what happened between you and my sister, I don't want to hear it."

"And if you're going to tell me you weren't high when it happened, don't bother. I already know you were."

Lainey stared at me from the bottom row of the bleachers, waiting for a response.

Of course this entire conversation was going to be about Penelope. And how I'd felt. And what had actually gone down that day.

Why would Lainey think otherwise?

Penelope was the reason we were sitting so far apart right now.

She was the reason Lainey and I had gone fifteen years without speaking.

She was the reason there was so much hurt between us.

She was the reason why just being here and looking at Lainey made my fingers clench nonstop and made my heart fucking ache.

I rubbed my hands over my pant legs for what felt like the millionth time as the silence between us grew.

I needed to find a starting point.

I needed to proceed carefully because once I went there, I had to go all the way. I couldn't back out; I couldn't hold anything from her.

I had to make her see a side she'd never considered.

A side she hadn't heard.

And that was my fault.

Fuck.

But what tripped me up was the shiver that I watched pass through her body.

I grabbed my suit jacket and stepped over the bleacher between us and wrapped the jacket around her shoulders. "You probably don't want it, but I can't sit here and watch you shake."

"I'm not cold. I ... don't know what I am." She held the lapels, turning her face to run her nose across one. "It smells just like you."

"I would hope so. I've been wearing it all morning."

"I mean, your scent. It hasn't changed at all."

Neither had hers.

I could smell her rose perfume as though my face were nuzzled in her neck.

A spot that I missed, that I would fucking beg for.

I put my feet on the metal in front of me and rested my elbows on my knees. "After all these years, why would you return to LA?"

She began to rock again, holding her bent legs close to her

chest. "I've been telling people I missed home. To me, that sounds like a good enough reason."

"I'm not people, Lainey. There's no need to hide anything from me."

There was the slightest nod of her head before her eyes slowly found mine. "I'm tired of running." Her body stilled. "Have you ever felt like you were going a hundred miles per hour, but you weren't moving at all?"

"Every day of my goddamn life."

I recognized the expression—it was the comfort in knowing you weren't alone.

"That was me in London. My feet were barely moving, but I felt like I'd tackled a marathon by every nightfall."

"Is that why you came to this track? So you could actually walk that marathon?"

"No." She glanced toward the school, which made her look over her shoulder, and the wind carried her whisper to me. "I came so I could remember ..."

TWENTY-THREE

Rhett

Fifteen Years Ago

As I stared at Penelope while she sat in the bow of the boat, my mind spinning with far too many thoughts, something made me lift my phone from my side. Something made my thumb swipe the screen. And something made me point the camera at Penelope and hit Record.

I'd just hung up with Lainey, and she'd asked me to take photos. I was going to give her something even better.

A fucking video.

And the star was her twin sister, holding the rolled-up bill to her nose, snorting each line of the powder she'd cut.

I let several seconds of footage roll before I ended the recording and shoved my phone into my pocket.

I wasn't going to yell at her even though I wanted to.

I wasn't going to take the mirror and the bag of blow and

throw them into the water because, knowing her, she probably had a lot more with her.

I wasn't going to tell her that watching her do drugs on the floor of my family's boat when we weren't even partying confirmed everything I'd feared.

Penelope Taylor was a fucking mess.

As I continued to stand here, reeling, I thought about what Penelope had said just a few minutes ago.

"No, you're shit out of luck because I don't share."

The coke—that was what she had been talking about. If I'd had some, she'd have snorted mine. But since I didn't—and I didn't mess around with that stuff—she'd use what she'd brought, and she wouldn't share it with me.

She didn't need to.

But what she needed to do was stop, so I walked over to her and said, "Penelope, you need to slow down with that shit."

She finished the last line and cupped the end of her nose, rubbing it, like the insides were burning. "I'm having some fun. You should try it, you snore."

The baggie of white powder that sat on her lap was still practically full.

"Put it away, Pen."

"It? That's what we're calling it?" She bit her lip, releasing it to smile. "The same title as Timothy? Now, that's just mean."

My patience was running out. "Pen—"

"Because this isn't an *it*." She held up the baggie. "This is expensive-ass—"

"I don't care what it is. Put it away."

"God, you really are a snore." She slipped the mirror into her bag, along with the coke and rolled-up bill, and stood. "All right, captain, I'm all yours." Her hands went to her hips. "What do you need me to do?"

She really thought I would assign her a task at this point?

Now, that was funny.

I pointed at the center double-wide captain's chair in the middle of the boat, which was unfortunately the only seating. "I need you to sit, and do not move."

"Don't you need me to tie something? Or untie something? Or start something? Hell, I can't remember what you said, that was, like, five hours ago." Her jaw was swinging, her pupils so big that I could see them from several feet away.

"No, I need you to sit. I'll do everything else."

She came toward me and put her hands on my shoulders, leaning up on her tiptoes to get closer to my face. "You sure? I can be super useful. I'm good at all kinds of things—"

"Go sit. Now."

She rolled her eyes. "You're the worst."

While she stomped her way over to the center console, like a child, I waited until the water around us was clear, and then I went to each of the cleats that faced the dock and untied the lines. With nothing holding us in place, I took a seat next to Penelope, and with the engines already running, I used the bow thruster to propel us away from the dock until I was satisfied with the clearance. I then put the boat in gear and maintained a speed that let off minimal wake as I made my way out of the marina.

When I bore down on the throttle, the engines revved, showing off their horsepower, and Penelope's hair began to fly, the pieces hitting my arms, her laughter blasting in my ears.

"Faster!"

I ignored her.

"Faster, Rhett!"

I still paid zero attention to what she was saying. This was my territory, not hers, and I didn't take orders on the boat.

But when she shook my arm and asked, "Why is this the

first time I've been on your boat?" she put me in a position where I had to reply.

This was a place where I came to chill. Where I came to get away. Penelope brought the loudness and drama, and I wanted relaxation and quietness.

That was why I never told Lainey to bring her sister.

But I couldn't say that to Penelope.

"Rhett! Answer me!"

Jesus Christ.

"What do you want to know, Penelope?" I asked, hoping the drugs would make her forget her question.

"Why haven't you ever taken me boating? This is so fun!"

"Lainey's only been a handful of times."

"So?"

I steered us into the open channel. "I don't know ... when I take her boating, we want to be alone."

"Fuck being alone. You need to start bringing me. I love this." She wrapped her arm around the top of the seat, her fingers on my back, and she put her bare feet on the dash, head tilted toward the sun. "Yep, this is paradise. And this is how I want to spend my *whole* summer with you and Lainey. Call me queen of the third wheel." She pulled down her glasses, looking at me over the rim, giving me a wink. "And you're one hot-ass captain."

She reached for the button for the music and cranked it up.

Within no time, she was dancing in the seat.

Not me. I was focused on the depth and how the boat was riding the plane, the very surface of the water, and how the chop was so mild that there was no reason to throttle back.

I tried to tune her out, but every time she shifted her hips, I swore she moved closer and somehow found a way to touch a part of me, whether it was my chest or hip or shoulder.

"Dance with me, lover boy."

I held the helm with my right hand, the same side she sat on, and kept my arm outstretched. I was using that arm like a shield, hoping it would block her, even though it didn't seem to since she was somehow still touching my chest.

"I'm driving the boat, Penelope."

"If you stand up, you can dance."

"No, I can't."

Which was a lie. I could dance while I was sitting, and I could dance if I was standing, and in either position, I could drive the boat. But I wasn't going to accept her invitation because giving that girl an inch was the last thing I needed to do.

"Rhett," she whined, "dance with me."

In the two years that my father had owned this boat, I'd never wished he'd gotten a bowrider—a style that had a lot more seating—until now. I would do anything for Penelope to be sitting in the bow, far from me, where she couldn't touch me whenever she fucking wanted.

"I know what will get you in the mood." She shifted to grab something from her pocket and held up a joint. "You can do the honors, captain."

"Nah, I'm good."

She took out a lighter. "You don't want to smoke?"

Of course I wanted to smoke. I wanted that entire joint to myself.

Once we got to the beach house, that would be a whole different story, but I sure as hell wasn't going to do anything to risk messing up Dad's million-dollar boat.

"No, I don't," I told her.

She nudged my shoulder. "What's gotten into you?" She put the joint between her lips and lit the end, taking a long drag. Her exhale blew right into my face. "Here." She tried handing it to me.

"I told you, I don't want it."

"Why not?"

I leaned my face away, keeping my eyes on the water. "Because I just don't want to smoke."

"But you always want to smoke."

"I just don't want to right now."

She groaned, "Ugh, you're getting worse by the second."

So was she.

"Just think, I'm leaving more for you. Isn't that what you want? To get even higher?" When I gave her a quick glance, her eyes were narrowed as she stared at me.

"No. I want to share it with you. I want us both to get so fucked up."

I turned back toward the water. "I'll make a deal with you. I'll smoke with you once we get to Timothy's. But not before."

"Promise?"

"Promise."

She wrapped her arms around my shoulders and rested her face on my arm. "I'm back to loving you."

I didn't know if that was a good thing or a bad thing.

I was leaning toward bad.

"But, Rhett, just so you know, you're going to dance with me. I'm not giving you any other choice."

A cloud of smoke rose over my face as she blew it toward me.

"I'm not dancing, Penelope. I told you, I can't."

"You just don't want to. But I'm going to change your mind."

She puffed down the rest of the weed and tossed the paper into the water. Then, she knelt on the seat, her palms pressed against the hard top above us.

"You need to sit, Penelope."

Instead of staying in that spot, she moved behind me,

wedging into the small space between my ass and the seat. Her thighs pushed against my back, her hands went to my shoulders, and she started to sing to whatever was playing.

"You've got to move," I ordered. I grabbed her hand, and I tried to return her to the seat beside me. "Pen, come on. This isn't funny. We're going fast, and this isn't safe."

She wouldn't budge.

She was only getting louder, grinding more of her body against mine.

"Penelope!"

Shouting her name did nothing; she wasn't listening, nor was she returning to her seat.

"You need to get off me!"

When nothing changed, I stood, hoping she'd back off from all the touching and dancing and calm down a bit.

"*Yesss*, Rhett! That's just where I want you!"

That hope completely died because, out of nowhere, one of her legs wrapped over my shoulder, the front of her pressed against the back of me, her other leg hung over my opposite shoulder, and she held my head for balance.

"Penelope! What the fuck?! Get off my shoulders right now!"

"I want to dance!"

And she did, like we were at a concert and she wanted a better view of the stage, bopping on top of me as if this were totally normal. She was completely ignoring the fact that we were in the middle of the ocean and this was one of the most dangerous things she could do.

I pulled back on the throttle, lowering our speed. It wasn't a super-busy day on the water, but there were enough vessels around that I needed to keep my focus.

But no matter what I did, she just wasn't having it. She couldn't stand that she wasn't getting all my attention. And the more I tried to blow her off—even though that was impossible since she was on my damn shoulders—the harder she rocked her hips.

It was like she was fucking the back of my head.

I couldn't take this.

She needed to stop.

But I knew I wouldn't be able to get her down if I was standing, not without her falling, and I didn't want to hurt her in any way. So, while I held the helm with both hands, I took a seat, and I tried wiggling out of her grip.

She only clung on tighter.

"Penelope—"

"Come on, lover boy. Dance! Dance! Dance!"

"Get off."

"No!"

"I'm driving the fucking boat, Pen! Why won't you take no for an answer and chill the fuck out?!"

When she still didn't move, I released the helm and pushed one of her legs off and switched hands on the wheel to do the same thing with her other leg.

"You're not getting away from me that easily, lover boy." She tried to get on my shoulders again.

But I caught her leg midair and turned so I could glare into her eyes. "You need to cut this shit out. I have to drive the boat. You're out of fucking control right now. Stop!"

"God! You're such an asshole! I'm not even doing anything wrong!" Her eyes widened, and a weird smile came over her face, her finger raising and pointing toward the bow. "Bumper boats! Now, that'll be really fun!"

Bumper boats?

My head turned just in time to see the vessel she was pointing at.

I knew we were getting closer to it because right before I

looked at her, I moved us more to the side, adjusting our path, to avoid the boat and its wake.

I'd thought I'd given us plenty of clearance, that we weren't in line with that boat anymore.

But somehow, that was no longer the case.

Either the water had shifted us, the other boat had moved in the same direction as us, or I'd unknowingly turned the wheel.

Whatever it was, we were fucked.

Because not only were we directly behind that boat, but we were about to crash right into it.

TWENTY-FOUR

Rhett

Present Day

Lainey was still staring at our old high school, so I took a
quick glance at the building. A place where I'd spent the
best four years of my life.

"I don't come here to remember. I don't need to. I
remember while I'm at work, and when I'm forced to travel for
work, and when I'm driving, and when I'm home. Everywhere
and anywhere—that's where I remember." I waited until I
earned her gaze. "My mind likes to fuck with me. Torture me
really. Especially when I try to go to sleep. Whenever I close
my eyes, it likes to replay the past on an endless loop, and my
eyelids open right back up. I don't like what I see in that darkness ... and sleep never comes."

I didn't know why I was telling her this.

But I knew she could relate.

I could see it in her face.

Pain recognized pain.

It attached to it, it attracted it, it sympathized in its misery, and the ends looped around, like a ball of yarn that was too knotted to use.

She swiveled on the metal bleacher until she was fully facing me. "I need to know why you want to talk to me. Rhett, please, just rip off the Band-Aid already."

There was a lot to unload, and I still hadn't come up with a starting point.

Time wasn't helping.

Maybe if I showed her the proof, I could then work backward.

I took out my phone and stood from the bench. Crossing the one between us, I sat on it, which positioned her directly in front of me. "I want to show you something." I held my cell so we could both see it, flipping through the years of pictures. There wasn't much—I rarely took photographs. My life looked the same every day; there was no reason to document anything, no purpose in saving memories that were as dark as yesterday.

"Wait, go back," she said.

When I halted, her finger hit the screen, and she swiped a few times, stopping on a photo of Ridge and me. We were at the beach, and we'd just gotten out of the water, the ocean dripping from our bare chests.

"Ridge. My God, he's changed so much. He's all grown up." She shook her head. "Your tattoo, Rhett." Her voice was only a whisper. "I'm surprised you didn't cover it up with something else or get it lasered off."

The way my arm was extended in the shot, the tattoo I'd gotten for Lainey was in plain sight.

"No, I didn't do that." As she looked at me, I added, "And I never will."

She used her fingers to zoom in—she obviously wanted a better view of my ink. Her hand stayed on my phone for several seconds before she pulled it away and softly said, "Rhett, my name is on your body. Why wouldn't you want to remove it?"

That answer was so clear to me, and I was sure it would be shocking to her.

"Because I want your name on me, Lainey."

Without even looking, I sensed her chest rise, her lips mash, her brows furrowing.

"I don't understand. We broke up on the worst terms ever without any chance of reconciling. We haven't spoken. There's absolutely nothing between us."

I searched her eyes. "That's not true."

"What? How can you say that?"

A moment of silence passed.

Within it, I swore she saw the answer to her question.

I fucking swore she could feel it.

If she couldn't, then she wasn't the woman I thought she was.

I waited.

For what felt like a goddamn eternity.

And then I saw it—the glimmer, the recognition, the long, deep sigh that left her lips.

"Lainey ..." I'd been holding in these thoughts since the last time I had seen her, and I could finally speak them. Why did it feel so hard to get started? Why was my heart pounding so fucking hard? "Do you really think those fifteen years made me stop loving you?" I shook my head. "Not even close."

I let those words set in—not just within her, but within me.

"I would wait an entire lifetime to have another chance with you. That's how I felt when you walked away from me, and that's exactly how I feel now. Maybe there's nothing pulling you to me, but what pulls me to you is love. It's grown every single day that's passed."

My free hand clenched, preventing me from reaching out. From cupping her cheek. From brushing my thumb across the side of her mouth. From doing everything in my power to make her smile.

"I'll only ever have one why, Lainey, and you're the one."

TWENTY-FIVE

Rhett

Fifteen Years Ago

F ifteen yards.

That was how much space was between my boat and the one in front of us, a distance that could easily be closed in only a few seconds, which was all the time I had to try to avoid crashing my bow into their stern.

I never allowed spaces that were this tight.

Especially with the speed I was going.

I couldn't brake—brakes didn't exist on a boat.

I had little options, and I needed to move fast.

"What happens when we bump them?" Penelope's face was near mine when she spoke, excitement in her tone when there should have been fear. That was the coke; it turned everything into a fucking party.

I didn't have time to push her away or comment on the closeness of our bodies.

"You need to hold on tight," I warned. "Do it now!"

I swore I'd shifted my path so this wouldn't happen. And I swore there had been plenty of clearance before I looked at Penelope when she had really started to act wild and that it had been somewhat safe to take my eyes off the water.

But I had known better. I had known how wrong that was.

My father had trained me not to get distracted, to always keep my focus on what was around me—the boats, the waves, the depth. I'd acted like a damn idiot, and I was going to pay the price.

Adrenaline was pumping through my body, my hands shaking as I held the helm with one and the throttle with the other. I couldn't jerk the wheel—boats were nothing like a car; the movement wouldn't immediately turn us, there would be a slight delay, and then we'd be sent in a three-sixty. With boats behind us, gaining speed by the second, that would just get us into another accident.

"Go, Rhett! Go!" She squeezed my shoulder. "You've got this, captain."

She acted as though this were a race, not a catastrophe.

That I wouldn't be dead the second my father found out.

That I wouldn't be paying him back for the rest of my life and beyond.

"Stop," I growled.

I didn't know if I was talking to Penelope or to what was unfolding, but I needed both to happen.

"I want to help—"

"You can help by keeping fucking quiet and holding on."

The only things I could do—and hoped to hell they worked— was turn the wheel a little, praying it would be enough to clear the other boat's left side, and lower my speed without causing an accident with the boats behind me. But if the one in front of me continued at the same rate, that would add some space between us.

Seconds would tell, and so would patience.

With Penelope's hand on my shoulder, as she shouted words in my face, patience was becoming a real problem.

My boat instantly reacted as I pulled back on the throttle, and I held my breath as I assessed whether the change had helped. The tip of my anchor, which sat front and center of my boat, was what I used to judge our position. One thing I could tell right away was that we were no longer aligned with the middle of the other boat's engines. By turning, we'd shifted at least a foot.

But would it be enough?

If the depth of the water wasn't an issue, I would have pulled off onto the side and let everyone pass. But the markers that were dug deep into the sand—posts that stuck out from the surface of the ocean—clearly defined the channel, and anything outside those tall sticks would bottom out the boat, causing a whole other nightmare.

With each second that passed, the space between our two boats began to grow, and the tension in my chest slowly released since the threat of crashing was getting less and less. Somehow, I'd done the right thing, I'd fixed this. I just needed to maintain the same speed so the boats behind us didn't face the same issues I'd just had.

But just because the danger in front of us was diminishing, that didn't mean I was back to breathing normally.

That there wasn't a fucking monster clawing its way out of my chest.

I'd never been in a situation like this before. I didn't screw around when it came to driving my dad's boat; I took this shit seriously.

And what had happened with Penelope? That wasn't okay. Things had gotten out of control.

She hadn't listened to anything I'd said.

She'd turned what had already been a risky situation into something that could have been fatal.

I needed a second, so when I saw the opening up ahead—a widening between the markers that would allow me to idle in the water—I navigated toward the right. I decreased the horsepower until I could shift into neutral.

Once the boat was stopped, my head dropped, and I clutched what I was holding, letting the air come into my lungs, doing everything I could to bring down my pulse.

"Yay, you did it!" She threw her arms around me. "You're my hero."

A fucking hero?

That was what she was going to say to me? After what could have just happened?

I couldn't take any more of this.

"You need to get off me." My fingers clenched as she squeezed her face into the side of my neck. "Penelope, get the fuck away from me." When she still didn't respond, I found her wrists and pulled her hands off me. "Jesus Christ, why don't you listen?!"

She looked as if I'd just slapped her. "What the hell is wrong with you?"

"Do you have any idea what could have happened back there?" I threw my thumb over my shoulder, pointing at the scene of the almost crime. "We could have fucking died. We could have totaled the boat. Does that mean anything to you?"

Her eyes were turning feral as she chewed her nail. "It was your fault. You were the one driving." Her arms lifted in the air, and she danced. "I was just a hot accessory."

"You're kidding me." When she continued to dance, I

shouted, "You're fucking kidding me! You've been touching me, flirting with me nonstop. Climbing on my shoulders, begging me to dance with you. None of that is right, Penelope."

Her arms dropped, and her body stilled. "Asshole."

"I'm the asshole?" My eyebrows couldn't possibly get any higher. "You're the one who's been acting like an idiot since we got on the boat."

"That's a lie."

"A lie?"

She crossed her arms over her chest. "I've done nothing but help you, and all you've done is reject me."

I held on to the top of my hat, my head so hot that I thought the cap might melt. "You're not making any sense right now. It's all that coke you snorted and all that weed you smoked. It's getting to your fucking brain—"

"This is about her, isn't it?" Her top lip curled. "Just say it. Admit it. She's why you're acting this way."

"Who?"

"Lainey!"

I was lost.

So lost that no map could ever get me out.

"What does Lainey have to do with this?" I asked.

Her bare foot pounded on the floor of the boat. "She gets everything. Always. Whatever she wants, it's hers. What about me, Rhett? When is it my turn? When do I get what I want?"

Was I hearing her correctly?

Or was I in a completely different conversation than the one she was having?

Because none of this was adding up.

"What does that have to do with what happened today? Because Lainey isn't the reason you were all over me, and Lainey isn't the reason you're all coked out, and Lainey certainly isn't the reason you put us in harm's way."

"Don't you get it?" Her eyes dipped all the way down to my legs and gradually glared back up. "This is Lainey's world. I'm just living in it."

"No, I don't get it."

She put her hands on her head, shaking her hair so each piece loosened from the curls and stood out. "I deserve all the things too!"

"What aren't you getting?"

Her sigh was long and drawn out. "Everything."

"You're going to NYU, the only school you wanted to go to —are you forgetting that? And the guys in our high school you wanted to date or hook up with, you got them too. What do you want that you don't have?"

A burst of air came out of her nose, and she rubbed it until the end was red. "God, you're so stupid."

"You're right. I must be." I nodded toward the water. "We have another twenty minutes until we're at the beach house. Can you control yourself long enough to not almost get us into another accident? I'd like to get there already so I can forget about this shitstorm of a day."

She pointed at me. "Fuck you."

Fuck me?

Why was I getting attacked?

What had I done?

This—whatever the hell this was—had spiraled into something so far from where it should have been. Somehow, I needed to get her back to a place where she was at least settled enough to handle the rest of this boat trip, and I'd deal with the aftermath once we were on land.

I kept my voice low and somewhat soft. "Penelope—"

"Leave me the fuck alone." She backed up to the right side, leaning against the fiberglass edge.

I waved her over and opened my arms, doing anything to

calm her down. "Come here. We'll hug it out, and then we'll get going. Don't forget, we have a joint to share once we get to Timothy's."

"You can go fuck yourself!" She flipped me off.

My hands balled into fists, and I turned toward the helm, slamming them onto the cold metal wheel.

She was impossible.

There was nothing I could do.

My anger was peaking.

My frustration was reaching a whole new level.

I didn't know if this was the person she really was or if it was the drugs making her act this way. It didn't matter because I didn't know what to do.

She'd lost her shit, and I saw no way out of this.

She hadn't reacted well to my yelling—something I should have held in, but I couldn't—and she'd had the same response when I tried to play Mr. Nice Guy.

Do I pick her up and put her in the seat?

Do I beg for her forgiveness?

Do I—

"I'm fucking out of here." She rocked the boat as she stormed toward the stern.

Awesome. Just what I needed, for her to stomp around like a damn child.

I pulled my hands off the helm and began to turn around. My body was only halfway pointed toward the stern, just approaching the starboard side, when I heard the sound.

A sound that made my heart suddenly stop.

A sound that made every bit of breath hitch in my lungs.

A sound that consumed every part of my body.

TWENTY-SIX

Rhett

Present Day

"I'm ... your why," Lainey whispered, the emotion deepening in her eyes, in her posture, in the softness of her voice. "I'm ... your one. *Oh God.*" She rested her forehead against her knees, hiding her face from me. "I can't, Rhett." She finally tilted her head to look at me. "I can't hear this. Not those words. Not from you."

I'd overstepped.

And I'd overshared.

I shouldn't have gone there—not now, not when there was so much to show her and tell her.

But I couldn't hold it all in. I couldn't lie and give her some bullshit reason for why I'd never had her name lasered off my skin.

A lie wouldn't help things.

It certainly wouldn't heal things.

The only thing that could do that was more truth.

"It's time you see this." Still holding my phone, I swiped past the picture of Ridge and me that she had been looking at, and I scrolled back fifteen years, almost to the end of my archives. When I reached the video, I handed her my cell. "Hit Play."

The phone rested in her palm, and she stared at the screen. "What is this?"

"Something I should have shown you a very long time ago."

The volume was loud enough that I knew when she played the video.

But if the sound hadn't told me she was watching it, her face would have.

Her mouth opened, her jaw hanging in shock.

Her head shook, like she didn't believe what she was seeing.

I could hear the tremble in her breath, and the quivering in her chest, and the tiny groan of pain every time she drew in air and released it.

"What is this?" she asked again. "Rhett, what am I looking at right now?"

The first question of what I suspected would be many more.

"Do you remember when I called you from the boat? You were getting your hair done, and Penelope and I were about to take off for Timothy's beach house."

"Of course I remember."

"I took that video as soon as you and I hung up."

"You're telling me my sister was doing coke?"

Penelope's erratic behavior and her using were things I'd never discussed with Lainey.

Until now.

"I'm not telling you, Lainey. I'm showing you."

She pointed at the screen. "And that's her, sitting on the floor of your boat, right before you guys took off for the beach house?"

I got why she needed the information repeated.

This was a fucking lot.

I nodded. "Yes."

I heard the video play again, and when those twelve seconds ended, the video repeated for a third time.

The phone dropped from her hand as though it were on fire, landing on the bleacher, and the sound of it hitting the metal vibrated between us as she glanced up.

"I don't understand. Why are you showing this to me now?"

"And why didn't I show it to you then? I should have. I should have forced you to watch it. I know that now. But I wanted to protect her. And I wanted to protect you and your parents from the truth. That makes little sense—I get that—but I didn't want any of you to think she was a cokehead and ..."

"Fuck!" Her hands went to the sides of her cheeks and pushed back until they were holding her hair. "There's more, isn't there? More I don't know and more you haven't told me?"

"Yes."

Her head shook again. But this time, it was like she wasn't letting the thoughts inside. "But there was another couple. They saw you. They heard you."

"They did, you're right. But there were things they didn't see and things they didn't hear. And those things, Lainey ... they were vital."

TWENTY-SEVEN

Rhett

Fifteen Years Ago

I 'd never heard that kind of noise, but it was unforgettable.

Like when you first fell off your bicycle and your bare knees scraped the gritty pavement, the road rash giving off that sandpaper vibration. One that made you wince whenever you thought about it, even years later. Or the first time you got into a car accident, never forgetting the sound of the crunching bumper and the squealing tires.

Once this noise hit my ears, I knew I'd never be able to get it out of my head.

The adrenaline from the almost crash was still pumping through my veins as I turned toward the back of my father's boat.

My body hadn't even come close to coming down from the nonsense Penelope had just spewed at me.

But now, since the noise, it was all amplified.

My breathing.

My heart rate.

My worry.

There was one rule my father had emphasized from the very beginning. The day he had purchased the boat, he had said it to me, and he repeated it every time I told him I was going out onto the water.

A rule every boater knew.

One that was so important and so obvious at the same time.

But today, there hadn't been a need to say that rule out loud.

Because I'd never thought ... I'd never anticipated ...

This.

As the noise pulsed in my ears, I hit the button on the dash, my hands trembling as I pressed it with all my strength, and I rushed out from the captain's seat.

The noise didn't get louder, but in my head, it was screaming.

Echoing.

That was all I could hear.

My body turned numb.

My hands unclenched, my arms lifting over my head as I took a step and then another.

My eyes started to close.

But before they shut, before I met the darkness behind my lids, I heard it again.

The sound.

But this time, it came from me.

TWENTY-EIGHT

Rhett

Present Day

Lainey had turned completely silent. Her gaze shifted from my phone—which still sat on the bleacher, where it had fallen from her hand—to my eyes. Back and forth in a constant, continuous sweep. Even when her stare wasn't locked with mine, I could sense everything that was going through her head.

The questions.

The confusion.

The accusations.

By showing her the video of Penelope doing coke on my boat, I'd laid the groundwork. Now, I needed to rewind to the beginning.

I stretched out my leg, my foot landing on the spot next to her, and I sat up straight, rubbing my palm over my knee. "Your sister ..." My voice cut off as her expression changed. The misery. I could feel it as though it were a living, breathing thing. As though it came with a set of arms that were fucking wrapping around me. "There were times—many times, in fact—that she said things and did things that she shouldn't have."

She pulled at the sides of my jacket, wrapping it around her, lost in its size. "What do you mean?"

"Like when she told me she loved me."

Her eyes widened before instantly returning to normal. "That was just how she was, Rhett."

"Maybe. But each occasion really stood out and felt highly inappropriate."

"Were there other things that she said?"

I let out some air, hearing the way it hit the wind, turning into a sound that was almost like a whistle. "That I should have chosen her instead of you."

Her mouth opened and closed. When it opened again, she whispered, "She flirted with everyone in high school."

"She took it further than flirting, Lainey. She sought out attention without considering the ramifications. The things she said, the way she touched me"—I paused, knowing this was hard for her, but it was just as hard for me—"little by little, it added up. Building, you could say, until ..."

Until it turned into something far different.

TWENTY-NINE

Rhett

Fifteen Years Ago

The noise that came across the water wasn't the only thing that was unforgettable. The color of the ocean was too.

I was used to the Pacific changing shades. Storms made the medium blue deepen to navy with murky, dark green hues. On days when there was a period of low current and consecutive sunshine, the water was teal with random patches that were so light that it reminded me of ice.

But as I stood at the stern of my boat, with my hands above my head, seconds away from my eyes closing, I didn't see blue.

All I saw was red.

THIRTY

Rhett

Present Day

As Lainey glanced back at the school, strands of her light-brown hair stretched across her face, blown in by the wind. Years ago, I would have tucked them away. It fucking killed me that I didn't have that permission anymore.

When her stare returned, her legs dropped from her chest. With her arms no longer wrapped around them, her hands clung to the edge of the metal seat.

Something had changed since she'd joined me on the bleachers.

When she'd first sat down, I hadn't gotten the feeling that she wanted to let in the truth. She was fighting it. But something I'd said had made her more aware, and it seemed like she was open to it.

Which was ironic because the longer I sat here, the more I struggled giving it to her.

"You know, when I came here, I planned on saying what I wanted to say and not giving you a choice about hearing it. I was going to get it all out, regardless of what that looked like. I don't feel that way anymore."

Because I loved her.

And if that meant dying with these secrets, then I would. If that meant going against the whole reason why I was there, I was all right with that. I'd gone this long without saying these words to her. I could go the rest of my life if I needed to.

"Rhett ..."

"Once you hear the rest of this, Lainey, you can't unhear it. And when that happens, there are consequences. Your dreams will change. So will your nightmares."

"I know." Her hand went to her heart. "They can't be worse than what they already are."

"Trust me, they can."

"Say it, Rhett." Her voice wasn't louder than a shallow breath. "Rip off the fucking Band-Aid."

I pulled my leg back from where it had been resting next to her and clasped my hands together. "At the end of our senior year, I wanted to tell you about the way Penelope was acting. The way she was with me—the things she said, the touchy-feely bullshit, I mean. But it just didn't feel like the right time. I wanted to wait until we were off at college and away from her. I knew how you felt about you two being on opposite sides of the country, and I didn't want to take those moments away from you."

"I wish you hadn't made that decision."

"What difference would it have made?"

Her eyes instantly filled with tears. "You can't ask me that. Not now."

"You're right. I'm sorry." *Fuck*. There were so many wrongs here, and I didn't know how to say the right thing. "Now that I've had years and years to piece it all together, I think, ultimately, it came down to jealousy. She was jealous of you, Lainey. She was jealous of what we had, and that came to a head the day we were on the boat. That much was very obvious."

She wiped her eyes. "I know there was yelling. I know you tossed her bag overboard. But I didn't know there was jealousy —of me or of us."

"She was coked out of her mind, Lainey. She'd smoked a joint all by herself."

"You said nothing about that."

"I was protecting her."

"Why?"

I'd get there.

I needed to explain several things first.

I filled my lungs even though it felt fucking impossible. "During that boat ride, she was all over me. Clinging to me, climbing on me. She got on top of my shoulders while I was driving. And when I finally came to a stop, after we almost crashed into another boat because I'd taken my eyes off the water for a few seconds to deal with her, she started to say things."

I stretched my fingers out, glancing at my palm, remembering the way I hadn't been able to feel my hands that day, how everything had gone so fucking numb.

"She said you got everything you wanted and she didn't and asked when it was going to be her turn. I couldn't make any sense of it. It all sounded like gibberish at the time. I just wanted to get to the beach house and see you and not have to deal with her one-on-one. After the almost accident, my patience was running extra thin, and once she laid on the touching and the jealousy talk and brought you into it, I lost it. I yelled. And when I saw how she reacted to that, I pulled back and changed course, and I asked her to hug it out." My fingers tightened, but this time, I was looking at Lainey. "That didn't work either. She was too far gone at that point."

"I don't understand." She rocked back and forth over the seat, each pass sending me more of her rose scent. It was fucking with my head—all of this was. "How do things go from yelling to ..."

Fifteen years later, and she still couldn't say it.

"I know you blame me. Your parents blame me too." The silence in this moment was the worst sound I'd ever heard. "What I'm trying to tell you is that ... it wasn't my fault."

THIRTY-ONE

Rhett

Fifteen Years Ago

I no longer heard the sound of the engines. I'd turned them off—that was the button I'd slammed on the dash. But still, I looked down at the four motors, making sure there wasn't any water being churned around them. And while I did, the sound of my father's voice was in my head.

The rule he recited each time I took out the boat.

The rule that changed everything.

The rule I hadn't voiced today.

With no time to drop anchor, I stood at the stern with my arms outstretched, my hands overlapped and over my head, my heart thumping in a way I'd never felt before.

Words were coming out of me—I had no idea what they were.

I couldn't hear myself, not with the way my ears were ringing and my heart was thumping.

As I dived off the stern, I didn't bother to take a breath.

I wasn't sure I remembered how. I wasn't sure I even could at this point.

When the Pacific surrounded me, it felt like ice. That was the first thing I noticed—how cold my skin felt despite the rest of me feeling so numb. The second was the feeling inside my body. There was no numbness there. It felt like electricity was shooting from my head to my toes, zapping each muscle and vein.

Those snaps weren't fiery, like the first time I had seen Lainey and every time I'd looked at her since.

They were like an offensive lineman heading right for me, hoping to cause a season-ending injury.

But worse.

I surfaced, shaking my head to clear the hair and saltwater out of my eyes.

The current had moved me; it had shifted the boat. I needed to get my bearings.

I treaded around in a circle, searching until I spotted her.

Screaming, "Penelope!"

Noticing all the fucking red, a path that led me right to her.

"Penelope!"

I didn't just feel my tongue and lips move, my throat tightening from the volume; I heard myself too. I felt the fear. I processed the urgency to get to her.

The water had moved her away from the boat, and she wasn't swimming to stay close; she wasn't trying to fight the current.

"Penelope!"

She was just ... floating.

But away from me and getting farther every second.

Five yards.

Ten yards.

My face dipped into the water, my arms rotating like a windmill, my legs kicking with every bit of strength I had.

I was almost there.

Her arm was within reach, and ... I got her.

"Talk to me, Pen. Tell me what's hurting."

Nothing.

"Pen!"

I turned her over, and her eyes were closed. There was a gash on her forehead, another on her lip.

And there was red.

It was everywhere—on her face, running down her chest, covering my hands.

"I'm going to get you back to the boat. Come on."

I wrapped an arm across her chest and side-stroked toward the boat. Each kick felt like I was maxing out on the leg press. The water was suddenly thick, like sand. My lungs didn't want to take in any air, and my single arm was straining as it reached forward, swiping the water toward me before stretching again.

When I reached the edge of the boat, I didn't know how I was going to get us on board.

The opening was only large enough for one, and I had to lift us out of the water with just one arm since the other was holding her. The ground was too far away, too deep to use that to push off.

The ladder.

Yes, the ladder.

There was one. I could use it.

I fumbled around until I found the latch, and the metal stairs descended.

"I've got you, Pen. Only a few more seconds."

With my foot on the first step, I pulled our upper bodies out of the water, gravity weighing down and working against me. I fought like hell to add my other foot to the rung above.

"Ah! Fuck!"

I was there.

I just needed one more, and I could straddle the opening and get us inside the boat.

I rocked my lower body in the water, building up the energy to lift my foot off the bottom rung and raise it to the top of the ladder while holding the side of the boat with just one hand.

Every part of me was shaking; even my shouting was strained.

One, two, three—push.

I fully breached the surface.

Now, I had to get us inside.

I rotated off the thin piece of metal that was beneath my foot and stretched my free leg over the opening, my toes hitting the SeaDek. The jump caught me off guard with Penelope's added weight, and I lost my balance.

Even midair, I knew she couldn't take it if I fell on top of her. So, I turned us and landed on my shoulder with her back pressed against the front of me. I quickly rolled her onto the floor and knelt beside her.

Fuck. The blood. There was so much.

A wound in her stomach, where the blade of the motor had sliced across the length of her abdomen.

It was deep.

Too fucking deep.

There was another one on her chest, where I could see bone.

I didn't know how to make her stop bleeding.

I didn't know how to fix her.

"Penelope!" I shook her arm. Her shoulder. Her face. Why was her skin so pale? "Open your eyes and look at me!"

I needed to do something.

I needed to get her to wake up.

Is she breathing?

I put my ear to her nose.

The softest puff of air hit my earlobe.

I could help.

I could get her breathing.

I'd taken a CPR class in high school.

I knew that I needed to open her mouth and angle her neck back and press my lips against hers. I pinched her nose and exhaled all the air from my body into hers.

I waited.

Seconds that felt like a fucking eternity.

Nothing.

No airflow.

No opening of her eyes.

No waking up.

I gave her a second breath. This one was even longer—I was sure of it because I'd filled my lungs to capacity and let it all out.

Come on, Pen.

Wake up.

Open your eyes.

Open them for Lainey.

I started compressions, counting out loud after each one. "One, two, three."

"Do you need help?" someone asked. "Should I call the Coast Guard?"

I didn't know where the voice was coming from. I didn't know who was speaking.

But I replied, "Yes! I need help! Call the Coast Guard right now!" My hands had frozen while I responded, but they were back to pulsing against her chest. "Four. Five. Six."

There was more red.

It wouldn't stop.

It just kept coming.

"Seven, eight, nine," I counted.

"Mayday, mayday, mayday," the same voice said. "This is vessel ..."

"Pen," I said, tuning them out, "help is coming. They'll be here soon."

Ten, eleven, twelve.

"Pen!"

PART 2

When I finally had the courage to close my hand, eliminating the
spaces between each finger, I knew.
I'd never have to reach for nothingness again.
I'd never have to clutch empty air.
Beautifully broken.
But in love.

THIRTY-TWO

Lainey

One Day Ago

I lifted a few strands of Penelope's hair and twirled it around my finger. In the thirty-three years I'd been alive, my hair color had changed many times. The palate cleanser was the light brown with golden highlights that I'd been born with, returning to it between my adventurous attempts of red and black and even platinum blonde. But Pen's color never changed. Neither did her style. Straight, the frizz controlled with loose beach waves that hung low down her back.

"What's going on in that head of yours?" she asked.

I smiled, looking down. "Nothing."

"Bullshit. I know when nothing is bothering you, and I know when something is bothering you, and I know when everything is bothering you. In this case, it's something." She shook my shoulder, causing me to glance back up. "Spill it."

She gazed toward the kitchen. "Or I'll just get the bottle of vodka that's in the freezer, and that'll get you to confess it all."

I grabbed the pillow that was behind me on the couch and tossed it at her. She caught the fluffy cream-colored square and held it to her chest, wrapping her arms over it.

"Vodka isn't the answer to everything," I said.

"It isn't?"

"Okay, you might have a point there."

She stretched an arm across the back of the couch. "This something wouldn't have anything to do with the date you went on last night, would it?"

"What makes you think that?" I tried to pull my brows out of their furrow.

"When I asked earlier if you had a good time, you mumbled something incoherent and walked into the bathroom and shut the door. If you'd had a good time on the date, I would have expected more. A smile. Some excitement. Anything."

"It sucked."

She sighed. "Finally, I'm getting somewhere. Why was it so bad?"

"There was nothing there. No chemistry. No spark—if that's what it's called."

I glanced toward the dark hallway that separated the bedrooms from the living room, remembering how I'd stood there for a few minutes last night before leaving my apartment for the date, wondering if I should just cancel. I'd had no desire to meet up with the man who'd asked me out at my gym a few days before. Maybe that was half my problem. I was dating because I was supposed to, not because I wanted to.

She lifted her arms, dancing as though there were music playing. In Pen's head, music constantly played. After a few beats, she stilled and said, "Your first date since you've been back in LA. That's kind of a big deal."

"Why is that?"

"I don't know. Maybe because LA reminds you of a certain someone, which is the reason you left the States in the first place."

A wave of confusion came across me. I couldn't place where it had come from or what it meant. I just knew something suddenly didn't feel right.

"I didn't leave because of Rhett—*fuck*."

"The name you never mention." She rubbed her hands together. "Oh, this is about to get good."

I got up and walked into the kitchen, grabbing the bottle of vodka from the freezer and two glasses from the cabinet, and returned to the living room. I poured some into each cup and handed one to Pen. I didn't clink them together and do a cheers. I just brought the glass right up to my mouth and took a sip.

Rhett.

I waited to feel better about that name.

For the tightness to break free from my chest and my breathing to return to normal.

I downed the rest of the vodka and poured myself some more.

Even that didn't help.

Pen eyed me. "You all right there, sister?"

"Yep."

"Let's talk about Rhett."

I glared at her from the next couch cushion. "Let's not."

"Have you seen him since you've been back?"

I nodded. "Once. By accident." The memory of that random meetup felt odd. The place, the timing, the feeling that had come over me when I found Rhett asleep. I wouldn't get into that. I wasn't sure why; it just felt like something I shouldn't talk about.

At least with my sister.

"And?" She bent her arm, resting her elbow on one of the pillows, her hand pressed against her cheek.

We were identical, yet Pen had gotten the better genes and, like my father, never aged. No gray hair. No wrinkles. I'd just gotten my first Botox treatment since returning to California, and my forehead still wasn't as smooth as hers.

"There is no *and*, Pen. We saw each other, we parted ways. End of story."

"Why does it need to be the end?"

My eyes narrowed, the confusion building within me. "Why does it feel strange, hearing those words come from *your* mouth?"

She smiled. "I don't know. Call me a hopeless romantic?"

I laughed. "You're hardly one of those."

"Then, let's say, I'm rooting for the guy."

"You're ... *what*?"

She shrugged. "Call me crazy."

I laughed. "Hands down, the craziest thing you've ever said." She went to voice something else, and I put my hand on her arm. "Some things are irreparable, and that's okay. Not everyone is meant to be together. And just because I was in love in the past doesn't mean I won't find it in the future."

"Have you found it?"

I rubbed my other hand over the couch. Its newness still making the fabric a little stiff, but the softness was there. So was the slickness of my skin that this conversation was creating. "No."

"Exactly."

"But I haven't been looking."

"But you kinda were during all those years abroad. Spain, Switzerland, until you settled in London."

Those years. Fifteen of them. When I thought back, they'd

gone by so quickly. The sights I'd seen. The friends I'd met along the way. A job that allowed me to work remotely, so it didn't matter if I was backpacking through Asia or standing outside the pyramids of Egypt; I could still support myself.

Until nothing was keeping me there. Until my fingers were tired of booking travel and my feet were exhausted from running. The walls of my flat in London had felt like they were closing in.

No one was my reason for staying.

"Regardless ..." I exhaled. "I'm back. Probably for good. And who knows? Maybe I'll find love at Whole Foods or something."

"You'll be reaching for a cheese sample, and so will he. Your fingers will briefly touch, and you'll pull yours back first— with a smile, of course. You'll live happily ever after."

"Except the one thing I did get while I was in Europe was a dairy allergy." I tilted my head while I took in her face. "I didn't tell you?"

She slowly looked away from me and moved her legs out from beneath her, extending them on the ottoman, her bare feet crossing. "Love is what's missing from your life."

"There are a lot of things missing."

"Like?"

I held her hand tighter. "Like—"

I drew in a gasp, my entire body tensing right before my eyes flicked open.

They were closed?

While the light from the lamp beside me shone in my face, I quickly glanced around the room. The art on the walls, the pictures on top of the bookcase, the plants in the corner, a TV that I'd never even turned on.

My apartment in West Hollywood.

The back of my head was snuggled into a fluffy cream-colored square pillow, and I was cuddled into the couch.

I'd fallen asleep. It had all been a dream.

But there was a bottle of vodka on the tray that sat on the ottoman. There were two glasses next to it; one was full ... the other was empty.

THIRTY-THREE

Lainey

Fifteen Years Ago

Cold.

That was how I felt. The hot water of a shower couldn't warm me. The blasting heat from the vent on the passenger side of the car couldn't dent my temperature.

And numb.

I couldn't feel a knife if it stabbed straight through my heart.

It wasn't just my skin that was frozen.

It was my insides.

My blood.

Organs.

Muscles.

As though I'd been dipped in water and placed in the ice

chest of a garage. A forgotten place where I didn't know when hours passed. When days moved from one to the next.

What I saw was darkness.

In my room with the blinds shut.

In my bed with the comforter over my head.

In the hallway when I paced from my bedroom to the bathroom and back.

Even when I ran outside.

But out here, when I glanced up, raindrops hit my forehead. The drips cascaded down my cheeks and inside my open mouth, my lungs releasing every sound I could scream.

The rain couldn't warm me.

It tried.

Everything tried.

Wet hair was plastered against my skin. My clothes stuck to me. The feelings of wetness and confinement were present, and I did nothing to stop it.

Because I couldn't.

Because I was ice.

Because I was hoping the rain would bring me back. It would rewind time. It would wash away the memories—not all, just the recent ones.

Like when I had walked out of my hair appointment and my phone rang.

Like when I threw up outside my car.

Like when I left my car running in front of the hospital so I could run inside.

Like every moment that had followed.

Even now.

Oh God, especially now.

The ground looked soft from all the rain. The grass squishy. The smell of white flowers was so thick in the air. The white ones had a different aroma from the red and purple and yellow.

All I saw was white.

I hated them.

Every stem.

Every petal.

A hand was holding mine. I could feel the dryness of their skin.

But I was too cold to know if they were as freezing as me or if their warmth couldn't soothe my chill.

On the other side, an arm was looped through mine. I felt fabric instead of skin. Thick, stiff, uncomfortable material.

And there were words—spoken by a man, in an attempt to fill my ears.

But I heard nothing he said.

I wanted him to be quiet.

I wanted ... to forget.

I wanted the hand and the arm off me.

I wanted out of my skin.

I wanted out of this body.

I wanted to stop feeling so cold.

I pulled my fingers away from the hand that held them and wiggled my arm free.

I was on my own.

Alone.

Still cold.

Still unbelievably numb.

My legs were loose. Unstable. The earth was moving, and so was I.

My knees hit the grass.

I felt nothing.

There was a gasp, followed by, "Oh, honey," that didn't come from me.

Hands were suddenly on my shoulder. Under my armpits. On my back.

I waved them away. "Leave me alone." And when that didn't make the hands retreat, I added, "Don't touch me."

I couldn't hear myself.

I couldn't remember the words I'd just spoken.

I didn't care if there was a single set of eyes on me.

I was so cold.

The grass stuck to my palms as I lifted my hands and lowered them, inching forward, the pointy toes of my heels pushing against the mud.

The murmuring around me sounded like raindrops hitting a windshield.

The statement, "Lainey, baby, come back," went ignored.

I didn't try to walk, I couldn't. Crawling would get me there just as fast.

My destination was only a couple of feet away, and when I reached it, I took in the wood. Even that felt cold. Hard and unforgiving. Shiny and difficult to grasp with all the grass and mud stuck to me.

I held on as if the surface were squeezing me back.

As if I could wrap my arms around it like it was a set of shoulders.

As if I could press my cheek against it as though it were another cheek.

My hands balled into fists, and I pounded the wood. "No!" I hit it again. "No! No!"

I know you're in there.

I can feel you.

I hit the back of my hands against the box. "No!"

You're so cold.

I wish you weren't so cold.

I wanted someone to wake me up.

I wanted someone to pull me out of this nightmare.

"Pen!" My voice startled me. I could hear it for the first

time in a while, and I hadn't realized I'd spoken out loud. "Pen!" Something was on my lips. Rain? Spit? Tears? "Come back to me, Pen!"

I wanted her to hold me. I wanted her to clench my fingers. I wanted her to tell me how much she loved me.

My sister.

I wanted to look at my beautiful twin, an almost-mirror image of myself, and say one last thing to her.

Just one more moment.

One more minute.

"Pen!"

Arms wrapped around me and hugged me from behind. "Baby, it's okay! It's going to be okay!"

But they couldn't drag me away.

Because I wouldn't leave Penelope.

I couldn't let her be all by herself in this cold.

Alone in a box that would now be her home.

Lowered into a hole that had been dug just for her.

A spot within the hills of a cemetery on Murphy Drive, where she'd spend the rest of eternity.

Far away from me.

"Pen," I whispered. I glanced up at the sky, and another raindrop hit my face. I tasted it. A small explosion of salt on my tongue, telling me it was a tear as I pleaded with the dark sky. "Please, Pen. Please don't leave me."

THIRTY-FOUR

Rhett

Fifteen Years Ago

L ike a flip of a switch, everything had suddenly gone dark.
My entire life had changed.

And just when I'd thought it couldn't get any worse, it did.

Because four days had passed since I'd talked to Lainey. My calls to her cell went unanswered. When I tried her parents' house, my call would either go to their answering machine or the phone would be picked up and then slammed down.

Lainey's parents were making it clear they didn't want to hear from me.

Which had started when Mr. Taylor thrust his head into the room at the police station where I was being interviewed.

He had pointed his finger at me from the doorway and said,

"I never want you to see or talk to Lainey ever again—do you hear me?" before a police officer pulled him away.

According to the law, I was innocent. I'd passed the breathalyzer test. The preliminary blood test showed small traces of THC in my system from when I'd smoked the day before—a level not high enough to prove I'd smoked around the time of the incident. The witnesses—the ones who had called the Coast Guard—had confirmed that Penelope had jumped on her own, that I was in the captain's seat when it happened, therefore I hadn't physically forced her into the water.

Still, Mr. Taylor believed I deserved the death penalty. He'd said as much when he shouted, "Give him the electric chair," in the hallway after the police pulled him away from my interview room.

Whatever I'd said to Penelope that made her jump off my boat was on me. I would have to live with that for the rest of my life.

Just like I'd have to live with the memory of this morning when, while hiding in the back of the cemetery, far from her parents' line of sight but with a clear view of Lainey, I'd watched my girl pull free from her parents' grip. I'd watched her crawl to Penelope's casket. And I'd watched her beg for Penelope to come back. I'd never seen anything more gut-wrenching or heartbreaking.

An image that would forever live in my fucking head.

While she had pressed her face to the casket, holding it as though she were trying to hug it, I'd just wanted to put my arms around her. I'd wanted to whisper in her ear that everything—somehow, someway—would be all right. I didn't know if that was true, if she'd ever be able to move on after a loss like this, but they were words Lainey needed to hear.

And I was determined to say them to her.

Which was why, hours after the funeral, I was at her front door, ringing the bell.

I clenched my fingers, listening to the sound of stomping feet on the hardwood floor, each step getting louder. I held my breath as Mr. Taylor's face appeared in the doorway. He still had on the black suit he'd worn to the funeral, the same way I still had on mine.

"I told you to stay away! Get off my front step and get the hell out of here!" Every time he emphasized a word, a piece of spit came flying toward me.

I didn't care how angry he got; I wouldn't back down, nor would I let him push me away.

"I need to talk to Lainey, sir."

He held the top of the door, looking at me with complete disgust. "I don't care what you need! Leave! Now!"

"You don't understand. I need to talk to her. Please. A couple of minutes—that's all I'm asking for."

"*I* don't understand?" He took a step toward me. "I understand that I put my daughter in your care, and according to the witnesses, there was yelling and screaming on your boat before she stormed off and jumped into the water. Your engines should have been off if you were idling and there was concern that she might jump—"

"I didn't know she was going to jump."

I couldn't even count how many times I'd said that over the last four days.

When the Coast Guard had arrived at the boat.

At the police station.

To my parents.

To my siblings.

"It doesn't matter what you knew or what you didn't. You do not take a risk like that when there are other people on your boat!"

I slipped my hands into my pockets to stop them from fisting. "But we weren't anchored, sir. I was just pulled over in the water so we could talk—"

"Argue."

"Regardless, the circumstances aren't what you're describing. If I was going to anchor, the engines would have been off. That wasn't the case. I was only stopping for a second—"

"I don't give a fuck what your circumstances were, young man. What you did on that boat killed my daughter!" He put his hand in front of his mouth, like he was trying to either hold himself together or prevent himself from exploding.

I took a deep breath.

And then another.

"She was my responsibility. I fully accept that. But there's nothing I could have done to stop her from jumping—"

"As the captain, she was under your care, and whatever you said to her led to her jumping." He took another step, the door staying open as he released it, his finger aimed and pointed at me. "You failed her, son. You failed her, you failed my wife, you failed me, and you failed Lainey." His face was turning red, the veins in his forehead sticking out.

He was right. Since I had been the captain, Penelope had been under my care—a role I took seriously. A promise I'd made to him when I spoke to him on Lainey's phone before I even got on the boat.

I'd failed him. He was right about that too.

"I'm sorry." Words that weren't strong enough. Words that had little impact as he stared at me. "I don't know how to express how sorry—"

"That's not fucking good enough."

"What can I do—"

"You could have not argued with my daughter—that's what

you could have done. You're the reason, Rhett. You're the goddamn reason!"

He was putting this all on me.

He was making me out to feel like a murderer.

I shook my head. "That's not it. It's not what you think."

"The report I read from the police said there was an argument between you and my daughter about getting to the beach house. Why didn't you just put the boat in gear and drive the rest of the way there? Why did you stop in the first place?"

I had been careful about what I told the police.

Not for myself, but for Penelope.

"I wanted to get going, but she was—"

"She was what?" He waited. "Are you going to blame something on an eighteen-year-old girl who's no longer here? Who should be heading off to NYU in a few months, but isn't? Who I just watched get lowered into the fucking ground?"

Jesus.

I couldn't ... I couldn't stop the shaking.

In my knees. In my hands. In my entire body.

His finger got close to my chest, but it didn't touch me. "When the witnesses got on your boat to help you with the CPR and wrap her wounds, they saw you throw Penelope's bag overboard. Who the hell does something like that? Someone who's pissed off—that's who."

I knew how that'd looked. I knew how it could be interpreted.

But I'd had a reason.

And that reason was hanging on the edge of my tongue.

But as our stares stayed locked, my throat closed.

My lips shut.

My eyes burned with emotion.

My chest felt like it was going to cave inward.

"I was upset," I said to him.

"*You* were upset?"

"And, yes, I was angry, but—"

"*You* were angry?"

My hands were sweating so badly in my pockets. I took them out, and they fell at my sides. "I'd just pulled Penelope out of the water and performed CPR—"

"I don't need a goddamn play-by-play. I already know how you killed my daughter!"

He stepped toward me, and I backed up a few paces, the accusation vibrating through me.

"Do you know what you've done to this family since you came into Lainey's life? You brainwashed her into becoming obsessed with you. She couldn't ever feel settled in New York and begged me every day for two years to move back to LA. And once we got here, USC was all I heard about. My daughter should have picked Stanford, but, no, you convinced her otherwise. Not anymore, Rhett. You're out of her life, out of our lives, and none of us will, thankfully, ever see you again. And if you try, I'll fucking kill you!"

What?

I'm ... out of her life?

But how?

And if I try ... he'll kill me?

Lainey was leaving for college in a few months.

Where we were going to be together.

"Lainey isn't going to USC?" I asked.

"No."

No?

"She isn't going anywhere near you!"

That couldn't be true.

It ... wasn't possible.

I needed to talk to her. I needed to see if she was okay. I

needed to know why she wasn't speaking to me. I needed to hear if what her dad was saying was true.

Mr. Taylor wasn't going to allow me to see Lainey.

So, I was left with no other choice.

While he aimed his finger right at my heart as though it were the end of a gun, shouting, "Now, get the fuck off my property," I used my skills as the fastest wide receiver in my high school's division and quickly swerved around him, running for the stairs.

"Get back here right now!" he yelled from behind me. "I'm going to call the police!"

I took two stairs at a time, and at the landing, I rushed down the hallway until I reached her room, opening the door without knocking. I scanned the inside until I found her. I didn't expect for her to be on the floor, tucked in the corner between the window and her dresser, the shades drawn and the light off.

She didn't look up at me.

She made no reaction as I stood there, her pale face a combination of appearing like she wanted to throw up and on the verge of crying and so empty that there was nothing left inside her.

"Lainey ..."

My heart had shattered at the funeral.

But here, right now, was a sight I could barely handle.

I locked the door behind me, knowing it would only be a few seconds until Mr. Taylor would try to tear me out of this room.

"Lainey ..."

Still no response.

I crossed the carpet and knelt in front of her. She was in the black dress she'd worn to the funeral. The mud was still caked to her knees. It was on her fingers. And there was a smear of it across her cheek.

"Lainey—"

"Stop." Her voice was just above a whisper as she finally glanced up, pushing my hands away as I set them on the sides of her knees. "Don't touch me."

"But I want to hold you—"

"No." Her head shook so violently that hair moved into her face.

No?

Oh my God, this was worse than I could have even imagined.

"Lainey, I love you."

Her head continued to shake. "No."

"I've been calling you. Your cell, the house. I just want to talk to you about what happened."

She pulled her bent knees against her chest. "No."

Mr. Taylor's fist pounded on the door. "Get out of my house right fucking now!"

"Lainey, I just want you to hear me out. Please."

The look in her eyes scared me. It sent a shiver through my whole body. What I'd thought was emptiness was not that at all. Emotions were in there; they just weren't directed at me. And at me, she was cold, turned off.

Finished.

"Rhett, I trusted you."

"You can trust me, baby." I put a hand beside each of her bare feet. "I didn't want this to happen. I didn't know she was going to jump off the boat. We were going back and forth in conversation, and she told me she was out of there. I had no idea that meant out of the boat and then ..." I couldn't say what happened next. That would be too much for her ears.

She folded like a smashed Oreo. "You had one job. To take care of her like I would have if I'd been there. And look what you let happen—" Her hand slapped over her mouth right after a sob escaped her lips.

"I did, Lainey. I took perfect care of her—"

"You can't say that." A single tear rolled down her face. "Because she's not here with me right now. She's not in her room. She's"—another cry came out of her, but this time, she didn't try and cover it with her palm—"dead."

"Get out of my daughter's room right now before I rip off this goddamn door!" Mr. Taylor shouted.

My eyes squeezed shut until her father stopped screaming, and I looked at Lainey. "There's so much I need to tell you about the boat. Your sister—"

"I don't care what you have to tell me. I'll never be able to look at you the same ever again. I'll never be able to forgive you." Her hands covered her face. "Get out, Rhett."

"Lainey—"

"It doesn't matter what you say." Her hands dropped. "It'll never bring her back."

"No, but it will show you that none of this was my fault."

As she held the tops of her knees, the pieces of mud that were there turned to dust and hit the air. "Were you driving the boat?"

I exhaled, the defeat eating at me. "Yes."

"Did you stop her from jumping?"

The inside of my body was moving so fast, yet the outside felt as though it were frozen. "I couldn't have, I didn't know she was going to do it. I wasn't even looking at her."

"Exactly! You weren't watching her, and that's all I wanted from you—for you to be me if I wasn't there."

It didn't matter that Penelope had been on coke.

Or that she had been out of control.

Or that she had been all over me.

All Lainey and her father cared about was that I'd failed them.

The realization of what I was facing was too much.

The truth was too much.

The thoughts in my head were too much.

"We can get past this," I urged, desperate to make her remember that she'd loved me before this. "You can find a way to forgive me, and we can go to USC and be together, and—"

"I'm not going to USC."

There was wetness in my eyes, and I pushed it away, my hand staying because another round of tears was on its way. "What do you mean, Lainey? What about us?"

"Rhett, there is no us." Her head slowly moved to the right and then the left, her throat bouncing when she swallowed. "Us ended when"—she glanced up at the ceiling, and the drips fell from her chin—"my sister died."

"Lainey, no—"

She pointed at the door. "Go!"

I sucked in a breath, feeling the blood drain from my body. "Lainey, I love you. I'll do anything to make this right. But please, don't do this. Don't push me away. Don't end what we have. You're my why—"

"After you leave this room, you will never see me again." Tears were streaming down her cheeks, but there wasn't any softness in her expression. No love as she stared back at me. "Now, go!"

"Lainey, can we talk about this? Will you please just hear my side of things—"

She got up, stepping around me, and kicked my hand away when I tried to touch her ankle. She unlocked the door, and as her father rushed in, heading right for me, Lainey gave me one last look.

I knew then.
I felt it.
I saw it.
She was gone from my life forever.

THIRTY-FIVE

Lainey

Present Day

I couldn't stop rocking back and forth on the cold metal bleacher. I couldn't stop gazing at Rhett even though, at times, his face was too much to look at. So was the feel of his presence. The way he stared at me, just like he had all those years ago, brought me right back to the summer after our senior year.

Rhett!

My mind was this wild mix of: *I can't believe I'm here, I can't believe I'm sitting so close to him, I can't believe I'm giving him a chance to tell me about that dreaded day, I can't believe I'm listening, and I can't believe I want to.*

Not just want to. I needed to.

I'd just gotten done telling him I didn't understand how

things between Pen and him had gone from yelling to ... and then my voice had cut off.

I couldn't finish.

Why was it still so difficult to say she was dead? Even in my dreams—which occurred several times a week, like the one I'd had last night—there were signs that I'd lived far more life than her. But saying it out loud was just too difficult. Too definitive.

"I know you blame me. Your parents blame me too. What I'm trying to tell you is that ... it wasn't my fault."

Rhett and I were sitting in silence while the words he'd just spoken resonated through me.

Someone had to be at fault. It was the only way to make sense of what had happened, so my parents and I had turned him into the enemy.

That was how we survived.

But was that fair?

Was that title even accurate?

Rhett's account was pushing together the missing pieces of a tragic puzzle, filling the gaping holes that had never made sense.

Did I blame him? Still?

"It wasn't your fault," I whispered, repeating his last statement. A shiver ran through me, and I held myself tighter, balling up to stop anything from getting in. "I have so many questions."

I needed to back up. I needed to make sure I understood this all correctly.

But, damn it, why did he have to have the most gorgeous icy-blue eyes? A color I'd seen in the waters of Italy and again when I'd gone to Portugal. Every time I'd visited those countries, I would take in the view of the ocean, and I would think of him.

And each time, I'd have to look away.

Just like I was doing now.

"I'd hoped you would have questions. Ask them. Ask me anything."

My brain was a giant spinner, separated into slices, like the Wheel of Fortune game, the arrow waiting to land on a question.

There were so many.

Where do I even start?

"The police," I said, a place that felt obviously comfortable. "You told them you and Pen were arguing about going to the beach house. That was what had caused her to jump. Was that true?"

"Partly."

I stilled after shaking my head. "You lied to them?"

"I just didn't tell them everything."

"Why?"

He held his hands together, his thumbs upward, a lion tattoo on one. It was so precisely done; I could even see the whiskers.

"I knew you and your family would see the police report. I didn't want you all to know what she had really been like in that moment."

My stomach sank.

Cocaine.

I had never suspected it. Was I naive? Ignorant? Or had it been obvious and I just hadn't wanted to see it?

"High, you mean?" I clarified.

"High as fuck and out of control."

His head dropped enough to show me more of the blackness of his hair. I swore it had thickened since high school, had even gotten curlier. His beard, too, had completely filled in, the open, splotchy patches no longer present.

"I didn't mention the almost accident to the police either. I didn't want it on record that she had been all over me."

When he glanced up, the whites of his eyes were turning a slight shade of red.

"The whole time I spoke to them, all I could think about was you. What it would feel like to read those things about your sister. I didn't want to shit all over the memory of her. Not when you and your family would be grieving for the rest of your lives. So, I honored her in the only way I knew how, and that was by giving the police enough, but not giving them the whole story."

"What if a witness had seen her on your shoulders and the almost accident that happened? What if they'd reported it?"

He shrugged. "I would have come up with something."

"And her bag? The divers weren't able to recover it, it was lost at sea. But you told the police you threw it overboard out of anger. Was that true?"

His exhale was loud and emotional. "I threw it because there was coke inside. I knew the police would search it and find the blow, along with the dirty mirror and the powdered bill she'd stuck up her nose, and I couldn't let that happen. Lainey ..." He quieted while he gazed into my eyes, the silence building before he said, "Again, I was just trying to protect her memory and you and your family from knowing that part of the truth. A truth that I was sure would only hurt all of you."

My head fell back, my throat open to the wind.

I'd come up with so many reasons. He had thrown it because he couldn't stand the sight of one more thing of hers. He had thrown it because there was something inside that would incriminate him. He had thrown it because he couldn't throw her—she'd angered him that badly.

But protecting her? And us?

I'd never considered that.

"I have to admit something that isn't easy."

"None of this has been easy, Lainey."

I waited, begging my heart to calm down, which was a laughable request because I knew it wouldn't. "There were so many times I wanted to reach out and talk to you about what had happened. I found your Instagram account. It's the only social media I could locate, unless the rest is under a pseudonym."

"Instagram is all I have."

I nodded. "I was going to message you on there, but the account looked dead. You never posted a single photo."

"Is that really the reason you didn't reach out? Because the account looked dead?"

"No."

"I didn't think so."

"The real reason is that I didn't have the nerve to." My voice softened as I said, "I was afraid, Rhett." I rubbed my lips together, the wind making them so dry. "There was so much I didn't know from that day on the boat. So much that I couldn't piece together. Parts that just didn't make sense in my head. An argument? About going to the beach house? It wasn't adding up."

"I didn't think you'd accept that as an answer ... but then you did, and you didn't want to hear anything else. Neither did your father."

My hands touched my earlobes, remembering back then how every sound had pounded my eardrums, even an almost-silent dribble. "I couldn't hear anything else." The knot was so thick in my throat that I could barely swallow. "All I kept thinking about was how much she adored you. How she loved spending time with you and being around you. What could have possibly made her want to get away from you? And then my brain would spiral. Did she know the engines were on? Did she jump on purpose—"

"No. She didn't know."

"I don't think so either. Pen wasn't suicidal. She didn't have suicidal ideation either—but if she had, would I have known? Because I'd missed so many other things, like her using. I don't trust my awareness at all."

"You're coming up with scenarios because that's what we do. We analyze. We interpret. We try to understand even if it doesn't make sense and it's impossible to understand." His hands moved to the metal, gripping the edge on either side of him. "I can hear every word she spoke as though it happened seconds ago."

"You mean of that day? Right before she jumped?"

He nodded. "Yes."

I heard myself gasp. And then I heard myself say, "Tell me. I want to hear it."

"Lainey, the last few minutes I spent with Penelope are imprinted on my brain in a way you can't even imagine, in a way that I'll never forget." He took a breath. "Are you sure you want to hear it all, word for word?"

"Yes. More than anything."

He let out a deep, loud breath. "The boat was stopped. I'd pulled over to a clear spot, and we were idling since we'd almost just gotten into the accident.

"We'd gone back and forth about you, and she said, 'I deserve all the things too.'"

"When I asked her what she wasn't getting, she responded with, 'Everything!'"

He huffed, rubbing a hand over the top of his head.

"So, I said to her, 'You're going to NYU, the only school you wanted to go to—are you forgetting that? And the guys in our high school you wanted to date or hook up with, you got them too. What do you want that you don't have?'" He was staring straight ahead, toward the track that I'd been walking on, as though he was watching the scene play out in his head.

"'God, you're so stupid,'" she said to me.

"Then, I replied, 'You're right. I must be. We have another twenty minutes until we're at the beach house. Can you control yourself long enough to not almost get us into another accident? I'd like to get there already so I can forget about this shitstorm of a day.'" He ran his tongue over his teeth, his eyes getting redder.

"She pointed at me and said, 'Fuck you.'"

"Rhett ..."

If he sensed the emotion in my voice, he didn't acknowledge it. If, from the corner of his eye, he saw me wipe my tears, he didn't look at me.

"I tried to say her name, and she said, 'Leave me the fuck alone.'"

"I opened my arms, Lainey, knowing I'd crossed some kind of boundary, and said, 'Come here. We'll hug it out, and then we'll get going. Don't forget, we have a joint to share once we get to Timothy's.'"

"She'd tried to get me to smoke on the boat, and I wouldn't. I'd promised her we'd share a joint at the beach house just to get her off my back. And the hug was to change her mood, but it caused her to flip me off and tell me to go fuck myself." He finally looked at me.

The expression on his face was haunting.

Harrowing.

But that wasn't the only thing that sent me over an edge that I hadn't realized I was teetering on.

The truth had done that. Penelope's last moments, which were unlike anything I'd ever imagined.

The tears were suddenly dripping freely down my face, my chin quivering, my breathing coming out in pants.

"The last thing she said was, 'I'm fucking out of here.'"

"Seconds later, I heard the engines. That sound ..." His hand went to his chest, and his eyes shut. "I'll never get over that noise, Lainey. It was a torture that ripped right through me."

His eyes opened, and a chill covered my body.

"But there was another noise that followed the engines that I'll never recover from either." He waited several beats before he said, "And that was her scream."

I held up a finger, searching for the words, but my throat was so tight that air wasn't even moving through it. "I need a second."

Emotion was pouring through me. It poured over me. And it poured out of me.

I bent toward my lap and covered my face, and as soon as I was hidden, I sobbed. I let out everything that was inside me. The years of sorrow, the pain, the unknown that had eaten at me. I cried for what Pen had experienced the second her feet left the boat, how those engines had beaten her to the point of ...

Out of nowhere, I felt heat.

An arm.

And then another.

Rhett was hugging me so hard, changing my coldness to warmth, and I didn't ask him to let me go.

"I'm sorry, Lainey," he whispered into the back of my neck. "I'm so fucking sorry."

THIRTY-SIX

Rhett

Fifteen Years Ago

"Rhett?" my father said from the other side of my
bedroom door.

I ignored his knock and pulled the blanket up to my neck.

I wanted it all to stop.

The noise.

The memories.

The sound of Penelope hitting the engines and the scream
that had escaped her lips.

Fuck!

"Rhett!" he yelled again. "Can I come in?"

I put my hands over my ears, my body swaying over the
bed, like I was still in the boat and the waves were causing me
to rock.

Seconds later, from the corner of my eye, I saw the door

open, my dad moving through my room and taking a seat beside me.

He put his hand on mine, pulling to free my ear. "Are you all right, son?"

"No." The pain was so severe in my chest; a sob came out of my lips. "I'm not fucking okay."

He rubbed my hand. "Your sister's been asleep outside your door for over an hour." He nodded toward the hallway. "Right out there, on the carpet. She's afraid to bother you, but she wants to be close to you. And your brother's been pacing the upstairs, waiting for you to open your door. We're all very worried about you."

"I don't want to see anyone. I just want to be left alone."

"I know, son." He paused. "It was a horrible tragedy."

"A tragedy? It was worse than that! Penelope is fucking dead!"

I put my hands over my face, the tears making my palms so wet.

"It's going to be okay, Rhett. I promise."

I was tired of hearing that.

From my father.

From my mother.

From the friends I'd talked to.

That was all anyone said.

But they were wrong. How could any of this ever be okay?

How could things ever go back to normal?

My hands dropped and balled into fists. "You told me one rule when it came to boating. One rule I always had to follow, and that was to make sure the engines were off before anyone got in the water. I didn't follow the rule. I didn't say it to Penelope, and look what happened!"

"You didn't know she was going to jump in, Rhett."

"I should have turned off the engines!"

"But you were idling," Dad said, "and about to take off at any second. There was no reason to turn them off."

Air wasn't moving through my lungs. I was a mess of words, and wet lips, and a runny nose, and an ache so bad that every part of my face was throbbing.

"She's not coming back, Dad!" I pounded my fists against the bed. "And now, Lainey never wants to see me again, and her father wants to kill me and ..."

There was nothing left to say.

It was all over ...

Penelope's life.

My relationship with Lainey.

The plans we'd made, the dreams we'd had.

"It hurts, Dad." I hit my chest with the back of my hand. "It hurts so fucking bad, and I don't know how to make it stop."

Rowan appeared in the doorway, holding the side of it while rubbing her eye. "I heard you and woke up." She made her way through my room and crawled onto my bed, grabbing a pillow on her way to my side, her head resting on my shoulder. "Don't cry, Rhett." Her arm looped through mine. "You're my favorite person in this whole world. You and Ridge both are. You would never do anything bad or hurt anyone. This wasn't your fault. Lainey knows that. I swear she does."

But Lainey didn't know that.

She'd said she put me in charge of her sister and look what had happened.

"Your sister's right, Rhett."

"Regardless, she won't take my calls. I tried again a few minutes ago," I admitted. "She's not going to USC. She's done with me."

Dad rubbed my hair. "That doesn't mean she's done forever. She just needs a time-out, and that's okay. Lots of people take breaks and get back together."

"This is different," I barked.

"She won't answer my calls either," Ridge said.

I glanced at the doorway, where he was now standing. "You called her?"

He nodded. "I know how much you're hurting. I just wanted to do something to make it better." His arms straightened, his fists hitting the air. "I just wanted to tell her how much you love her."

"Ridge ..." I whispered.

"It's true," he said. "I didn't know how else to help."

As my brother joined us on the bed, my father said, "Listen to me, Rhett. If you need to take a few days and bury yourself in this room, fine. But you're going to enjoy the summer with your friends, like you planned to do before this all happened, and you're going to go off to USC. Who knows? Maybe Lainey will show up a little later in the year or your sophomore year."

What the hell is he talking about?

Did he really think I could go to the beach with the rest of the guys and ride the waves, like a catastrophe hadn't happened in that ocean? And find myself at parties, laughing, drinking, smoking, having fun, when all I could think about were the sounds from that day on the boat?

And the blood.

Oh fuck, all that blood ...

I held the top of my headboard and banged my skull against it. "Lainey's not coming back."

"You don't know that, Rhett—"

"Yes, I do, Dad. You should have seen the way she looked at me when she left me with Mr. Taylor and walked out of her room. I could feel her glare all the way in my stomach. She's ... done."

Rowan squeezed my arm.

"She's upset, son. That's understandable."

"But it wasn't my fault." My voice was so soft.

"No, it wasn't," Dad said. "Right now, they're too upset to see that."

"Well, they should see it," Ridge said. "Rhett's the guy everyone loves. How could they treat him like this?"

"The loss that family just experienced is unimaginable," Dad explained. "If anything happened to any of you"—he cut himself off and shook his head—"I don't know how I'd ever be able to move on. But you know what? Somehow, someway, I would—because I have other children I need to live for, just like Mr. Taylor does."

His hand moved to my cheek. "I need you to stay strong, son. I need you to keep going. That's all you can do." He tapped my chin with his fist. "You're a Cole. We don't give up, we fight. That's just what you're going to do."

THIRTY-SEVEN

Lainey

Fifteen Years Ago

As I rode in the backseat, I stared at the backpack on my lap. I didn't know what was inside of it. I couldn't remember putting a single thing in it or zipping it up. And as I glanced down at my outfit, I couldn't even recall getting dressed or climbing into this seat or how long we'd been in the car.

The radio was off, and Mom and Dad, sitting in the front, were silent.

Have they been quiet the whole time?

My stomach tightened every time we went over a bump, my breakfast threatening to come up. Nothing settled anymore. My gut was a bundle of sadness and acid; some days, the acid stayed put, and other days, it came spewing from my mouth.

Have I even eaten breakfast?

When was the last time I ate?

The sky was darkening. I wasn't sure if it was Tuesday or Wednesday, even though it was probably Thursday, and coffee was all I'd ingested in the last week.

I clutched the bar on the door and watched LA fly by through the window.

There was one thing that I did remember—when I'd sat just like this, folded into the corner of the seat, gripping the door that my father had locked, wishing for the car to turn around and go back to our house instead of Manhattan.

This time, we were headed to the airport, and I didn't have that hope.

I had given up on hope.

Fuck hope.

The car came to a stop outside of Departures. Both front doors opened, and I took that as my cue to get out. I put the straps of my backpack on my shoulders and stepped onto the curb. My parents joined me, their faces looking so different as I studied each one.

My dad, always a thin man, had hollow cheeks and a gaunt neck. Mom looked like she hadn't slept in a year; the bags under her eyes were turning dark, and her eyes were rimmed in red.

"Your passport," Dad said as he handed me the small navy leather-bound booklet. "And here's enough cash for at least a week or two. I didn't have time to get it converted. Use your credit card. This is just for incidentals."

I shoved the hundreds into my pocket. "Where am I even going?"

"I pulled a few strings and got you into a school in Spain," he said. "You'll be starting classes in two months. A driver will be at the airport, holding a sign with your name on it. He'll take you to your apartment."

"My apartment?" I whispered.

I remembered when we'd talked about this.

USC was off the table.

I couldn't go there ... with him.

But I wanted school. I needed the schedule and routine and to stay busy. My parents supported that decision.

Different states were thrown out during that conversation. All possible options. I told them I wanted to go as far away as I could and I wanted to go right now. I didn't want to wait until classes started. I needed to escape everything that reminded me of Pen.

My parents didn't want me to leave so soon. They'd lost one daughter; they weren't ready to say goodbye to another.

But I'd begged.

I needed to be alone with my grief.

I couldn't hear Mom cry another tear. I couldn't hear Dad pace the kitchen all night, unable to sleep.

If Dad had told me where he was sending me—which he probably had—it hadn't registered.

I was as empty now as I had been when I rushed into the hospital and was told she was no longer breathing.

Nothing was sticking.

I was a slick, oily slide, and everything that came in rolled right off me.

"Do I have clothes?" I asked.

"We'll ship them to you, honey." Mom tucked some hair behind my ear. "This all happened a little fast, and I didn't want you to have to worry about lugging around suitcases. You have enough in your backpack for a couple of days, and there's laundry in your apartment if you need to wash what you have."

I nodded. "Okay."

"We're going to miss you." Mom's voice cracked. Tears welled in her eyes.

I'd never seen my family cry more in the last I didn't know how many days than I had in my whole life.

"I'll miss you," I replied.

Arms were around me. The scent of Mom was so off; there were hints of wine and even smoke, something she'd quit when I was a kid. The hug grew stronger when Dad joined us, his chin resting on top of my head. He hadn't shaved in a while, and the whiskers stabbed through my hair and into my skull.

I didn't pull away.

The pain felt oddly comforting. It gave me something to focus on.

Instead of ... her.

When the hug ended, I said, "I'll call." Did I even have my phone? I felt my pocket, and it was in there, taking up the whole space. "Will my phone work there?"

"I almost forgot." Dad rushed back to the car and returned to us. "I got you a new one." He handed me a phone. "Why don't you give me your old one?"

I reached into my pocket and switched devices with him.

"Our house line and both of our cell phones are saved in there," he said, nodding toward the one now in my hand.

"What about all the other numbers?" I asked. "I don't know them by heart. And the texts that are all there ..."

From her.

From ... him.

"Do you need their numbers?" Dad asked. "You're leaving, Lainey. You're starting fresh. That life ... it's behind you."

I nodded. "I suppose you're right."

"We'll be coming to visit soon, baby." Mom hadn't stopped touching my hair. "A couple of weeks, tops."

"I have a colleague who lives not far from where you'll be," Dad said. "She's worked for my company for as long as I have. I trust her. I put her number in there, and she's going to be in touch when you land. If you need anything, ask her. Don't be afraid."

I nodded again.

Because it felt like I was supposed to.

"We love you," Mom said.

I could barely hear her over all the noise outside the terminal.

"We're only a phone call away." Dad's eyes were filling with tears. "We love you very much."

I didn't know if I had any tears left. I'd shed so many that I felt dry.

I was holding each of their hands. Both felt different. Like the grief had even changed their skin.

I gave them a squeeze. "See you soon."

I walked into the airport, moving in a daze, so disassociated that by the time I came to, I was in the window seat, looking out onto the wing of the plane.

We were already in the air.

And in my hand was a photograph. I didn't remember putting it in my bag and taking it out. But there was a picture of Rhett and me. We were on the beach. His arm was around me in a way where his tattoo was showing, and the *R* necklace dangled from my throat. I was looking at the camera, but he wasn't. He was gazing at me.

The smile on his face ... for me.

Warmth.

When all I felt now was coldness.

"Can I get you anything?" someone said.

I looked across the two seats beside me, not realizing they were empty, and at the flight attendant standing in the aisle.

"You were sleeping when I came by during the drink service," she said. "You slept right through dinner too. I'm happy to get you something now that you're awake."

I'd been ... sleeping?

Did I want anything?

The thought of putting something in my body made my stomach churn.

"I'm okay."

She nodded. "Just let me know if you change your mind."

"Wait," I said as she started to walk away. "Can I ask you for a favor?"

"Of course."

I handed her the photo. "Can you put this somewhere I'll never have to see it again?"

She took the picture from me and glanced at it. A soft, understanding smile came over her face. "Are you sure? He looks like he really loves you."

I touched my throat, where the necklace still sat, and mashed my lips together, holding back a cry. "Yes, I'm sure."

THIRTY-EIGHT

Present Day

W hy did a hug feel as personal as a kiss? Why did it have the power to make me feel things that should have stayed dormant? Why, while Rhett had his arms around me, did I want him to squeeze me tighter?

Did I want him to not let me go?

"I'm sorry, Lainey."

I didn't know how many times he'd repeated that statement, but it was many. I got the feeling he was saying it for himself as much as he was for me. I also didn't know how long we sat here, folded together on the bleacher, the wind whipping past us as fast as the memories were taking hold in my brain. But at some point, he released me, and I uncurled from the ball I'd been in.

"You want to know why she jumped off my boat." He

straightened his tie, letting the silk eventually fall from his hand. "You want a definitive answer."

"My heart would like one, yes."

He traced his thumb over his bottom lip. "What I think is that Penelope wanted attention. She wanted it from me, and she wanted it from everyone. She also wanted what you had. That was the noise and chaos she lived with. I think she jumped because she wasn't getting enough attention, and she had no idea that on her way into the water, she would hit the blades of four engines."

While he'd been hugging me, his jacket had dropped from my shoulders, and I lifted it off the metal, draping it around me.

"The attention—yes, that makes sense. But you ... she knew she was never getting you."

"I don't think she wanted me. I think it was the idea that she couldn't have me."

I considered his theory. "Probably." I let some time settle before I sighed, "God."

He leaned in closer, putting his arms on his thighs. "I opened that Instagram account to watch you. That's the only reason it exists. I never hit the Follow button on your page or liked a single photo or dared to comment on one, but every few days, I'd check on you. I'd see the friends you posed with and the places you visited. I'd take in your smile, and a pang of jealousy would stab at me, wishing I were who you were smiling for."

"Even after all these years," I whispered.

His skin flushed, the red coming in and leaving just as fast. "Time changed nothing, aside from making me older. My feelings—those went untouched." His leg bounced. "That's not true. They were touched because they became stronger."

This was so much to hear, so much to take in. Today was an

emotional trauma dump, and I didn't know how much more I could handle.

Rhett's hand lifted and got as high as my face. But before he touched me, it dropped back to his lap. "You know what else I know? Those smiles in your pictures weren't out of happiness, they were out of obligation."

I'd always wondered if he'd looked at my photos.

I'd never thought that, if he had, he saw right through my purpose, which was convincing myself I was happy with my life.

"Why didn't you ever reach out?" I asked.

"When I left your house the day of the funeral, I called you and sent you texts for about a week straight. Your phone was eventually disconnected. I assumed you had gotten a new number, and I tried to get it from your friends, but no one had it. When your social media profiles were deactivated, I thought you just didn't want to be found. You went completely off the grid. And then about six months later, you appeared on Instagram under a different account."

"All of that is true." I nodded. "But you still haven't answered my question."

He smiled. "You're asking why I gave up ..."

"Did you?"

"Giving up would mean I'd moved on. I haven't done that, Lainey. I've thought about you every day for the last fifteen years. But if you're asking why I never reached out, that's because I didn't think you were ready to hear my side. I was thinking of you. Not me." He looked at me through his long, thick lashes. "Since Penelope jumped, nothing I've done was for me."

The report he had given to the police. The conversation he'd had with my father, never pushing to air his side of what had happened. The talk he'd had with me on the floor of my bedroom. His lack of contacting me, even though he was watching, even though he was always there.

He'd been living in limbo until I found him asleep at the cemetery.

"The day I saw you at Pen's grave," I started, "I was supposed to fly in earlier that evening, but my flight was delayed. I didn't get in until after ten, and I threw my stuff in my old room and went straight there."

"And found me passed out."

The memories prickled my skin, like tiny nails were tapping me. "All I could think about the entire flight was that I was going to get there past midnight. That I was potentially going to miss the anniversary and disappoint Pen. I wanted to talk to her. I miss her so much."

His gaze intensified. "Disappoint her? Lainey, come on ..."

"She doesn't ask anything of me anymore. She doesn't need me. You would think, after all these years, I'd have adjusted to that. I haven't. So, at the very least, I can show up on the day of and not the day after."

I pulled his jacket closer, the scent getting stronger from the movement. I wish my nose didn't trigger thoughts. I wish scents didn't stir up emotions. But every time I'd gotten a whiff that had similar notes of Rhett's cologne, I would freeze, instantly looking for him. He was never there, of course. But the fact that I didn't have to scan the space around me, that he was right here in front of me, made the air leave my lungs. I took several deep breaths.

"I couldn't believe you were at her grave. I never, not in a million years, expected that. And I didn't exactly give you the warmest welcome."

"It's okay. I deserved it." He dragged his hand down the side of his beard. "I go to see her often."

"You do?"

"I tell her things about me. I talk to her about you and what I've seen on your Instagram. I apologize to her."

Tears were threatening to build in my eyes, especially as his last admission hit me. "Apologize for what, Rhett?"

"For not giving her what she needed. I should have been more understanding and not so fucking angry with her. I should have been patient. She wasn't sober, she wasn't thinking clearly." He rubbed the tattoo on his thumb. "I know that as an adult. I didn't know that as an eighteen-year-old kid."

"You've put so much into this, haven't you?"

He pointed the lion at me. "It started with this. I needed the reminder to find the courage. It would have been easy to let the darkness consume me. And I'll be honest—it does at times. The week around the anniversary isn't a pretty sight. I do everything in my power to bury myself, and I let the thoughts win. But after that week, I get pulled out, and I try my damnedest to stay on a good path." He chuckled. "My family and friends will tell you I'm a raging asshole ninety-nine percent of the time." He ended the laugh with a small grin. "They've learned to love me for it."

I could understand why.

He was irresistible. Even more so now than before.

"God ..." I glanced up at the sky, at the clouds, at the sun that was peeking between them. "This is ..."

"More than you bargained for."

I held the air in my lungs, my chin slowly dropping, and I nodded. "I think I need a giant glass of vodka, and the quietness of my apartment, and a minute to let my thoughts win."

"I get that."

I took a few moments before I said, "Thank you for coming here. I don't know if I ever would have asked you for your side or if our second meet up would have looked any different, if I would have listened."

"I can't say these words often, but I finally did the right thing."

I squeezed the lapels of his jacket, and I handed it back to him, the wind causing a shiver to run through me. I stood from the bleacher, my fingers clutching at my side, the thoughts in my head spanning from my freshman year of high school to now.

We'd probably been sitting there for an hour, yet it felt like half a lifetime.

I took a step toward the track and whispered, "Rhett ... I ..."

"You don't have to say any more, Lainey. I know how hard this was."

The knot in my throat wouldn't let me say any more. Not without another tear falling.

My fingers lifted a few inches and wiggled in the air, giving him a soft wave, and I turned my back to him and walked to the parking lot.

THIRTY-NINE

Lainey

One Year Ago

As I sat at a small table outside the café in Rome, my laptop open with my latest work project on the screen, my hand gripping my second cappuccino, my cell vibrated from a call coming through.

I put down the coffee and lifted my phone, smiling as I brought it to my ear and said, "Hi, Mom."

"Hi, honey. How's Rome?"

The street in front of me was bustling with cars and bikes, the sidewalk full of pedestrians. Since Americans spent their late summers abroad, right before the kids returned to school, I was hitting Italy during a peak time. Had I waited a few weeks, the city would have been a bit quieter.

Quiet was what I had been after, and loud was what I had gotten.

"It's ... Rome." I laughed. "You'll be very jealous to hear I'm at a café, having a cappuccino with a whole plate of biscotti in front of me." I lifted one of the cookies and took a bite, savoring the way it crumbled in my mouth. The heavy flavor of vanilla—which no other country, aside from Italy, could perfect—made me moan. "How are things at home? How's Dad?"

"Oh, you know your father, he's stressed with work, as usual. He thinks he's still your age and won't even discuss retirement."

"He craves a busy brain, like me. You need to book him a vacation with a hotel that has a no-refund policy and make him get massages and drink mai tais. If that doesn't relax him, nothing will."

"Which is why I'm calling. Your father and I are off to Hawaii in a few days. Our neighbors just got back from Kauai and said it was the best vacation they'd ever taken, so that's where we're going. I surprised your father last night with the info. He grumbled at first, but I think he'll come around once we get on the plane."

I closed my laptop and leaned back in my chair. "That's fabulous news, Mom. I'm proud of you for taking charge. Dad will absolutely love it. Where are you staying?"

She was silent for a moment, and I glanced at the screen of my phone to make sure she hadn't hung up.

"The Cole and Spade Hotel on the South Shore of the island." Another second of silence ticked by. "I don't know if you've heard, but Cole International merged with Spade Hotels. They've got quite a monopoly in the hotel industry."

My eyes closed, the pounding of my heart causing my breathing to speed up.

Of course I'd heard.

Rhett's family already had hotels across the globe, and when combined with the Spades' empire, their name was everywhere, including most of the places I'd traveled to over the last fourteen years.

"Yes, I'm aware." My voice was far too soft. "Is Dad okay with staying at a Cole hotel, or was that the reason for his grumbling?"

After I'd left for Europe, my father had never mentioned Rhett's name to me again. That wasn't the case with my mom. She approached those conversations delicately, allowing me to discuss him when I could handle it. And during the first year, I could barely talk about him.

"Your father's initial response is always a grumble, especially when it involves money. But if he had an issue with the hotel, he didn't say anything to me about it."

A flutter moved through my chest.

I didn't know where it had come from or what had caused it or why it wasn't leaving.

But I placed my hand there, feeling the thumping of my heart, and said, "I'm sure it's a beautiful resort. From what I've seen of their ones in Europe, they're five-star accommodations. Rhett's family—and I'm sure the Spades are the same—don't do anything that isn't luxurious."

"Now, that's a name I haven't heard you say in a while."

Just because I hadn't said it didn't mean I hadn't thought about him.

I'd done plenty of that.

I'd also Googled his name and found an Instagram account that seemed to be his, even though he'd never posted a single photo. During my last trip home to visit my parents, I'd even driven by his house. There was a gate that blocked his entrance from the street, so I could only see parts of his mansion that stuck up beyond the line of hedges.

Why I Googled him every few months, I didn't know. Why I'd looked up his address and driven by his home, I didn't know that either. There was no explanation for my desire to want to see where he lived and what his life looked like now and to know details that I couldn't find online.

There was just something inside me that wanted those answers. But even if I got them, I wouldn't know what to do with them because my feelings for Rhett Cole were such a complete and utter mess.

I licked my lips, wishing the coffee was an Aperol Spritz. "Well, his name didn't come out of nowhere. This conversation had prompted it." I paused. "You haven't seen him or his family out and about in LA, have you?"

"Honey, we don't run in the same circles as the Coles."

"Right." I took a breath. "I was just curious."

"I can understand why. You loved that boy for a long time."

Mom ... I still do.

FORTY

Present Day

Hart Weston waited until the entire conference room turned quiet before he stood from his chair, earning everyone's attention, and said, "Ladies and gentlemen, in one week, we'll be breaking ground on the Charred restaurant in the Cole and Spade Hotel in Bangkok."

The other four Weston siblings; the three Spades; their cousin, Jo, along with her husband, Jenner Dalton; and the three of us Coles erupted in applause.

We were a full house today, all packed into the conference room of our corporate office.

The Bangkok hotel, our newest build-out and a project led by Brady Spade, was halfway through completion. That meant it was time for the Weston family to go in and do their thing. They were a group of five siblings who had been longtime partners with the Spades. When our families merged into one company, they became business partners with my family as well. They owned steak houses, seafood and raw bars, and clubs across the world. Charred—their award-winning, Michelin-rated steak house—would be just off the lobby in our hotel in Bangkok.

I didn't think the Westons' only purpose in coming today was to celebrate the upcoming construction. I was positive they were also here to discuss where we were building next. They didn't want to miss out on any new opportunities, and with their reputation and following, we wanted them just as badly as they wanted us.

"So, spill the news," Hart continued once everyone turned silent. "Where's the next project?"

I chuckled. "I would have bet my life that was the next thing coming out of your mouth."

"Your life?" Hart grinned, his green eyes shining like fucking gems. "I need to start making myself less obvious."

Brady glanced at the other six partners of our company and said, "Should we tell them?" When he finished speaking, he focused his stare on Jenner, our attorney.

"From a legal standpoint, I don't see any reason to keep it a secret," Jenner replied.

"Iceland," Rowan announced. "Specifically Reykjavik."

"Tell me more," Beck cooed.

Beck Weston was an NHL star for the LA Whales. He didn't have an active daily role within their company. But during offseason, he was extremely involved, and he personally financed many of their projects.

"We're building a three-hundred-room, six-level hotel and spa in the heart of the capital," Macon replied. "There will be space for two restaurants and a coffee shop, a rooftop bar that will be enclosed with a retractable glass roof, and a patio that'll wrap around half of the top floor."

"Envision an overly modern build," Cooper explained. "A level of modernism we've never explored and an interior that will have the same feel—completely off-brand from anything we've done. We're known for our warmth and inviting designs. This won't be that."

"But it will fit the aesthetics of Iceland," Jo offered. "We've put a lot of time, a lot of effort, and a lot of research into this hotel. With the recent boom of tourists traveling there and the cost visitors are willing to spend, we believe this could be one of our most successful properties."

"And we will do everything in our power to make it so," Ridge said.

I could see the enthusiasm on Hart's face. He was practically foaming at the fucking mouth.

"What do you say?" he asked his siblings, rubbing his hands together as he waited for their responses.

Walker—the oldest in the family and the creator of every recipe and dish on their menus—was one of the most praised chefs in the business. He replied, "Locally sourced. Farm to table. Authentic flavors. I'm ready to start cooking now." He nodded toward Hart. "I think it's a hell of an idea, but"—he glanced at his sister, Eden, who sat next to him—"from a financial standpoint, is it doable?"

She swept her long hair away from her face and put her hand on Walker's shoulder. "The logistics of getting supplies to Iceland isn't as easy as other countries in Europe. Everything, aside from food, will have to be imported. We'll have to use an Icelandic wholesaler, and there will be a value-added tax." She glanced at Colson, their COO. "Doable? Yes. Complicated? Very much so. But exciting?" She smiled at the group. "Absolutely."

Colson seemed to ponder everything his siblings had said. The five of them had equal roles and voices, like the seven of us did, but his opinion tended to push things forward if the others were undecided. "This is a big decision," he said. "I'd like time to pull some numbers and see how profitable this restaurant could be, but"—he held his hand out to Ridge, who sat next to him—"we could very well have a deal."

Ridge shook his hand. "Excellent."

"Who will be spearheading this project?" Hart asked.

The room went silent.

And within that quietness, I took a deep breath. "Me."

When the darkness threatened to pull me under and I needed to get the fuck out of Dodge, I didn't want to go to one of our hotels, where every employee tried to impress me and did everything in their power to please me. I wanted to go somewhere I didn't know anyone.

The last time, I'd ended up in Iceland.

And I immediately fell for the island. The moodiness of the weather, the Viking mindset, the architecture that was cold and sharp, clean air that allowed me to breathe.

That was when the idea had come to me, and that had been almost a year ago.

I would be leaving for Reykjavik in the next few months.

A thought that had once excited me.

But that just wasn't the case anymore.

"We've never worked on a project with you before," Hart replied.

"I promise to make it a memorable experience." I winked.

Hart let out a laugh. "My man, I have no doubt you will."

Everyone got up from the table, the room full of murmurs as we made our way out into the hallway. I was only a few steps from my office when someone grabbed my hand.

I glanced to my side, meeting Rowan's stare, her fingers now linked with mine.

"Let's talk," she said.

Before I could decline her offer, she was pulling me into her office, where Ridge was already waiting.

"What is this? A fucking ambush?"

She shut the door and took a seat behind her desk. "Call it a family meeting." She nodded toward the chair next to the one Ridge was sitting in. "Take a seat."

I sighed. "I know you're not barking orders at me."

She pressed her hands together and placed them under her chin. "Rhett, please, will you sit?"

I slumped down in the chair, my leg bouncing, my hands gripping the armrests. "What is it you want to talk about?"

"Trista's back at work, which tells me you're no longer having her follow Lainey," Rowan said.

"You're correct," I replied.

Ridge eyed me with a smile. "Are you going to tell us what you and Lainey talked about?"

"I never said we talked."

"You don't have to," Rowan responded. "We can see it in your face. Besides, isn't that where you ran off to the last time we were discussing her?"

It had only been days ago when they were drilling me about Lainey and I rushed out of the office to go to our old high school.

It felt like a goddamn lifetime.

"I told her"—I took a long, deep inhale—"everything."

"*Everything*, everything?" Ridge asked. When I nodded, he added, "Oh shit."

"And?" Rowan leaned on her desk. "How did she take it?"

I shook my head. "I don't know."

"Did she hear you out?" Rowan pushed.

"Yes."

"Did she tell you to fuck off and storm out?" Rowan continued.

"No."

"Rhett ..." She flattened her hands against her desk and pounded them down a few times. "Talk to us. You're giving us nothing."

I shifted in my seat, unable to sit still. I had all this pent-up energy, and I didn't know what to do with it. "She listened to everything I told her. She didn't fight me. She didn't tell me I was wrong or that this was my opinion and she believed otherwise. She wanted to hear it, and she was ready to."

"Wow," Rowan whispered.

"I didn't hold back, Row. I told her I'd never stopped loving her. That I'd thought of her every day for the last fifteen years. When she left that track—she was walking at our old high school—she knew exactly where I stood and how I felt."

"Fuck. You went all in." Ridge clasped my arm. "I'm proud of you."

Rowan nodded. "Me too."

"I've stayed silent for far too long," I admitted.

"Fifteen years too long," Rowan offered.

"Holding in those secrets did nothing to fucking help me. They gave me nightmares when I actually did fall asleep. They put me in the worst headspace." I dragged my fingers through the side of my hair. "No more. I'm done with that bullshit."

"I don't know who you are right now, but I'm loving every word of this," Rowan said.

We all turned silent, and I broke it with, "Lainey Taylor isn't mine. I had nothing to lose by being honest with her."

"She's not yours *yet*," Ridge corrected.

I released a hiss. "You know ... that's the best thing you've ever said to me."

FORTY-ONE

Lainey

Six Months Ago

My third time in Bangkok, and like my previous two visits, I was learning that there was something so special about this city. Food that I craved each time I returned to London, an energy I could almost smell in the air. A sensation that overcame me when I inserted myself in the center of all the busyness and let Bangkok move around me.

I hadn't come for the quiet—that didn't exist here.

I had come to get lost.

To forget.

And that was exactly what I was doing.

I'd logged over five miles this morning, following the loudness, the lights, turning onto streets where the activity drew me in. The only reason I'd stopped was because my stomach was growling and the smells from the different restaurants and street vendors were making it worse.

I happened to walk by one that I'd eaten at before, and I grabbed a table outside, ordering a Thai iced tea and a papaya salad. While I waited for my drink and food to arrive, I took out my phone. Not to provide entertainment. After years of traveling by myself—something I preferred—I didn't rely on technology to fill the silence. The view could hold my attention and keep it. But given that today was a workday, I needed to make sure I hadn't missed anything.

Of course, the first message I came across was from my mom. I could always count on her for a daily check-in. Since Dad wasn't a texter, she would relay our conversation to him.

MOM

Honey, how's Bangkok?

ME

I'm having a great time. I just sat down for some lunch. You and Dad should meet me here sometime. You would love it. So different from anywhere else you've ever been.

MOM

If I could convince your father, I would be there in a minute.

I miss you.

I could tell her how much I missed her or I could show her my face, which she'd appreciate more.

I clicked on my Camera app and hit the button to point the lens at myself. I then held the phone high in the air, and with my lips puckered in a kiss, I repositioned the phone until I found an angle that looked best in the light.

But for some reason, I couldn't focus on myself.

Because I couldn't stop looking in the background.

A man, walking on the sidewalk less than ten feet away, was owning my attention.

With a face ... that looked far too familiar.

I tilted the phone until the camera was only on him, his features coming into view and fully defined.

Black hair.

Icy-blue eyes.

A face I would never be able to forget.

I heard myself gasp as my entire body became frozen. Those handsome, haunting features confirmed everything I'd feared.

Rhett Cole ...

Why is he in Bangkok?

On the same street?

At the same time?

After fourteen long years of not seeing him?

Why ... now?

Oh God.

Before he caught a glimpse of me, I lowered my phone. My hand shook so badly that I almost dropped it.

I held my breath as he got closer.

I turned my face before he reached the side of me and waited for him to pass to carefully gaze forward.

Rhett's here, was what I kept repeating in my head.

I should look away.

I shouldn't care.

I should be completely unaffected.

But I couldn't look away.

I couldn't stop caring.

I couldn't help but feel everything.

I took in the way his jeans hugged his thighs, his ass, his waist, and then I looked up to the broadness of his shoulders, the darkness of his hair.

He wasn't the boy I remembered—that was for sure. What I was looking at now was a man.

My heart.

Why was it pounding so hard? Why was my stomach flipping as though I were circling the loops of a roller coaster?

Why was my mind filling with so many questions?

I watched him until I couldn't, until he disappeared into the buzzing of Bangkok.

And the moment he was gone, when I could no longer see even a stitch of his black hair, I felt this overwhelming loss.

An emptiness, similar to the one I'd felt on the plane ride from LA to Spain.

A feeling that had never gone away.

But that feeling had changed over the years, sometimes by the day, like it was a tide. The depth rising and falling, where some moments would feel endlessly hollow and others only toe deep.

Today, I was hitting the bottom.

Why?

What am I missing?

Is it love?

LA?

Or is it Rhett Cole?

I picked up my phone and stared at Mom's message.

Something had been in the back of my mind for the last several months. Something that had been weighing on me. Nagging at me.

Because, goddamn it, I was tired of running.

ME

Miss you too, Mom. You know, I've been thinking ... it might be time for me to come home.

FORTY-TWO

Lainey

Present Day

My phone buzzed on the counter in my kitchen as I was washing the collection of glasses in my sink. Just glasses—no plates, no silverware. The last few days, I'd been drinking my dinner and skipping lunch.

That was something that needed to come to an end—and it would. But there were times in my life that were just about survival.

I knew those periods well.

I was in the middle of one.

I wiped my hands on my jeans and lifted my phone.

> UNKNOWN
> So ... how about date two? Are you game?

I had absolutely no idea who this text was from.

Unless it was Rhett.

But how would he have gotten my number? And would he have considered our meetup at the high school a date?

ME

Who is this?

UNKNOWN

Are you going out with that many people that you don't know who I am?

ME

No.

UNKNOWN

This also tells me you didn't save my number or our previous text exchange.

It's Charlie. From the gym. You know, the guy you had dinner with last week.

Oh.

Him.

A date I'd almost canceled because I didn't want to go. That dinner had proven we had zero chemistry; the evening had been dull, the conversation as uneventful as a trip to an empty mailbox.

I needed to find a new gym.

Crap.

While my fingers hovered above the screen, I contemplated an excuse. Work, travel—anything. It was too much for my brain. I was just going to give him the truth.

ME

> Hi, Charlie. I'm just going to be honest and tell you that I'm in a very weird place in my life. I'm grieving many things, and although I thought I might be ready to date, I'm not. I just can't mentally handle it. I'm sorry. I hope I didn't mislead you. You're a nice guy, and you're going to find someone amazing.

UNKNOWN

> Wow. A woman who is finally honest about her feelings. I respect that. Best of luck, Lainey.

ME

> Best of luck to you too.

That had gone better than I'd thought.

I slipped my phone into the back pocket of my jeans and finished washing the rest of the glasses, remembering the dream I'd had of Penelope, when we talked about Charlie and Rhett.

"He wanted a second date. Can you believe that, Pen?"

I wiped my hands on a dish towel, laughing at how often I talked to my sister. How, in my head, it felt like a completely normal thing to do. I wasn't looking for a response. I certainly never heard one.

But in some wild way, it gave me comfort to say my thoughts to her out loud.

I walked out of the kitchen and into a mess of a living room. Boxes that I'd shipped from London were stacked against the wall. Pictures and art still needed to be hung. A dining room that had no table and a living room that needed a rug.

I sighed, bypassing the disaster and heading into my bedroom. There were more boxes in here. Fifteen years' worth of clothes and memorabilia and things I'd collected during my travels had made its way across the pond.

"One at a time, right?"

The boxes were in stacks of four, and I grabbed one, placing it on the dresser—a homecoming gift from my parents, along with my bed, two nightstands, and a chaise lounge. They'd wanted me to feel cozy in my new apartment, ensuring I'd stay in the States and not move back abroad.

I pulled the tape free from the box and reached in, my hand digging past the paper that I'd stuffed in for protection. My nails hit something hard. I took out the small wooden jewelry box and set it in the center of the dresser. I'd bought it in India at one of the markets. It was hand-carved, the design along the top an intricate swirl of raised wood. I ran my fingers over it, tracing the dips and curves, and when I opened the lid, those same fingers went over my mouth.

With the jewelry box now in my hands, I backed up until the edge of the bed hit my legs, and I took a seat, holding it on top of my thighs. There were earrings and rings, necklaces, and bracelets filling the entire interior. None of them were overly expensive, just items I'd collected over the span of my life.

All except for one necklace that sat in the middle.

The diamond R that Rhett had gifted to me.

There were times in the past when I'd tried to toss it or leave it in my old flat before I moved to a new one, making it someone else's treasure.

But I never could.

That man would always be a part of me, and getting rid of the necklace wouldn't change that.

Oh God, Rhett.

We were tied together by ropes and binds that were far stronger than the pain that had separated us.

I lifted the necklace out of the box and held it in my palm, remembering the day I'd finally taken it off.

It wasn't on the plane to Spain or within the first few months of living in the apartment my parents had rented me, lost in a city, because I'd crawled from one dark life to another. It happened during the first week of school when a classmate asked me who R was.

A question that had completely thrown me off guard.

A question I couldn't answer because saying *the love of my life* and *my ex-boyfriend* in the same sentence was far too much for me to bear.

"I love him, Pen. Every day. He's all I think about." I turned the initial around. "My heart wasn't broken the day you died. It was taken from me. And when I saw Rhett in Bangkok, I heard it beat again for the first time in a long while. And when I saw him at the track of our high school, I watched him hold my heart out to me as if he was returning it."

My chin tilted up, my neck reclining. "Pen, what am I doing? Why am I holding back?"

Love wasn't stopping me.

There was more than enough of that.

It was always him—there was no question.

"Have you seen the way he looks at you? Because I have, and I can tell you right now, he's obsessed with you." I could hear Pen whispering those words even though she'd said them fifteen years ago.

I could see her in my bedroom at our parents' house, telling me to put on the dress to impress Rhett at the party.

"You're forgetting, as your twin, I have the ability to feel everything you're feeling. When you're nervous, I know. When you're happy, I know. When you're doubting yourself, I'm doubting myself."

"What am I feeling now, Pen? Like an emotional train wreck?" I let out a small laugh. "That would be an accurate description."

I watched the way the sunlight hit the diamonds in the letter.

"Do you blame him for what happened?" I clasped my fingers around the necklace while I stared at the ceiling. "Now that I know everything, I don't. I'm not sure I even did then ..." My eyes closed.

My mind returned to the dream, to when she'd said, "Why does it need to be the end?"

God, that had felt real.

"Let's say I'm rooting for the guy."

A statement that had surprised me even though she'd adored Rhett. I couldn't yet process the way she'd acted with him—the flirting, the touching. One day, I would, but right now, I was at capacity.

"Love is what's missing from your life."

But that was where she was wrong.

Love wasn't missing. Love was there. Love had been there. Love had never lightened for even a second.

"You wouldn't blame him, Pen. I know you wouldn't."

So, if she doesn't blame him and neither do I, why am I not with him?

My eyes opened, and a single tear from each side fell down to the center of my cheeks. I took a deep breath, holding in the air, waiting to see if it made me feel different. If a second pause would change my mind.

But it didn't.

I reached into my back pocket and took out my phone, pulling up the Camera app. With my other hand, I put the necklace back in the box, and I positioned the phone over it, snapping a picture, the light capturing the diamonds even though it was surrounded by wood.

I tapped my Instagram app and loaded the photo. I didn't add a filter—the picture didn't need one—and under the caption, I typed, *Unpacking memories.*

As I filled my lungs, there was a thumping in my chest.

A feeling.

A realization.

I was getting back what I'd lost, and for the first time in a very long time, the smile wasn't there because it should be. It was there for him.

I hit Share and posted the photo.

FORTY-THREE

Rhett

Present Day

My stomach was a fucking mess as I stood outside Lainey's apartment building, scrolling through the call box until I found her name, pressing the number beside it.

Two rings passed before she picked up. "Hi."

"It's Rhett."

"I know. I can see you." She laughed. "I'm in apartment 611."

"I know."

"Of course you do. I'll buzz you in."

When the front entrance unlocked, I walked to the elevator, taking it to the sixth floor, my hand barely knocking on the door when it opened.

Lainey stood in the entryway, holding the frame, and her eyes locked with mine. Her chest rose and fell and rose again before she finally said, "I just posted the photo to Instagram last night. I'm assuming you saw it, and that's why you're here?"

She was certainly creative.

I'd barely held my shit together when I saw it, the urge to come here almost outweighing my responsibilities.

"If I hadn't had important meetings all day today, I would have skipped work and come this morning."

"But you came." Her expression was soft, her voice light.

And I knew in that moment, I'd read her post on Instagram the way she had intended.

A post that hit me so goddamn hard, I felt my entire life change.

I loosened my tie. I hadn't even bothered to go home; I'd just come straight here from the office. "And miss an opportunity to spend time with you? Fuck that." I smiled.

She smiled back and opened the door wider. "Come in."

I stepped inside the apartment, a little taken aback that I was in Lainey's space. For so many years, I'd wondered what her life looked like. That I was here, that I was getting a glimpse —that was hard to wrap my head around.

"I haven't finished unpacking and decorating." She joined me in the foyer. "Please ignore the disaster. I know how bad it looks, and I really wish you weren't seeing it this way—"

"It's perfect."

"You're being nice."

"It's perfect," I emphasized again. "I mean it. I can see you all over the room. Whether your shit is in boxes or your art is sitting on the floor, that doesn't matter. It smells like you in here, and it feels like you in here."

"Smells?"

While she was looking toward the living room, my focus was on her. My gaze dipped to her toes before slowly rising to her face. The yoga pants and tank top were showing every curve I'd been missing.

"Roses."

"Ah. That. Yes." She hugged her stomach and looked at me. "A scent I haven't been able to give up."

I wanted so fucking badly to reach for her, but I shoved my hands in my pockets instead. "I hope you never do."

She grinned.

"There it is." I nodded toward her face, my fingers fighting to stay tucked inside. "God, I've fucking missed that."

She slowly took a breath. "Can I get you a drink?"

"Yes."

"What do you want?"

You.

"Whatever you have is fine."

"Take a seat in the living room. I'll be there in a second."

She left me in the foyer to go into the kitchen, and I watched the way she moved around the small room. My mind pictured her in my kitchen, her light-brown hair flying every time she turned, the early sunlight catching the golden streaks. Her hands on my countertops, mine wrapped around her stomach.

Fuck yes.

As I took a seat toward the center of the couch, I heard glasses hitting the countertop and the fridge open. The rattle of ice. The beautiful noise of her bare feet hitting the hardwood floor as she walked into the living room.

She handed me a tumbler. "It's vodka."

When she sat, putting a cushion between us, I held my glass out to her. "To unpacking memories."

Her inhale was loud. "I'll cheers to that." She took a quick sip. "I feel like we have fifteen years to catch up on. I barely know anything about your life now. Just that you're an executive for Cole and Spade Hotels." Her eyes went wide. "Rhett, you followed your dream. You made it happen. I'm so proud of you."

"It's not exactly hard when your dad owned the company. But, yeah, I'm one of the head guys there now. When I first started out, I worked a bit in each department, getting a feel for the way everything ran, until I slid into an executive role. Now that we've merged with the Spades, the seven of us—we're all equal partners—manage the daily operations. And aside from that, each one of us works on a hotel from start to finish, meaning we find the land, we help design the building, we're there during construction, and we stay until it's open."

"Which hotel is yours?"

"Iceland."

"Iceland, huh? I've been. It's unbelievable. I mean that quite literally. The whole time I was there, I kept saying to myself, *I can't believe I'm here, and I'm seeing this.*"

I chuckled. "My experience was similar."

"I didn't realize there was a Cole and Spade Hotel on the island. I don't remember seeing that as a choice when I stayed there."

"It's not built yet. We'll be breaking ground in a few months." I took a deep breath. "And I'll be moving there."

Her brows rose and stayed high. "Moving there?"

"For six to eight months."

She took another drink. "That's ... amazing."

I slowly nodded. "You can call it that, I suppose."

The room turned silent for several moments before she said, "What about your family? How's Rowan? Ridge? Mom? Dad?"

"Rowan has a little girl now. Her name is Rayner. She's just a tiny thing and so cute. She's with Cooper Spade—one of our partners—and they're getting married. Ridge is a single dad to

Daisy. Well, he's not so single anymore, he's dating Daisy's first-grade teacher." I pulled out my phone and showed her my lock screen, which was Daisy and me at Disney. "That kid is my whole world."

"She's quite possibly the most beautiful little girl I've ever seen."

"She is, and she has me wrapped around her sparkly pink-polished finger." I chuckled and put the phone back in my pocket. "Fingers she recently had manicured when I took her to the nail salon." I pointed down at my feet. "She demanded that we have matching toes."

"Are you telling me you have sparkly pink polish on your feet?"

My head rocked up and down, and I ran my hand over the top of it. "That's what I'm telling you."

"I'm dying right now."

I smiled. "Mom's good, but Dad ..." I drew in some air and held it in. "He passed not too long ago. When the doctor gave him only a couple of months, he fought like hell and blew through their projection. Eventually, the cancer got him." I paused. "One of the worst days of my whole life."

"Rhett, I had no idea." She touched my arm, leaving her fingers there.

"Losing him ... it's been so rough. Dad was my best friend. We went through so much shit together. So many times, I wouldn't have made it if it wasn't for him. I still can't believe he's gone."

Only someone who truly understood what that loss felt like could nod the way she was nodding now. "He was a wonderful man. Always so kind to me."

I brought the glass up to my lips, keeping it close to my mouth while I said, "That's pretty much it. Work, family, travel."

"And trips to the cemetery."

I swallowed the vodka. "Plenty of those, yes."

"I bet Pen appreciates that." She looked down at her lap. "Even now, I'm sure she wants all the attention." Her voice was turning quieter. "I went the other day and brought her hot-pink flowers. The loudest-looking flowers in the whole cemetery, and all I could think was how much she'd approve."

When she eventually gazed up, I asked, "How's nursing? I assume that's what you're doing? Some type of traveling program and that's why you've seen so much of the world?"

She rolled her shoulders forward in a shrug. "You would think so, but no."

"No?"

"Once Pen died, that passion completely left me. I couldn't stomach the thought of being around loss of any kind. But I still wanted to work in the medical field in some capacity, just not directly with the patients, so I shifted into health care administration. I work for a company that staffs and schedules for hospitals across the UK. All of it's done online, which is why I can be anywhere in the world and do my job."

Penelope's death had affected every single part of her.

It hurt to hear that.

At the same time, I could relate.

"Do you like it?" I asked.

"I do. Except, without an office, there's no culture, no stopping by someone's desk and chatting, no meeting up in the kitchen to gossip. The closest employee lived about forty-five minutes from me in London. We'd sometimes meet halfway for lunch, but not often enough." She tucked her legs beneath her. "That's why I would travel so much. The walls of my flat would cave in." She rubbed her hands against her thighs. "It's funny, even though I wanted quietness, I couldn't handle the silence at home."

"Fuck, do I get that."

"You do?"

I stretched my arm across the back of the couch and crossed my legs. "The quieter the room, the louder my thoughts."

"Yes."

"And those thoughts can bring me to a place where nothing feels right. Where I don't feel right. Where I'm questioning if I'll ever feel right again." I filled my cheeks with air. "Then, the fear kicks in. *Is this permanent? Will normal ever be within reach?* It's a spiral with no end, just millions of beginnings."

"God, you do get it." She mashed her lips together, her head falling back.

"When you found me at the cemetery, that's where I was. Crawling out of my fucking skin. My senses on overload. Miserable. I was dreaming about Penelope. She kept telling me to wake up and open my eyes. I couldn't understand why she was saying that. And then I did and ..." I let those words hang there, taking my time to sip the vodka. "I couldn't have opened my eyes to a better sight. It didn't matter what you said to me, just hearing your voice, being around you, looking you in the eyes—that was enough. Even though, honestly, it wasn't even close to enough."

"Rhett, I wasn't prepared for you to be there."

I scanned her eyes, back and forth. "What were you thinking about when you saw me?"

"You mean, were the things I said to you that night one hundred percent true?"

I chuckled. "Sure, we can start there."

"Where you were mentally, I was there too. And seeing you, that took me to a place I hadn't expected." She positioned her elbow on the back cushion and rested her face against her palm. "Instead of letting you in—which is something that probably would have benefited both of us in that moment—I tried my hardest to push you out." Her head tilted to the side. "Saying to you that what you did was unforgivable, that wasn't fair, it wasn't true, and I'm sorry."

When I tried to tell her I accepted her apology, she held up a finger.

"What's ironic is that I told you it wasn't an opportunity, it was just a coincidence that the both of us were there. But it wasn't the only coincidence from our past, and technically, it was an opportunity."

"I don't know what you mean."

"Six months ago, I saw you in Bangkok."

I shifted on the couch to face her more. "You saw me ... in Bangkok?"

She nodded. "I was sitting outside a restaurant, and you walked by."

My heart began to fucking pound. "Why didn't you stop me? Why didn't you say something?"

"I"—her head shook—"don't know. It felt like too much. The way my emotions suddenly took over and my heart was beating—the whole thing felt so surreal, so out of body in a way. But what it did was show me that it was possible to actually feel something." She turned silent. "I'd gone so long without feeling anything."

I lifted her hand and held it to my chest, right over my heart so she could feel what was happening within me.

"Yes, Rhett, just like that."

I didn't release her fingers, and she didn't pull them away. And when I tightened my grip, she still didn't pull away then either.

"That's when I made the decision to move home," she admitted. "I'd been thinking about it, toying with the idea. Like I told you, I was tired of running. I just didn't know if LA was where I wanted to plant my feet."

I couldn't believe she had seen me there.

That I'd walked right by her and hadn't seen her.

That, somehow, I hadn't felt her.

"Why did seeing me in Bangkok solidify your decision to come back?"

She drained the rest of her vodka and set the empty glass on a tray in the middle of the ottoman. "You know that whole *out of sight, out of mind* thing? That's how it was, except it wasn't like that at all." She laughed. "I thought about you all the time. I just couldn't see you, especially since you don't have a presence online. I guess, in a way, that made things easier on me. My brain filled in the blanks, satisfying my curiosity. But then I saw you, and I completely spiraled. You started to consume me again, just like when I'd left to move to Europe." She stopped to take several breaths. "I had no idea what would happen between us. If there was even a possibility of something happening. If I even wanted there to be one. I just knew I needed to come back."

"You know there's a possibility. You heard that in my words when I found you at the track, you're seeing that right now on my face."

This was going to be the most important question I ever asked, and everything in me was fucking shaking. It didn't matter what she'd posted on Instagram or that the darkness had finally lifted or that I felt a bit of hope. What mattered was how she answered this.

"Do you want us?"

I needed to feel her. I needed her to feel me. I touched her cheek, my heart melting the moment I came in contact with her skin.

"Because I want to give you everything, Lainey. I want to be with you. I want to love you forever. I want to marry you. I want to have children with you. And I don't want to ever spend a second away from you." I halted. "But I don't know what you want."

"You." There was no hesitation in her reply. "Rhett, you're all I've ever wanted. But I need to take things slow. I'm not talking a date once a week and speaking to each other every few days. Nothing at all like that." She shook her head. "I'm also not saying we should move in together next week."

I chuckled. Because I fucking would.

"I loved the eighteen-year-old you," she continued. "I loved the nineteen and twenty and all the way up to thirty-three-year-old you. But a lot of time has passed, and I want to continue getting to know you all over again." Her hand went to her chest. "I want to fall, like I fell back then."

My other hand gripped the back of my neck, releasing the air I'd been holding in while she spoke. My gaze was getting a little blurry as I stared at her, the water making it hard to see the finer details of her face.

"Did I say something that upset you?"

"Upset me?" I forced the emotion down. "You just made me the happiest man alive." My hand lowered to her neck. "I've dreamed about this day, Lainey. Shit, I've dreamed of many things when it came to you, but this ..." I bit my bottom lip. "I didn't think it was ever going to happen. I thought I was going to spend the rest of my life loving you from afar, silently wishing you happy birthday every year, telling Penelope my hopes of marrying her sister ..." My nostrils flared as I exhaled. "And never getting to spend birthdays with you, or watching you walk down the aisle toward me, or seeing your belly swell with my baby inside."

Her eyes filled so fast; I didn't get there in time before the drips spilled over. "Our baby."

I caught the first few. "A little boy named Penn Ray Cole."

She let out a sob. "And if it's a girl?"

"There are too many baby girls in my family. We're having a boy." I reached across the couch, sliding forward just enough that I could pull her against me.

"I want all of that," she whispered. "I love you."

Her body fit in my arms and against my chest. Just as perfectly now as it had back then.

"Lainey, I love you." I held her back and the tops of her shoulders and the base of her neck, and when I pulled away, my palms slid to her cheeks. I kept her steady, gazing into her eyes. "It's always been you. Nothing has ever changed that; nothing will ever change that."

As I closed the distance between our faces, her eyes shut, and her lips parted.

There wasn't a sight in this world that was as beautiful as Lainey Taylor.

My mouth surrounded her top lip, my tongue touched hers, and I moaned as I tasted her. My movements were slow as I memorized this new feel, even though, technically, it wasn't new at all. I let the sensations grow between us while getting reacquainted with a mouth that I'd missed so badly.

I pressed her cheeks, and I pulled even closer despite the fact that not even air was separating us.

And when I knew I was on the verge of taking it further, which I didn't want to do tonight, I gently released her lips.

There was silence.

A quietness where so much was said yet not a single word was spoken.

And I finally broke it with, "Have you eaten dinner?"

She smiled, and I could feel it on my hands as I continued to hold her. "Aside from vodka, no. Admittedly, that's been my dinner lately."

"We're going out."

Her eyes grew large. "Now?"

"Yes."

"I need to change. I'm a mess—"

"You look absolutely gorgeous, Lainey."

"But you're in a suit. I'm in yoga pants."

"And that's just how I want you. You never have to get all done up for me. I'm in love with you just the way you are." I traced my thumb over her lips. "There's a Thai place down the street from here. I'll be overdressed, not you. What do you say? Are you down?"

"I can't say no to noodles." As I laughed, she gripped my wrist. "Or you."

LAINEY

Thank you for an amazing dinner and the most incredibly unexpected night.

And for dropping me off at my apartment and being a complete gentleman. 😊

ME

It took a massive amount of effort. The gentleman part, I mean.

LAINEY

I can only imagine.

ME

I'll talk to you in the morning?

LAINEY

I hope so.

ME

Good night, Lainey.

LAINEY

Get some sleep. 💚

FORTY-FOUR

Lainey

Present Day

ME

I know you never sleep, so I'm just checking in to see if you got any last night.

RHETT

I don't know how, but I got about six hours. That's more than I've slept in years. You're doing something to me ...

I do know that when I finally get to fall asleep with you in my arms, knowing I'll wake up next to you, I'll sleep even more.

ME

I want that too. Trust me.

Are you at work?

313

RHETT

I've been here for over an hour. So much to do for this Iceland build-out.

Just throwing this out there ... I think you should come with me.

ME

To Iceland?

RHETT

Yes.

ME

You're not kidding, are you?

RHETT

Not even a little.

Listen, I know you just told me that you aren't going to move in with me within a week—LOL —but I'm not leaving for a few months. That gives you plenty of time to think about it. By then, who knows? Maybe you'll be ready to live with me.

ME

I'm smiling ... just thought you should know.

RHETT

Is that a yes?

ME

That's a strong maybe.

RHETT

I can live with that. I can't live without seeing you tonight.

ME

Then, you'd better come over after work.

RHETT

I'm on my way. Want me to grab dinner?
Don't worry, I'll make sure it doesn't have any
dairy.

ME

That would be amazing. See you soon.

RHETT

And more vodka?

ME

How about wine?

RHETT

Even better.

RHETT

You look so beautiful when you sleep—that's
why I didn't wake you. Just want you to know
I left for work.

ME

Thank you for the coffee—you made it
perfectly—and for the cutest note ever.

RHETT

Almond creamer with a dash of cinnamon.
Even I can't fuck that up.

Glad you liked it.

ME

I have to work tonight—a big project I have to
get done before the morning. Could you meet
for lunch instead of dinner?

RHETT

Are you asking me out on a date, Lainey?

ME

Ha! Yes, a day date.

RHETT

For you, I think I can make that happen. I'll text you an address where to meet me.

But don't expect me to put out. We're only on our third date. You've got at least a week to go before you can even think about getting in my pants.

ME

Dead.

For the record, I've thought about getting in your pants.

RHETT

I know. I can tell. 😊

ME

That lunch = sooo good. Thank you. And thank you for showing me the pictures of the Iceland hotel. I was already in awe of you, and now, I'm just blown away.

RHETT

Keep talking that way, and I'm going to think you want to move there with me.

ME

I just might.

ME

Rhett! The flowers! OMG, they're absolutely gorgeous. And huge! They take up almost the whole kitchen counter. I'm in love with them. Thank you. XO

RHETT

I'm glad you love them. Hopefully, they'll make this sting a little less ... I have to cancel our dinner plans tonight. The whole team is getting together with the Westons to talk about Iceland. If it wasn't my hotel, I'd bail, but I can't.

ME

Please don't worry. I completely understand.

RHETT

It'll probably be a late night—it usually is when it comes to those guys. I don't want to wake you when I get home, so I'll sleep at my place tonight.

ME

Wake me.

RHETT

You're sure?

ME

I'd rather sleep with you than without you.

RHETT

God, I fucking love you.

I'll go into work late tomorrow. Maybe we could hit up the track for a walk and go to breakfast?

ME

I would love that.

And I love you.

ME

I miss you already.

RHETT

Going into work late and having my mornings with you is something I could really get used to.

ME

I still can't believe I didn't hear you come in.

RHETT

I tried to be quiet.

ME

You were mouse quiet. But to be honest, I'm surprised you didn't wake me up ...

RHETT

We both know I wanted nothing more. But I'm trying to be a good boy, Lainey. Truth, that's become so hard and almost impossible.

ME

I didn't ask you to be a good boy, Rhett.

RHETT

You told me you wanted to fall. You're going to fucking fall.

ME

Rhett, I already am.

I got off the elevator on the executive-level floor of the Cole and Spade Hotels. My mind was blown by the grandness of the high-rise and the amount of people working here and how professional it all was. Rhett had described the company on several occasions, but seeing it with my own eyes was an entirely different experience.

I approached the receptionist's desk and said, "You must be Trista." I stuck out my hand and smiled. "I'm Lainey."

"It's so nice to meet you, Lainey." She stood and shook my hand.

"I appreciate you taking my call and helping me with this. Iceland is keeping Rhett pretty busy, so I didn't even know where to start."

"Oh, please, it's my pleasure." She straightened the bottom of her blazer. "You're right, the project has certainly kept him busy, but I've carved out an hour for you without him knowing. That's the good news. The bad news is that I couldn't keep his office free. It seems Rowan and Ridge are in there now with him." She lifted the receiver of her phone. "Should I call him and make some kind of excuse to get him alone?"

I adjusted the bag on my arm. "No need. I'd love to see them too."

She placed the receiver back down. "Great. Then, I'll take you to his office. Please follow me."

Trista approached a large glass door that was behind her desk, hitting several buttons beside it and swiping a card before it opened. I followed her through and into the hallway. There were doors every several feet—some ajar, some fully closed, name plaques next to each one, most that I recognized from conversations I'd had with Rhett.

"He's going to be so happy to see you," Trista said.

"He's usually the one surprising me." I hesitated before I continued, "You know, like the time he showed up at the track at our old high school." I laughed and put my hand on her arm. "Rhett mentioned you helped him find me."

She slowed her pace. "I had a feeling he would tell you." Her face was turning red. "I'm so embarrassed—"

"Please don't be. You were doing what your boss asked of you. And look what it did—you brought us together."

She gave me a soft grin. "Lainey, I can't even say I've never seen him happier because I've never seen that man happy until you came back into his life. He's an entirely different person than who I've known for all these years."

"We're both different people now. That's the power we have over each other."

She stopped outside a door, Rhett's name on the side of it. "It's been quite an honor to watch. Have a wonderful lunch. Please let me know if you need anything."

I thanked her and gently knocked on the thick wood, waiting a few seconds before I opened it just enough to peek my face in.

Rhett's expression went from confusion to a smile once he realized it was me. "Baby," he said from behind his desk. "Come in, come in. What are you doing here?"

"I wasn't sure if you'd have time to eat with all your meetings, so I wanted to bring you lunch. Trista helped coordinate it."

I gave him a grin and looked at Rowan and Ridge, who sat in front of Rhett's desk. Rhett had shown me pictures of both, but nothing could have prepared me for what it felt like to see them in person, all dressed up in their corporate attire, looking like true executives.

"Lainey," Rowan said softly, pressing her hands together and holding them at her chest. "I can't believe it—it's you."

I held open my arms. "Girl, you were around fourteen years old the last time I saw you. Look at you now. You're gorgeous."

"No, you're gorgeous," she said as she got up and hugged me. "Aw, Lainey, it's so, so good to have you back."

I squeezed her tightly. "You have no idea how good it feels to be back."

"You've made him the happiest man alive," she whispered before we released each other, our hands clasping at the end of our hug.

"Get over here," Ridge said as he reached for me. "Lainey fucking Taylor. My God, I never thought I'd see the day."

I slipped my hands out of Rowan's grip and walked into Ridge's grasp. "Honestly, I didn't either, but I can't believe I stayed away for so long. I wish I hadn't."

He rocked me and pulled back. "You haven't changed a bit."

I laughed. "Well, you two have. I know the age difference between us isn't massive, but I feel like you went from babies to corporate badasses. And parents! Rhett has told me all about Rayner and Daisy. I cannot wait to meet them. They're both so beautiful, you guys. Congratulations."

"We'll have to plan a family dinner soon so we can all spend some time together," Rowan suggested.

"Yes," I replied. "It's a must."

She looked at Ridge and said, "Let's leave these two so they can enjoy their lunch." Before she headed for the door, she gave me a small hug again. "Let's catch up. Maybe we can grab dinner."

"I would love that, yes."

She smiled. "Me too."

Ridge patted my shoulder on his way to the door and said, "You're the best thing that's happened to this family in a long time."

I watched them leave, and when the door closed, I turned toward Rhett. "They're just as wonderful as they used to be. Maybe even more so."

"Get over here."

I laughed as I walked around his desk, setting the bag on the floor before I climbed on his lap. "Hi. Surprise."

He kissed me. Slowly. And then he nuzzled into my neck. "Lunch, huh? How did I become such a lucky man?"

My head tilted back as he kissed up to my ear and over my throat, his lips making it difficult to think. "I felt like cooking, and you get to be my guinea pig. Since I can't eat it, I have no idea how good it is—or how bad."

"You can't eat it?" His mouth stalled on my collarbone, his exhales causing shivers to run through my body.

"Lasagna with real cheese as opposed to the vegan cheese I would normally use."

"I'm going to devour it, the same way I want to devour you right now," he breathed out before he pulled his mouth off my skin. "What I wouldn't do to swipe everything off my desk and put you on top of it, getting you naked so I could eat you for fucking lunch." His exhale sounded like a moan while he looked at me. "*Mmm.*"

"Rhett, you're at work." I gently slapped his chest, but the truth was, I wanted everything he'd just described.

"I'm the boss. What I do in my office is my business." He rubbed his thumb back and forth over my lips. "But you're right, I need to let this hard-on die because the first time I taste you after all these years isn't going to be on top of my desk or in a room where anyone else can hear you scream."

FORTY-FIVE

Rhett

Present Day

LAINEY

So ... I did something today.

ME

You stopped taking your birth control.

LAINEY

Ha! NO. Nice try though. 😌

ME

Tell me.

LAINEY

How about I show you instead?

A picture came through, and I pressed on it to blow up the image. It took a second before I realized I was looking at

Lainey's wrist. In the center, a black infinity symbol had been tattooed, and in the middle of the loop was an *R*.

> LAINEY
>
> I'm your why. But you're my why too, Rhett. Forever.

I balanced the bottom of my phone on my desk, and after rereading her words several times, I looked at her tattoo once more. At the symbolism she'd permanently inked on her body. At the letter she not only wore around her neck again, but now on her hand that was closest to her heart.

This woman ... did she know what she was doing to me?

Every gesture, every surprise, every word she spoke.

It all made me love her even more—when more wasn't even possible.

> ME
>
> Baby, you put me on your body.

> LAINEY
>
> I can't see the necklace unless I look in a mirror. But this? I can look at it whenever I want. That's important to me. Having you there. Always.

> ME
>
> I can't wait to kiss it.

> LAINEY
>
> I can't wait to kiss you tonight.

FORTY-SIX

Lainey

Present Day

Mom held the coffee cup with both hands, the ceramic balancing on her breasts as she looked at me from the other side of the couch. One of the advantages of moving back to LA was that I got to have breakfast with my mother whenever I wanted.

But this morning, when I'd walked into my parents' house, knowing Dad would be at work, I'd told her to stop cutting up the grapefruit she'd been carving, that we needed to chat.

Almost a week had passed since Rhett had come to my apartment, and we'd had the conversation about what we wanted. In most scenarios, that was a time frame far too premature to even discuss it with the parents.

Not in my case.

And not when it came to the love between Rhett and me.

There was no question in my mind; this was only the beginning of us.

So, while Mom and I sat on the couch and I held my untouched coffee, I told her everything that had transpired, starting from when I'd seen Rhett in Bangkok to the unexpected meetup at the cemetery. I went into detail about the things Rhett had told me about Pen while we were at the track. I purged everything. I kept nothing from her. And when I finished, I explained the Instagram post I'd made—since she'd seen it—and how I'd shared that photo, knowing it would get Rhett to come over.

There was emotion on Mom's face when I covered the parts about Pen. When I told her how my sister had acted with Rhett and what had really gone down that day on the boat in comparison to the police report. But once Mom's tears cleared, she looked at me like my best friend, listening to me pour my heart out.

And when I wrapped up the last bit, explaining the handful of days and nights Rhett and I had spent together, I put my hand on her knee, which was the closest part of her I could reach, and said, "What do you think about all of this, Mom?"

"What do I think?" She drew in a huge breath, slowly letting it out. "As far as your sister is concerned, these are things we didn't know about. Honey, it's a lot to unpack."

"I know."

"Cocaine?" She put her hand on her chest. "Dear God, that hurts to hear, Lainey."

"There were times ... times she was so messed up that I wondered if she was just drinking or if she was mixing things. I never asked her. And I never saw her doing anything other than drinking and smoking. But the thought was there, especially the nights when she blacked out." I paused. "Did you know about those nights? Or how much she was drinking? Or partying?"

"When she would come downstairs in the morning, white as a ghost, still three sheets to the wind, yes, of course I knew. But she was such a good kid. She was home on time. She got exceptional grades. She got into NYU. I just ..." As she went silent, she sighed. "I turned a blind eye. I know now that I shouldn't have."

When I pulled my hand back, she continued, "I have to ask. Is there any part of you that's questioning whether Rhett is telling you the truth about Penelope?"

"No." My head shook. "Not even a little. Because toward the end, when Pen was hanging out with the lacrosse team, I knew their reputation and that they were into coke and pills, and I knew she should stay away from them. But instead of learning that lesson, she just got deeper involved with them." I rested the cup on the couch and stared at the top of it. "I should have done something too. I should have ... I don't know."

"Carrying that guilt won't bring her back, honey. There's a strong possibility we'd still be here now, having almost the same conversation, had you tried to do something about it. Because whether Pen was high or not, she might have still jumped."

"I know."

She gave a weak grin. "What *I* know is that you're the reason she was home on time. That when you were with her, nothing ever happened. You took care of your sister, baby. But that wasn't your responsibility, and it's not something you could have done forever." Her smile strengthened. "My goodness, didn't she look up to you? She admired you. And given what Rhett said, she envied you."

"I envied her, Mom. She could walk into a room and not know a single person and leave with ten new best friends. She wasn't afraid of anything or anyone. She could create a spotlight out of total darkness and have it shine right over her." I folded my legs up to my chest and leaned my shoulder into the back cushion of the couch. "Rhett waited all these years to tell me. He didn't think I was ready." I exhaled. "He didn't know if I'd ever be ready." I paused. "He had nothing to lose, Mom."

"He certainly didn't."

I went quiet for several moments before I whispered, "I love him."

"You always have." She finally took a sip of her coffee and set the mug on the small table beside her. With her hands free, she moved forward a whole seat and clasped my fingers within hers. "Since you were a freshman in high school, and I knew you going to Europe wouldn't change that."

"I want to be with him." My eyes were welling with tears. I couldn't stop the emotion. "I have to be with him—for me. And I don't know how you and Dad feel about that, especially Dad, but I can't go another day without Rhett in my life."

"My girl," she said so softly. "Over the years, every time we spoke about him, I knew you still loved him. I heard it in your voice, honey." She released my hand to brush some hair out of my face, holding my cheek and then my chin. "You're thirty-three years old. You've only been in love once, and now, that love is back and ..." Her head tilted, an adoring expression spreading over her face. "I understand."

I didn't want to ask this question.

It made me sick to my stomach thinking of what her response could be.

But I was extremely close to my parents. It was only the three of us. And I couldn't go on without knowing how she felt.

"Do you support this, Mom?"

She swiped away several of my tears. "After some time passed, I think it became clear in all of our heads that Rhett wasn't the reason Penelope died. Sure, he was the captain of the boat, and something happened under his watch, but he couldn't have stopped her from jumping. He couldn't have prevented it either. And as someone who now knows far too much about boating without ever being behind the wheel of one, I can say that there was no reason, given the situation, that he should have turned off those engines."

She looked down for a moment. "It made it easier on our hearts to blame him."

When she gazed back up, I saw the pain in her eyes. "The way your father treated that boy when he came to our house after the funeral ... it was wrong. Your father knows that. I know that."

Her touch turned so gentle. "Yes, honey, I support you."

Every time I nodded, a tear fell. "I'm going to marry him, Mom."

"Are you going to give me grandbabies? Dear God, please say yes."

ME

> I just left Mom and Dad's house. Mom says hi.

I sent the text to Rhett, and as I was pulling out of my parents' driveway, I wasn't surprised at all when my dashboard showed an incoming call from him. I hit a button on my steering wheel to answer and said, "Hi," once it connected.

"Lainey ... we haven't talked about your parents. Jesus, that's a topic I wasn't ready to tackle. I figured I'd approach it in a couple of weeks. You know, after you already moved in," he joked.

I laughed. "I didn't want to bring them up either."

"I was afraid they wouldn't support us being together. And then that would become a whole other situation."

I turned off their street, accelerating as I replied, "The thought was in my mind too. I couldn't obsess over it for a second more."

"So, you ripped off the Band-Aid."

I remembered when I'd said something similar to him at the track. "I did. But I only told Mom. I wanted to start with her. She's the easier one to talk to."

"How'd it go?"

"By telling her about you, I had to tell her everything about Pen and the day of the accident. It was a lot—saying those words to my mom, watching her process. But fifteen years have passed, and although things are still sensitive in some spots, other spots have healed." I smiled as I thought of her response. "She wants me happy, Rhett, and she knows you're my happiness."

"You're saying ... she's okay with us?"

"Yes."

He exhaled. "Was she surprised to find out we're back together?"

"I think, deep down, she was expecting it. Just like she's expecting grandchildren."

He laughed. "She said that?"

"In a roundabout way."

He was still laughing. "Perfect. We'll start trying tonight."

My gasp ended in laughter. "The thing is, you're serious."

"I've never been more serious in my life."

I came to a stop at the red light. "Maybe we could wait a few weeks?" The smile owned my entire face. "Or say, a year? Or even two? We just got each other back. I want to enjoy this time before we have to share each other with a little one who is going to take up every second of us."

"Fair."

I tapped the steering wheel. "Note to self: double up on my birth control when I get home."

"I haven't even touched you yet."

"But when you do, I just have this strange feeling you're going to get me pregnant."

"That's some powerful shit right there."

I chewed my lip. "For some people, yes. But not for Rhett Cole."

He went silent for a second. "Lainey, I want to talk to your parents. I think it's important that they not only hear it from you, but they also hear it from me."

My eyes fluttered closed, and I silently nodded. "I think that's a really good idea."

FORTY-SEVEN

Rhett

Present Day

Lainey turned toward me while we sat beside each other on the beach, a blanket beneath us that I'd spread over the sand, a cooler behind us that we'd just finished picking through. Plastic flutes, full of champagne, in our hands.

"Why does this spot look so familiar?" she asked.

It was sunset, and the warmth of the sky was reflecting over her glowing skin.

She was even more gorgeous now than the day we'd sat here all those years ago.

I loosened my grip from her shoulders and moved my fingers to her face. "Because we've been in this exact spot before."

Her eyes narrowed. "Wait ..."

"You remember. I know you do."

She glanced toward the water and pointed. "Pen was right over there with Timothy." She paused. "And I told you I didn't want to spend the day at the beach." She gazed back at me. "So, we left and went to your house ... and that was when I lost my virginity to you."

"Yes."

She snuggled back in, pressing her cheek into my neck. "That feels like a million lifetimes ago." She took a sip.

"Because it was."

She rubbed her hand over my thigh, the sound of the waves a language we enjoyed listening to until she said, "I talked to my parents. They told me all about your visit."

I put my lips on her forehead and breathed her in. But when I exhaled, it was relief that I felt on a level I hadn't experienced in a long time. If ever. "I've waited a decade and a half to talk to them."

"For God's sake, the man had told you he would kill you if you ever came near me again. And you walked into that home, not only to tell him the truth about what had happened on the boat, but to tell him you're still in love with his daughter. Rhett"—she pulled away to look at me—"that's courageous, and that's ..."

"That's love."

Her nod was exaggerated. "Yes."

"What helped was that your father was willing to listen. Our conversation went much differently this time than the last time we spoke."

"Dad has been grieving for the last fifteen years. It was time for him to know the truth."

I fanned my fingers across her cheek. "He told me he was proud of the man I'd become and that, in his heart, he knew I'd take care of his baby." I pressed my forehead to hers. "To hear him say that … after what happened with his other baby. Lainey …"

"I know." Her hand flattened against mine. "I know."

"We have his blessing."

She leaned back a few inches and stroked my beard. "He told me."

I kissed her slowly, and when I felt a vibration in my pocket, which had to be the text I'd been expecting, I pulled back. I waited for her to look at the water before I peeked at the screen.

TRISTA

All set. You're a good guy, Rhett. She's going to love it.

And thank you for the gift—that was unexpected and so nice of you.

I put the phone back, set the champagne on the sand, and wrapped my arms around her waist. As I was nuzzling her neck, I lifted her onto my lap, her legs straddling mine. My hands went to her face, and I kissed her.

But this kiss was different from any of the others.

Because there wasn't a question; there was zero doubt.

Lainey Taylor was mine.

Again.

And nothing would ever come between us.

Not our past. Not her parents. Not the memories that threatened to pull us into the darkness.

Somehow, someway, we'd survived, and we'd come out on the other side.

When I separated our mouths, I kept us close, locking our gazes. "Do you see that house behind me with all the lights on? The two-story one with the balcony off the second floor?"

"Yes."

"That's ours for the weekend."

Her brows rose. "What? We're staying there?"

I chuckled at how surprised she sounded. "We are."

"But I didn't know. I didn't bring anything. All I have is what I'm wearing."

"I brought everything you'll need. Even a bikini."

Since she'd also set down her drink at some point, both of her hands now rested on my shoulders. "Hold on a second. You brought me a bikini?"

"I did."

She was smiling so hard, and I fucking loved to see it. "Are you saying you went shopping? For me?"

"Baby, the Coles have a private shopper. I wouldn't call what I did shopping. I'd say I looked at a rack of clothing that had been picked out for you, and I pointed at the items I wanted. The thing is, I liked everything that the shopper had pulled, so I bought it all." I nodded toward the house. "It's inside, along with some toiletries—for the record, I didn't pick any of that out, but our shopper said it's the best shit. What the hell do I know about face cream? Nothing."

"I don't even know what to say right now." She traced my lip with the back of her thumb. "You brought me to a spot that's such a memorable place for us. You booked us a house for the weekend. You bought me everything I could possibly need for the stay. Do you ever forget anything?"

Even though the sky was darkening, filling with magenta and burnt orange, the diamonds in her *R* necklace still glimmered.

I held on to her ass, making sure her legs were positioned around me, and I stood. "You tell me," I said as I walked us to the beach house.

She laughed in my arms. "You left the blanket and the cooler and our shoes and champagne—"

"Don't worry, I'll get it all later."

I carried her up the flight of stairs and entered the code on the door before walking us inside. Since it was far too bright in here, I flipped the switch, turning the lights off, and the room became aglow with candles.

"Rhett, oh my God."

On the floor were rose petals, thousands of them scattered between the candles, the perfect contrast to the all-white room.

"Aside from your apartment, I've never been in a space that smells so much like you." I kissed her before I set her down, and I watched her face while she took in the sight.

"This is ... stunning. You did this all?"

I smiled. "I might have gotten a little help, but I put the plans in motion and picked it out."

"That's the most important part." She wrapped her arms around my neck.

"I want you to know—and this might not make any sense to you—part of the reason I haven't devoured you yet is because I needed to know where things stood with your dad. In my mind, there were two steps to this." I palmed her cheeks. "The first was getting you back, and the second was making sure your parents supported that decision. If we didn't have that, I didn't know if you would still be with me." I moved my lips close to hers. "And I didn't want to make things physical, knowing there was a chance I could lose you. That doesn't mean I didn't want to. That doesn't mean I didn't obsess about your body every minute of the fucking day. And that doesn't mean I didn't think about your pussy and how wet it was going to feel, how tight"— I kissed her—"and how badly I want to come inside you. Waiting has been straight-up fucking torture, but now, I have my answer."

"I had a feeling, and that's why I didn't push you." Her

fingers dived into the back of my hair. "But you have their support now ..."

My hands returned to her ass, and I lifted her feet off the floor and moved her legs around me before I walked her to the bedroom. "And I'm going to do everything I've been dreaming about for the last fifteen years."

She looked around the room, at the rose petals on the bed and the floor, the candles on every surface that was large enough to hold a votive. "Rhett, I'm blown away. This is exquisite."

"They're in the bath, too, where I'm going to take you once I'm done with you."

Her head shook in awe. "I'm so in love with you."

I felt the smile move across my lips.

And, damn it, it felt good.

"Show me," I ordered.

She laughed. "Gladly."

While she kissed me, I set her on the end of the bed, pulling the loose-fitting dress up her body and over her head. I knew she didn't have a bra on underneath—there was no room for one with the way it cut across her tits—and I'd been admiring the hardness of her nipples all night. Beneath, I found a thong, and I yanked it past her hips and down her legs, flinging it behind me.

Now that she was naked, I didn't rise off the floor. I stayed kneeling in front of her, looking at her body as the light from the candles lit up her skin. "My God, Lainey. Do you have any idea how beautiful you are?"

"I feel it by the way you're looking at me."

"And that fucking smile." I moved in between her legs until I was only inches from the bottom of the mattress. "It makes me so happy when I know you're grinning for me."

Her fingers raked through the top of my hair. "For the rest of my life, this smile will only be for you."

I knew that. I felt it.

But there was nothing like hearing it.

She rubbed her lips together, eyeing me. "What are you about to do to me?"

"I'm going to taste you."

"What if I tell you that you can do that later? That I need you inside me right now. That I can't wait another second—"

I dived my face into her pussy, my nose pressing against her clit. "This is for me. But don't you worry, I'm going to take care of you. I promise, you're going to get everything you want. I just fucking need this."

I could spend all night right here, inhaling her scent. But I wasn't going to drag this out—not the first time we were together after so long apart. So, I only allowed myself to breathe her in once, savoring that rose scent. Memorizing it again. Realizing just how much I'd missed it. And then I lifted my nose and licked her from top to bottom, tasting her wetness, the sweetness of her pussy exploding in my mouth.

"Rhett!"

Fuck, she tasted amazing.

Better than I remembered.

"That feels good, doesn't it, baby?"

"Yes!"

I moved my tongue in between her lips, flicking the flatness down the length of her, the tip of it against the bridge of her clit. And while I increased my speed, I rubbed her pussy with my thumb, spreading the wetness that was already there, my mouth only adding more. My thumb moved lower and lower until it was dipping inside. I gave her a few pumps up to my knuckle before replacing it with my pointer finger, gradually moving all the way in.

"Ah!" She rocked her hips forward. "Rhett!"

My lips were covered in her, my hard-on fucking pounding to be released from these tight boxer briefs, wanting to put my dick where my face was.

But I couldn't get enough.

And I wanted more.

I wrapped her thigh over my shoulder, the creaminess of her skin rubbing against my beard, giving me another wave of that gorgeous rose scent.

"Please," she gasped.

I didn't know if she was begging to come or if she wanted my cock.

Or both.

But I wasn't leaving this spot until she got off on my tongue.

I also knew that wasn't going to take very much. A few hard thrusts of my finger and licking her with an intensity she hadn't felt yet, and she'd be quivering.

Shit, I was right.

Within a few more swipes, she was screaming, "Rhett," so loud that my ears were ringing.

"That's it," I moaned. "Come on my tongue."

With my finger inside her, I could feel the tremors going off in her body, her orgasm blasting straight through her stomach. And then there was the wetness, a rush of it that went past my knuckle and onto my tongue.

"Oh my God! Fuck!"

I licked through each shudder, waiting for a stillness that told me it was over, and once she reached that place, I slowed my movements, licking the thickness and swallowing it.

"That taste, Lainey. Fuck me, it's everything I've wanted." I kissed her pussy while I gently pulled out my finger, and when I saw my skin glistening, I surrounded my finger with my lips and sucked that off too.

"That mouth." She stared at me in such a naughty way. "I don't know how, but you've only gotten better at that."

I chuckled as I stood from the floor, getting to work on my jeans, letting them fall with my boxer briefs, my dick springing free.

"*Mmm.* Yes. That's what I want." She put her lips over my tip, sucking my crown and pumping all the way to my base.

"Fuck," I groaned. I stepped out of my shoes, lifting my right foot to take off my sock and then my left foot and finished by tossing my shirt. I held the sides of her face, our eyes locked. "You'd better slow down there. You're blowing me like you want me to come."

I let her have a few more bobs before I popped my dick out of her mouth and moved her up the bed until her head was on the pillow. I held the outside of her thighs and positioned her legs around me. Our bodies pressed together, my lips over hers, our eyes focused on one another. The revelation that so much time had passed since we'd been here was evident in our stares.

Within one sweep, I was inside her.

"Lainey ... fuck!"

"I know." She was panting. "Trust me, I know."

The heat of her was what overcame me at first, completely taking over me. The wetness followed, her pussy hugging me like two arms squeezing my neck. My forehead rested against hers while I stayed there, frozen, her cunt pulsing around me. I felt every clench. Every fucking drip. Every degree of heat.

"You are so tight."

My teeth ground as I waited.

My body tensed.

I could come right now. That was how amazing she felt.

But I let the seconds pass, for her pussy to remember me, before I reared my hips back and sank in. And once those pumps started, they got deeper. They got harder. Every one of her moans driving me closer to that edge.

"Baby!" She was breathless, her nails in my shoulders, both legs now around me, her feet locked, keeping our bodies in position.

"Fuck yes," I hissed.

I circled within her, rotating to hit each of her walls, to add pressure to the parts of her that needed attention, leaning up just enough on my knees that I could use my hands.

To pinch her nipples.

To hold her cheek.

To rub my thumb over her clit.

"Oh! My! God!" she yelled.

She was getting close again—I could feel that by her wetness.

But the next time she came, we were going to do it in sync. And she was going to scream my fucking name while I filled her with my cum.

So, I lifted her off the bed and walked to the wall next to it, where there was a mirror directly across from us. With her back on the paint, her face was pointed at our reflection.

"I want you to watch me fuck you," I demanded. "I want you to see how beautiful your face looks when you're screaming from another orgasm."

"I'm almost there."

I angled her in a way that I could pull her hips forward, leaving just enough space that my finger could rub her clit. When she realized what I was doing, she moaned.

But that was only the beginning.

A sound that was far too light for my ears. I wanted that piercing scream to return.

I thrust into her, using a strength she hadn't yet felt tonight, and I maintained that stamina, but every time I bucked into her, I gave her a twist, adding friction to her G-spot.

She felt it.

Because every time I did it, her nails stabbed me even harder.

"Rhett!" She gasped in some air. "The muscles in your back. Your ass. You have no idea how hot this looks."

Within a few more pounces, I growled, "You're going to come ... I can fucking feel it."

And so was I.

The tingling was moving through my balls and into my shaft. It was bringing this wild wave of pleasure that was making everything turn numb.

"I love you," she cried.

I was slamming her so hard that her lips vibrated over mine.

"I love you more." Once the last word left me, the first stream of cum shot from my tip. "Fuck!"

She was there too.

Shuddering.

Screaming, "Rhett," just the way I'd wanted.

Our movements matched.

Our breaths intertwined.

Our voices turned hoarse from all the shouting.

It took several dips of her milking me before I was empty. Her body was already still at that point, and I joined her in that quietness, breathing over her lips, hers in a smile.

Her nails pulled back from my skin, and her arms tightened around me. "I missed you. I missed this."

"You're never going to have to miss it again." I gently kissed her. "You're mine now. And mine forever."

FORTY-EIGHT

Lainey

Present Day

Once I heard the knock, I rushed around my apartment, grabbing my jean jacket and purse and keys, and walked to the door. The smile was already on my face as I reached for the knob and opened it. But where I expected Rhett to be on the other side, there was someone else.

A beautiful little girl in pigtails and a baby-pink T-shirt with a matching tutu-style skirt and the most adorable pink Chucks. She was holding a bouquet of pink daisies that she handed to me. "For you."

Her grin was so large, and I felt my own lips pull even wider.

"Thank you. You must be Daisy."

"How did you know?"

I laughed. "I recognized your photo. Your uncle is very proud of you and has shown me many pictures of you."

"He has?" She gave off a devilish grin. "Uncle 'Ett is my best friend. Did you know that?"

"I would say you're his best friend too." I could feel Rhett's stare on me as he stood against the wall on the side of the door. I held out my hand to her. "I'm Lainey. It's so lovely to finally meet you, Daisy."

"Uncle 'Ett says your last name is Taylor. Do you know how cool that is? Taylor Swift is my favorite singer in the whole wide world. And since your name has Taylor in it, that makes me think you're so cool too." She shook my hand. "I'm Daisy"— she giggled—"but you already know that."

When I went to pull my hand back, she readjusted the way she was holding it, keeping our fingers together, and said, "Come on, Lainey. We're going to lunch. Uncle 'Ett says I'm buying. He-he."

With her fingers now looped through mine, I let the door shut behind me and joined them in the hallway.

"I don't think your uncle would ever let you buy," I replied, giving her a little squeeze.

"Hi," I said to Rhett. My cheeks flushed as I felt his gaze across my whole body.

"Hey, you." He was giving me the sexiest grin as he put his arm around my shoulders, which placed me in between them.

"You're right, Uncle 'Ett. Lainey is *sooo* pretty. Like, the prettiest, like Mommy and Auntie Row."

He kissed my forehead. "I told you she was gorgeous, Daisy."

"And she has the best hair ever." She reached for one of my curls and bounced it in her hand. "I love it so much."

"You two are making me blush," I said.

As we reached the elevator, Daisy voiced, "Uncle 'Ett said I'm a surprise. Were you surprised to see me?"

I lifted the flowers from my side and smelled the daisies. "Big time," I told her. "And I'm just as surprised that you gave me these. I love them. Thank you."

"I picked them out all by myself. I thought you would love pink, just like me."

"Hey, speaking of pink," I said, "I heard you were a big influence in your uncle getting his toes painted sparkly pink."

She put her hand over her mouth. "That was totally me."

"I'm a big fan of the color. You picked out the perfect shade." I winked at her.

"Uncle 'Ett showed you his toes?" Her eyes got big. "*Ewww.*"

I laughed. "He did."

"See, Uncle 'Ett, I did a good job! Even Lainey Taylor"— she giggled over my last name—"loves them!"

Daisy asked Rhett if she could hit the button.

Once she pushed it, Rhett said, "I think we need to go for another pedicure, Daisy, so I can get the color off. It's time."

"Another pink!" she replied. "Hot pink!"

"Oh, I bet hot pink would look amazing on you," I said to Rhett.

He shook his head at me, smiling.

"I want you to come next time we get our toes done," Daisy said, resting her face against my arm. "We can get matching ones too."

"I would love that," I told her. "So, tell me, Daisy, what are we eating for lunch?"

"Egg burritos!"

"That does sound delicious," I replied. "Is that your favorite lunch?"

"I eat egg burritos every day." She pushed a pigtail out of

her face. "I just love them with extra-gooey cheese that squirts out the bottom. I try really hard not to get it all over me, but sometimes, it happens, and I'm covered in cheese." She smiled. "That's kinda the best part."

"Sounds like a stomach disaster for Lainey," Rhett said, grinning.

I laughed at him and replied to Daisy, "Gooey cheese sounds incredible."

When the elevator dinged, Daisy released me and rushed inside to hit the button for the lobby. "Uncle 'Ett, you haven't told us where we're eating. Say burritos. Say burritos. Please!"

"I've got one more surprise up my sleeve," he said. "The both of you are just going to have to wait a little bit before you find out where we're going."

"*Okaaay*," Daisy sang. She looked at me as the doors closed. "His surprises are always the best."

"What makes them the best?" I asked.

She seemed to think about the question and shrugged. "He knows what I love the mostest."

"I know what you mean," I said softly. "It's like you don't even have to tell him. And then he gives it to you, and it's everything you've ever wanted." I touched my neck where the diamond *R* sat.

"It's 'cause he loves us," she said, and she rushed over to him and hugged his waist.

"And I love you. Come here, kiddo." He reached down and lifted her like she weighed no more than a feather and carried her out of the elevator to his car parked out front.

Even though he'd teased me about trying to get pregnant, I knew how badly he wanted a child.

We both did.

And seeing him with Daisy was something I couldn't have

prepared myself for. The patience he had with her, the way he looked at her, the way she looked at him.

She'd been his light since the day she had been born.

And for the years I couldn't be there for him, Daisy had. She'd held his hand and walked him straight out of the storm. The best part was, that little girl didn't even know it.

I could understand how Rhett could come across to people who didn't know him. Or for even those who did, there was a roughness to him, like a callus. One that, I assumed, had taken shape after losing Pen. Anyone who had experienced what we had—what my whole family had—would never be the same.

But what was inside that man was pure love.

Someone who would make the most remarkable father.

Someone who would stand by my side for the rest of my life.

And someone who would never make me question his love.

Because I didn't just feel it in my heart.

I felt it everywhere.

Once he got Daisy settled into the backseat, he opened my door for me, kissing me on the cheek. "I knew you'd be so motherly with her." His voice was low so only I could hear. "But seeing how much she loves you already, fuck, Lainey, I can't even explain how that's making me feel."

I smiled at him and held the flowers up to my face as I climbed into the passenger seat. I waited for him to close the door to put on my seat belt.

And as he started the car and pulled away from the curb, I said to Daisy, "Where do you think he's taking us?"

"Somewhere that's the best. I just know it."

"The best, huh?" Rhett said. "That's a lot of pressure, Daisy. I'd better be bringing you somewhere amazing." He reached across the seat and held my hand.

"You promised me a delicious lunch," I teased him. "So, I agree with Daisy. I hope we end up somewhere that's the best."

"You're jumping on the bandwagon, I see." He looked at me quickly to smile.

"Just a woman supporting another woman—that's all," I replied.

"That's right, Uncle 'Ett. We're besties already."

Rhett laughed, and I did too. I turned even more and waved Daisy closer. She could only bend so far with how tightly she was buckled in.

"I have to tell you a secret."

"Yay! Okay!"

I waited until she moved forward and whispered, "Will you tell your uncle something for me?"

She nodded.

I whispered out the message I wanted her to share and leaned back into the front seat, turning toward Rhett.

"What was that all about?" he asked.

"Daisy has something she needs to tell you." I looked at Daisy and said, "Girl, you're up."

"Uncle 'Ett, Lainey says she wants to move to Iceland with you."

The biggest grin was on Rhett's lips. "Is that so?"

"*Mmhmm.* She just told me. Is that another surprise, Uncle 'Ett?"

"It is," he said. "A giant one." He pulled my hand up to his mouth and kissed it. "I love you."

"I love you too," Daisy and I said at the same time.

Which made me laugh, and it made Rhett smile even harder—an expression I hadn't known was possible for that man.

"Iceland ..." He shook his head as though he couldn't believe I'd finally made the decision.

"I wanna go to Iceland," Daisy said. "Where's Iceland?"

"It's far, baby. But don't worry, you're coming too," he said. "When the hotel is finished, your dad is going to bring you, and we're going to have a massive party. Doesn't that sound like fun?"

"I can't wait, Uncle 'Ett."

Rhett was careful when he pointed out the windshield, making sure Daisy didn't see him, but I did, and as the sign came into view, I knew exactly why he wanted me to see it.

"Our first date," he said softly.

God, this man.

Sentimental in a way I'd certainly never expected.

"It's like you don't even have to tell him. And then he gives it to you, and it's everything you've ever wanted," I said quietly, repeating the words I'd said to Daisy earlier because they were already coming into play again.

"I knew you'd love it for that reason," he said. "The little one, she'll love it for an entirely different reason." He kissed along the back of my knuckles. "I think you should deliver the surprise."

"I would love to." I turned toward Daisy. "Before you go to Iceland, there's another land I think you should visit first."

Her eyes widened. "Where?"

I reached for her hand and squeezed her small, pink-painted fingers. "How about Disneyland?"

Her mouth dropped open. "We're going to Disneyland?"

"Yes, ma'am, and guess who's going to ride all the rides with you," Rhett said.

"Lainey TAYLOR!" Daisy screamed.

EPILOGUE

Rhett

Ten Months Later

Lainey looked so fucking beautiful. She had on a strapless red jumpsuit with the diamond R around her neck—an outfit that showed the dip of her chest and the cinch of her waist, the curve of her ass and the delicious muscle in her legs.

An outfit she'd purchased from a boutique in Reykjavik even though I'd had my shopper in LA send over a slew of things for us to wear this weekend. Lainey thought it was important to represent a local designer for the opening of my hotel. My shopper's selections were added to our walk-in closet, Lainey insisting they get returned when we moved back to LA in a few weeks.

She tried to limit how much I spoiled her.

Most of the time, I won.

But tonight, with how sexy she was in red, I was happy to cave.

"Come here." I turned her hand so she faced me at the mouth of the hallway, where we were about to do a final walk-through of the bottom level of the hotel—at least that was what she thought—followed by dinner with some officials of the island to celebrate the opening of the hotel. "I just want to tell you I love you. Spending the last eight months here with you by my side has been an experience I'll never forget. I couldn't have done this without you."

She flattened her hand against the lapel of my suit jacket. "You could have. You just would have had a very lonely bed at night and no one to eat dinner with at midnight when you finally returned home from work every day."

I wrapped my arms around her, holding on to her ass. "You did far more than keep me company, Lainey. You helped me make decisions. You picked out finishes. You weighed in on the hiring of certain staff." I chuckled. "Cole and Spade Hotels might need to put you on the payroll."

She gave me the smile that was reserved just for me. "It was an honor to stand by your side while you created this master-piece." Her hands went to my face, the R tattoo pressing against my cheek. "But maybe next time, you could pick a place that's a tad bit warmer?"

"Baby, are you telling me you're tired of shivering?" I squeezed her ass.

"And I thought London was cold. Jeez."

"As long as you come with me, I promise the next location will be warmer." I narrowed in on her mouth. "I want to kiss you, but that lipstick is just fucking cruel."

"The red, you mean?"

I nodded, knowing I would be kissing her soon, but that color was going to paint my lips and never come off.

"Ah, let me show you something fun." She dragged her thumb over each lip, and when she was done, her finger was free of red. "It's smudge-proof. It won't come off—"

That was all I needed to see.

I pulled her face to mine and surrounded her lips, teasing my tongue around hers. Her rose scent was all I smelled, and I couldn't get enough, drawing her in closer, pressing my body to hers.

"Whoa," she moaned a few seconds later. "Are we going to make it to that dinner?" She winked.

I chuckled. "Let's do the walk-through, then."

I linked her hand in mine, kissing the top of her knuckles as I walked her down the hallway, pointing out the different spaces where, in the last few days, some tweaks had been made. Because we wanted privacy, away from the construction and hotel employees, Lainey and I lived about a quarter of a mile away in a house I'd rented within the heart of the capital. So, even though she was here a lot, she didn't come daily to witness the progress.

We were only a few rooms down when I came to a stop outside a closed door. "Open it." I nodded toward the handle.

"Isn't this one of the ballrooms?"

"It is."

"Did you add the lighting that we talked about—" She stopped herself mid-question, her hand going over her mouth after she gasped. "Rhett, oh my God!"

I moved us inside the ballroom. The scent from the roses instantly filled my nose, so I knew it had to be doing the same for her. There were thousands of long-stemmed red roses inside. They covered the four walls; they were in tall, clear glass vases every few feet throughout the room; the floor was made entirely of petals.

This didn't feel like a space filled with flowers.

This felt as though we had stepped inside an actual rose.

And the only light inside were candles, the flickering flames creating an ambiance that I had been envisioning for weeks. There were hundreds of them, each wick ablaze, the white base the only color inside all the red.

I brought Lainey to the center and positioned her to face me. There wasn't any nervousness running through me. What I felt was a calm. Because this was the woman of my dreams. The woman I'd waited all these years to be with. The woman who I knew, in my heart, would be with me forever.

I reached inside the pocket of my suit jacket, and I took out the small velvet box, opening the lid while I got on one knee.

Lainey's eyes filled with tears, her hand finally dropping from her face as I reached for her left one to hold, her chin quivering now that it was uncovered.

"My Lainey." I smiled. "You came into my life to show me who I really was. You came in to teach me about love—a word I never knew the meaning of before. You came in to make my world a better place. You give me purpose. Passion."

I rubbed my thumb over the back of her hand. "I breathe because of you. I want because of you. I learn and I grow and I need—all because of you. You're more than my why, baby. You're my reason. My one."

I opened the lid of the box, the diamond nestled inside the velvet folds. "Our journey has been made up of three phases. Freshman year was one. Junior to senior year was two. And this has been our third. When I designed this ring, I wanted those stages to be present, like steps leading us to where we are now."

I took the diamond out and placed the eternity band in front of her finger. The five-carat center stone was oval, shaped like the inside of an infinity symbol. The two-carat rectangular stones beside it sat lower on the band, as if they were actual stairs leading to the main diamond, symbolizing our life now.

"I love you, Lainey. I've always loved you. I will love you until I take my last breath." The emotion was building in my throat. "Will you be my wife—"

"Yes!" She collapsed on top of my leg, sitting there while she threw her arms around my neck and squeezed. "I love you so much, Rhett."

Still holding the ring, I put it in my palm, and I hugged her back, tucking my face in her neck, breathing in a scent that a roomful of roses couldn't even compete with.

"My wife," I whispered. "Lainey, you've made me the happiest man."

I clutched her hair, clinging our bodies together. And when I finally let go, I placed the diamonds on her finger.

"Rhett, this is the most beautiful ring I've ever seen." She stared at it, her eyes wide and watery. "It's truly a staircase with an infinite amount of love."

I wiped a tear off her cheek and another that was starting to fall. "My baby." I kissed her tattoo. "Mine forever."

"My husband," she said softly. "I already call you that ... you just don't know."

"Then, kiss your husband, Lainey."

I got a smile, and then I got her mouth. I got her to exhale, and I got her to moan.

Her grin didn't fade when she pulled back. "I can't wait to tell everyone. Only two more days until they're all here. Won't they die when they come for the hotel opening and find out we're engaged?"

I palmed her cheek. "Baby, they already know."

She searched my eyes. "Did you tell them you were proposing?"

I leaned in until my lips were in front of hers. "No. But they just heard."

I snapped my fingers three times, and the wall across from

us began to open, a parting that revealed our group of family and friends on the other side of the ballroom.

"I wanted them to share this moment with us." While I stayed kneeling on the floor with her on me, I took in the faces that were smiling at us, the roar of applause, the shouting. "It was a long road of unhappiness for the both of us, Lainey. It's time to celebrate some love."

"Rhett, is that my mom and dad over there?" Her hands were on her face, steepled over her nose and mouth.

"I couldn't ask you to be my wife without having them here to hug you after."

She looked at me. "I love you. To the moon and back—endless times."

I wiped the bottoms of her eyes. "I love you more."

I guided her up to her feet, and my hand clasped around hers as we joined the party that had miraculously stayed silent while I proposed.

Everyone was here.

But the first trio we approached were the Taylors and my mom.

As my mom hugged me, she whispered, "I wish your dad were here to celebrate you and Lainey. He'd be so proud of you, Rhett."

"I wish he were here too," I replied, kissing her on the cheek.

I then hugged Mrs. Taylor before I shook hands with Mr. Taylor, who said, "Welcome to the family, son."

I knew he appreciated the conversation I'd had with him before Lainey and I moved to Iceland—when I'd asked for his blessing to marry his daughter. I'd called him several weeks ago to update him on the plan, letting him know the details of when our private jet would be taking off for Iceland so he and Mrs. Taylor could be on board.

"A family I'm thrilled to be a part of," I told him.

I waited for my mom to release Lainey before I led her over to the Daltons. Dominick, Jenner, Jo, Ford, Hannah, Camden, and their significant others were here to offer their congrats. Although Jenner worked for the Spade and Cole Hotel brand, his siblings and cousins, all lawyers as well, were a group we now knew on a personal basis.

Once I finished introducing them to Lainey, we approached the Westons, the five siblings hanging out in a circle, opening as we neared.

"Congrats, brother," Hart said, going in for a hug, slapping me on the back as we separated. "Couldn't be happier for you."

"Thanks for flying in early," I replied.

"I can see why you love it here," Hart responded. "I'm happy as hell we're joining you on this journey."

"I've sampled some of the food already." I shook my head, showing him how pleased I was. "That's one sick menu Walker put together for this restaurant."

"Yes, it is," Walker said, laughing. He shook my hand. "I'm glad you like it."

Beck, Colson, and Eden all offered their congratulations as well.

Lainey and I headed over to Macon, clasping his hand, before moving on to Brady and Cooper, who was holding my niece Rayner.

"Look at that rock," Macon said, lifting Lainey's hand to admire the ring. "Never thought I'd see this day." He laughed. "Like a pig in shit—that's how fucking pleased I am that I get to witness this."

I chuckled at him. "You fool."

"From one asshole to another," Brady said, knocking me on the chest with his fist—a man I hadn't always gotten along with in the past, but we were finally in a good place—"there's nothing like finding a good woman to bring out the best side of you." His hand stilled but stayed on me. "You deserve this."

"Back at you." I shifted over to Cooper and kissed Rayner on the cheek. "My baby girl," I whispered.

"Proud of you, my man," Cooper said. "Hopefully, now, your sister can stop obsessing over when you're going to pop the question."

I shook his shoulder, careful not to disrupt Rayner. "Now, she can obsess over our wedding."

Lainey held out her hands to Cooper. "Gimme that baby."

Cooper happily set Rayner in Lainey's arms.

Lainey rested their faces together, kissing the top of her head. "I swear you've doubled in size since I last saw you."

"She's getting big," Cooper agreed. "Which means it's time for another one."

"I heard that," Rowan groaned from a few feet away.

By the time I turned toward her, I heard, "Uncle 'Ett," screamed all the way across the room, my favorite pink-wearing, pigtailed girl running right for me.

I lifted her into my arms, kissing her cheek, and embraced Ridge and Rowan, saying, "I'm engaged. Is that wild or what?" While holding Daisy, I hugged each of them.

"It's about damn time," Rowan sighed.

"It's been the perfect amount of time," Ridge corrected her.

With Rayner in her arms, Lainey kissed my sister and brother.

"Uncle 'Ett, Daddy told me I get to be your flower girl."

"Is that so?" I looked at my brother, who was shrugging, and I laughed at him.

"It's a big-girl job, Uncle 'Ett. I have to sprinkle flowers everywhere. That's *sooo* important, Daddy says."

I put my hand over hers as she placed it on my chest. "I'd say that's one of the biggest roles in the wedding, Daisy."

"I know." She nodded, and a pigtail flopped in her face. "And guess what!"

"What?" Lainey said to her.

Daisy grinned at Lainey. "I'm going to sprinkle pink daisies because I know how much you love them."

Lainey leaned in and rubbed her nose against Daisy's. "You're right. I do love them. But, bestie, I think I might have an even bigger role for you than flower girl."

Daisy's eyes grew larger. "You do?"

"How would you like to be one of my bridesmaids?"

Daisy gasped.

"Do you know what that is?" Lainey asked her.

"Taylor was a bridesmaid, and Daddy showed me the picture of her in the wedding she was in. Is that what I get to be, Lainey? Just like Taylor? I get to be right by you at the wedding?"

"Yes," Lainey said, laughing. "You get to be right by me."

I looked at Lainey, knowing there was a smile on my face. I couldn't fucking hide it even if I wanted to. "You look pretty good with that baby in your arms, Mrs. Cole."

"Mrs. Cole," she replied with a wink. "We're going there already, huh?"

"I'd marry you tomorrow. You know that."

Lainey let out a long, deep breath, her face turning the slightest shade of red. I didn't know if anyone else could see it, but I could. "Are you just saying that because you want me to have your baby?"

"Well, there's that, yes," I told her. "But I'm saying it because you're my why and I'm ready for you to give up Taylor and become a Cole."

Daisy shouted, "But I want her to always be a Taylor!"

"I know, baby, but that's not going to happen," I whispered to my little one.

"No, it's definitely not," Lainey agreed.

Lainey gave me the smile—the one I had been after.

The one I would always try to keep on her face.

Forever.

Interested in reading the other books in the Spade Hotel Series?

Macon's book: *The Playboy*
Cooper's book: *The Rebel*
Brady's book: *The Sinner*
Ridge Cole's book: *The Heartbreaker*

Would you like to read more about the Weston family?

Hart Weston's book: *The Arrogant One*

And if you would like to check out the Dalton family ...

Dominick's book: *The Lawyer*
Jenner's book: *The Billionaire*
Ford's book: *The Single Dad*
Declan's book: *The Intern*
Camden's book: *The Bachelor*

ACKNOWLEDGMENTS

Nina Grinstead, we're at the end of another series—how is that even possible?!—and I still feel like it's only the beginning for us. You understand my moments better than anyone. The Zooms where I cry because we hit another goal. The Zooms where I tell you my deepest, darkest secrets. The Zooms where I'm more honest than I've ever been. And you look at me like how the proudest mom looks at her daughter, and you shake your head, and you remind me where we started. What brings even more tears is that I know so many more dreams are waiting for us, and I can't wait to hold your hand through each of them. I love you. Team B forever. XO

Jovana Shirley, one day, we're going to tally every deadline I've missed, and I'm going to get to hug you so hard for never making me feel bad about it, for always telling me it's going to be okay and that you'll make it work. You always do, and that feeling—that security of knowing I can count on you, no matter what—the weight of those words is immeasurable. I've said this before, but I mean it with my whole heart: I can't be me without you. Love you so, so hard.

Ratula Roy, it's hard to summarize us. To describe what you mean to me. You hold me together, you make me accountable, you push me, you make me reach when I can't stretch another inch. That's not an easy job, but you do it so seamlessly. And I know you do it because you truly love me. Because you get me. You're my person, and I'm so thankful, so grateful, and so honored to have you in my life. Love you forever.

Hang Le, my unicorn, you are just incredible in every way.

Judy Zweifel, as always, thank you for being so wonderful to work with and for taking such good care of my words. <3

Christine Estevez, I have so much appreciation for you. You're such a joy—on every level. I can't wait to squeeze you. Thank you, thank you, thank you.

Vicki Valente, you're the best—I hope you know that.

Nikki Terrill, my soul sister. Every tear, vent, virtual hug, life chaos, workout—you've been there through it all. I could never do this without you, and I would never want to. I've been saying this for years and I ALWAYS will: Love you.

Pang, I treasure you. In all the ways. And I'm so, so lucky to be able to work with you.

Melissa Doughty, you're such a light in my life. I'm so blessed to know you and get to work with you. <3

Sarah Symonds, my forever friend, I love you.

Brittney Sahin, I hope you know how much you mean to me. I hope you know that your words keep me going. I hope you know that you're stuck with me forever. In book world, out of book world, we're forever. Love you, B.

Kimmi Street, my sister from another mister. Thank you from the bottom of my heart. You saved me. You inspired me. You kept me standing in so many different ways. I love you more than love.

Kim Cermak, Kelley Beckham, Sarah Norris, Christine Miller, Valentine Grinstead, and Daisy—I love y'all so much.

To my ARC team—To the moon and back, I appreciate you all. <3

Mom and Dad, thanks for your unwavering belief in me and your constant encouragement. It means more than you'll ever know.

Brian, my words could never dent the love I feel for you. Trust me when I say, I love you more.

My Midnighters, you are such a supportive, loving, motivating group. Thanks for being such an inspiration, for holding my hand when I need it, and for always begging for more words. I love you all.

To all the influencers who read, review, share, post, TikTok —Thank you, thank you, thank you will never be enough. You do so much for our writing community, and we're so appreciative.

To my readers—I cherish each and every one of you. I'm so grateful for all the love you show my books, for taking the time to reach out to me, and for your passion and enthusiasm when it comes to my stories. I love, love, love you.

ABOUT THE AUTHOR

USA Today best-selling author Marni Mann knew she was going to be a writer since middle school. While other girls her age were daydreaming about teenage pop stars, Marni was fantasizing about penning her first novel. She crafts unique stories that weave together her love of darkness, mystery, passion, and human emotions. A New Englander at heart, she now lives with her husband in Sarasota, Florida. When she's not nose deep in her laptop, she's scouring for chocolate, sipping wine, traveling, boating, or devouring fabulous books.

Want to get in touch? Visit Marni at ...
www.marnismann.com
MarniMannBooks@gmail.com

ALSO BY MARNI MANN

THE WESTON GROUP SERIES—EROTIC ROMANCE

The Arrogant One (Spring 2025)

The Wildest One (Summer 2025)

The Mysterious One

The Irresistible One

The Forbidden One

SPADE HOTEL SERIES—EROTIC ROMANCE

The Playboy

The Rebel

The Sinner

The Heartbreaker

The One

THE DALTON FAMILY SERIES—EROTIC ROMANCE

The Lawyer

The Billionaire

The Single Dad

The Intern

The Bachelor

HOOKED SERIES—CONTEMPORARY ROMANCE

Mr. Hook-up

Mr. Wicked

THE AGENCY SERIES—EROTIC ROMANCE

Signed

Endorsed

Contracted

Negotiated

Dominated

STAND-ALONE NOVELS

Even If It Hurts (Contemporary Romance)

Before You (Contemporary Romance)

The Better Version of Me (Psychological Thriller)

Lover (Erotic Romance)

THE BEARDED SAVAGES SERIES—EROTIC ROMANCE

The Unblocked Collection

Wild Aces

MOMENTS IN BOSTON SERIES—CONTEMPORARY
ROMANCE

When Ashes Fall

When Darkness Ends

When We Met

THE PRISONED SERIES—DARK EROTIC THRILLER

Prisoned

Animal

Monster

THE SHADOWS DUET—EROTIC ROMANCE

Seductive Shadows

Seductive Secrecy

THE BAR HARBOR DUET—NEW ADULT

Pulled Beneath

Pulled Within

THE MEMOIR SERIES—DARK MAINSTREAM FICTION

Memoirs Aren't Fairytales

Scars from a Memoir

Printed in Great Britain
by Amazon

56095456R00214